T0304859

# THE LOST LIONESSES

# THE LOST LIONESSES

The incredible story
of England's forgotten
trailblazers

## GAIL EMMS

First published in Great Britain in 2024 by Cassell,
an imprint of Octopus Publishing Group Ltd
Carmelite House
50 Victoria Embankment
London EC4Y 0DZ
www.octopusbooks.co.uk

An Hachette UK Company
www.hachette.co.uk

The authorised representative in the EEA is Hachette Ireland,
8 Castlecourt Centre, Castleknock Road, Castleknock,
Dublin 15, D15 YF6A, Ireland

Text copyright © Gail Emms 2024

ISBN 978 1 78840 4969

A CIP catalogue record for this book is available from the British Library.

Typeset in 11.5/18pt Plantin MT Pro by Jouve (UK), Milton Keynes.

Printed and bound in Great Britain.

3 5 7 9 10 8 6 4 2

This FSC® label means that materials used for the product have been responsibly sourced.

Publisher: Trevor Davies
Senior Managing Editor: Sybella Stephens
Copy Editor: Chris Stone
Creative Director: Mel Four
Senior Production Manager: Katherine Hockley

To Harry and June Batt and their son, Keith.

To the Lost Lionesses (especially my mum ☺).

To my boys, Harry and Ollie.

# Contents

---

# Preface

___

**22 August 1971, Mexico City**

In the hallowed depths of the iconic Azteca Stadium, 14 girls clad in the purity of all-white football kits, occupy the cool embrace of the underground dressing room. Anxious and nervously casting glances at each other for support, their youthful faces mirror a mosaic of emotions – excitement, anticipation and energy pulsating through the air.

In a world where these girls dared to defy societal norms, all united by their love for football, their journey unfolds against the backdrop of persistent gender stereotypes. Growing up in an era when girls were told football was a sport reserved for boys, destiny leads them to this moment. It is here that, against all odds, they stand as England's representatives in the historic 1971 Women's World Cup.

Among them, Leah, a mere 13 years old, radiates impatience, her eagerness to step onto the grand stage evident. Meanwhile, Carol, the stalwart captain, breathes in the moment, attempting to subdue the jelly-like tremors creeping into her legs. The room, electric from tense whispers and silent encouragement, centres around Carol, the rock upon which the uncharted uncertainties of the moment rests. She imparts the final words of motivation and encouragement to the girls, gazing into the depths of each player's eyes, affirming her unwavering belief in them, a reflection of the trust she holds in their collective abilities.

In the midst of this nervous tension, Harry Batt, the sagacious 65-year-old manager, smartly dressed in a black suit and white shirt with thick-rimmed glasses, attempts to veil his excitement about the impending match. His calm voice imparts tactical wisdom, positioning each player strategically. Encouragement flows like a river, his words cascading over the fast-paced wingers Louise and Paula, advising them to conserve energy in the sweltering heat and unforgiving altitude. Then, turning to the whole team, he delivers final tactical instructions for the crucial clash against the host nation, Mexico.

Harry's words start to become a distant echo as the noise level rises, drowning out all else. The stadium thumps with anticipation, a symphony of 90,000 fervent fans echoing the heartbeat of a team determined to rewrite the narrative. Unable to resist the allure, centre back Jean, the tallest among the girls, clambers onto a bench, and peers out through a metal vent to catch a glimpse of what lies beyond. Her partner in defence, Trudy, a mere 16-year-old, clambers onto a toilet to steal a glimpse outside the high window, capturing a preview of the grandeur awaiting them. Not one unoccupied seat.

An official arrives, knocking on the dressing room door, interrupting the pre-match anticipation and beckoning the team to follow. It is time. In a procession, the girls, and Harry, traverse the dark underground corridors, arriving at the entrance of the tunnel where they await their moment to emerge into the shining spectacle of the stadium.

Through the tunnel's end, the midday sun blazes, casting an intense glow that heralds the forthcoming event. The noise intensifies, an anticipatory crescendo echoing the onset of a grand performance. As the Mexican climate's heat envelops them, droplets of sweat begin to emerge, catching the light and shimmering on the faces of the team. They stand, heads turned upward, ascending the stairs, poised to face the fate that awaits them in the world of football.

As the crowd roars with chants of 'Mexico! Mexico!', the atmosphere intensifies, marking a momentous occasion. No English women's team has ever stepped onto a stage of such magnitude, no English women's team has played in front of a bigger audience.

In a symbolic formation, Carol stands at the forefront, hand in hand with the team's mascot Keith, the 10-year-old son of Harry, who gazes up at her in bewilderment. A reassuring squeeze from Carol communicates strength, and as she breathes in the humid air, she glances back at the girls, offering a nod of unwavering reassurance. Battle-ready, this is their moment – the emergence of women's football, etched in the history of time. The echoes of cheers reach unprecedented levels.

This is it.

# Chapter 1
## Unveiling the Lost Lionesses

———

In the August of 1971, Harry Batt boldly led a cohort of English girls, determined to defy the prevailing notion that women were unsuitable to play football. In the face of stern opposition from footballing authorities, Harry fearlessly confronted those in power, challenging the status quo.

Amid adversities, the ensuing 14 girls embarked on a journey, overcoming obstacles merely to partake in the sport they passionately loved. Accepting Harry's invitation to play in Mexico, they willingly stepped onto the world stage, representing their country. Little did they know the profound consequences and battles that awaited them, both on and off the pitch. These resilient women were about to carve a path that would forever alter the landscape of women's football.

## Introducing the girls. . .

The girls' names will be mentioned frequently in the book, and to assist with this, here is a brief guide to the 14 players you'll meet, listed in the positions in which they most often played:

**Christine (Chris) Lockwood**
**DOB: 17.04.56**
**Position: Goalie / Any Position**

First up, Chris, the 15-year-old rebel with a cause and the undisputed fighter within the squad. Originally born in Yorkshire but raised in Luton, Chris may exude attitude on the surface, but beneath it all lies a remarkably different person. When it comes to her teammates, there's nothing she wouldn't do, embodying loyalty to the core.

A natural comedian with a fantastic sense of humour, Chris is the go-to source for laughter, constantly cracking jokes. Finding solace and self-discovery through sports, particularly as she understood she was gay, Chris sees football as a source of peace of mind. Despite her cheeky and crazy demeanour, she's incredibly kind-hearted.

Versatile on the field, Chris has played every position on the football team, serving as the backup goalkeeper in Mexico. With short, dark hair styled in a mullet, Chris stands as one of the taller players in the squad, at 1.73m (5ft 8in). A genuine character who occasionally feels the weight of the world against her, Chris remains friends with everyone and staunchly stands up for anyone in need.

## Lillian Harris
## DOB: 05.05.52
## Position: Goalie / Defence

Standing just a little over 1.52m (5ft), Lillian might not be the obvious choice for a goalkeeper, but the agility and reflexes of this spirited young lady are reminiscent of a cat. A dynamic ball of energy often compared to a ping pong ball, she embraces the audacity required to confront the strikes of the opposing team.

At 19 years old in Mexico, with her mousy-brown short-cropped hair, Lillian approaches defending as if engaged in a fierce battle. Hailing from Silverstone, Northamptonshire, she experienced her inaugural proper football match only months before, quickly grasping the rules. Despite her relative newcomer status, Lillian infuses the squad with fun and motivation, always donning her cute wide-rimmed glasses.

Off the football pitch, she maintains a quiet demeanour, but once on the field, Lillian unleashes her feisty side when needed. Determined and assertive, she knows her goals and stands her ground in challenging situations. Renowned for her bravery and fearlessness, Lillian courageously dives all over the penalty box in relentless pursuit of making saves.

**Jean (Big Jean) Breckon**
**DOB: 22.03.52**
**Position: Centre Back**

'Big Jean', a towering figure at nearly 1.83m (6ft) with a broad Yorkshire accent, is the epitome of a gentle giant. With a heart as big as her stature, Jean exudes immense love for her team and takes great pride in her Yorkshire and English roots. Sporting short brown hair, she holds down one of the pivotal centre back positions on the team, showcasing her strength and defensive prowess.

Jean also comes with a poignant story; she lost her ring finger in a freak accident while saving a shot from striker Jan during a warm-up for a match and her engagement ring became entangled in the goal-netting hook. A Royal Air Force recruit, Jean's Yorkshire grit and 'get on with it' attitude leaves no room for nonsense from anyone.

While impeccably down-to-earth, Jean is not one to be trifled with on the pitch, making her presence known with a formidable demeanour. An impressive defender, and incredibly strong, she remains fiercely protective of her team. Jean is always smiling, engaging in jokes that, although appreciated, sometimes challenge her squad mates in understanding her strong accent. Adored by all the girls, Jean stands as the salt of the earth.

## Carol Wilson (Captain)
## DOB: 27.12.51
## Position: Centre Back

Next there is Carol, the captain and Physical Training Instructor in the RAF, aged 19, and playing in defence. Sporting auburn shoulder-length hair, Carol approached her role with a dedicated and professional attitude, ensuring the squad's discipline and fitness remained at peak levels to navigate the challenges of Latin America.

A proud Geordie lass, Carol holds a deep affection for her teammates. Her commitment to their fitness is unwavering, pushing the girls to be in the best possible shape. As a true captain and natural leader, she serves as a great motivator, both on and off the pitch. Carol's dependability is a cornerstone of the team, always there for her teammates when needed.

Exuding oomph and zest, Carol thrives in her role as captain, displaying a remarkable ability to handle both people and pressure. Whether offering a helping hand or delivering a stern talking-to, she balances the responsibilities seamlessly. Carol's leadership qualities made her born for the role, and her teammates adore her, willingly following her lead in all endeavours.

**Jill Stockley**
**DOB: 11.08.54**
**Position: Defence**

Jill is a proud native of Nuneaton who marked her 17th birthday in the vibrant setting of Mexico. Both on and off the pitch, Jill exudes confidence, standing out as the natural powerhouse of the team. With her innate strength, she easily held the title of the strongest member of the squad.

Sporting short blonde hair, Jill showcases her versatility as an exceptional swimmer, actively participating in numerous competitions in that realm. Standing at 1.62m (5ft 4in), she assumes the role of a defensive player, embodying solidity and dependability. Despite not regularly playing alongside the rest of the girls, as she was based in Nuneaton, Jill seamlessly gels with the team, proving to be a great team player.

Her wealth of experience, gained from playing in many big stadiums, sets her apart from the rest. A hard worker with a kind-hearted nature, Jill is forthright in expressing her views. Her natural talent in football, coupled with her physicality, makes her a valuable asset on the pitch.

**Trudy McCaffery**
**DOB: 23.11.54**
**Position: Right Back**

Trudy, a spirited and feisty character, is a fiery blonde with an unwavering never-give-up attitude. Standing at 1.68m (5ft 6in) with shoulder-length blonde hair, Trudy made her mark at just 16 years old in Mexico. From a young age, she's known for speaking her mind, unapologetically expressing herself even if the recipient may not appreciate her candour – and this applies equally to officials.

Hailing from Lincoln and raised in a family that travelled the globe due to her referee father's Royal Air Force postings, Trudy is formidable in defence. Intelligent and insanely competitive, she possesses a keen understanding of what she wants. A dedicated football enthusiast, Trudy immerses herself in the sport, displaying tactical astuteness and an impressive ability to tackle with finesse. Her passion for football is evident in her knowledge and commitment, making her a brilliant and integral member of the team.

## Valerie (Val) Cheshire
## DOB: 12.02.47
## Position: Left Back

Meet Val, the eldest member of the squad at 24 years old, who occupies a crucial defensive role on the field. With shoulder-length brown hair, Val emanates a natural quietness that belies a wickedly dry sense of humour. Her smile has the power to uplift spirits but beware if you rile her on the football pitch, as sweetness transforms into a competitive passion that goes above and beyond.

Softly spoken yet fiercely grateful for her footballing journey, Val endured the longest and toughest struggle to find a girls' team in her youth. Despite this, she remains eternally appreciative of the sport. Acting as the closest ally to Harry Batt, the manager, Val serves as his inaugural captain – and confidante – for Chiltern Valley Ladies. Together with Marlene, she keeps a watchful eye on the younger girls, providing crucial support.

Harbouring an obsession with the Hitchin Town football pitch – 'The best pitch I've ever played on –it's flat and wide, just beautiful. You could play proper football on it, precise, silky passing, everything' – Val embodies good sense and dependability both on and off the field. She won't tolerate any hint of ego or arrogance within the squad, firmly establishing herself as a no-nonsense presence in the team.

**Marlene Rowe**
**DOB: 12.09.47**
**Position: Left Back**

Introducing Marlene, the second eldest in the squad at 23 years old. She assumes the role of the sensible figure, overseeing the well-being of the younger members. Often acting as a nurturing big sister, Marlene found her passion in the defensive realm on the pitch, becoming a crucial support pillar for the team.

A latecomer to football, Marlene, a skilled netballer, quickly adapted to the sport upon leaving school, leveraging her natural athletic abilities to catch up swiftly. Born and raised in Luton, the 1.68m (5ft 6in) player sports short-cropped brown hair and embodies the essence of a team player. While allowing the more extroverted characters to shine, Marlene maintains the squad's equilibrium, solidifying her reputation as a dependable and solid presence on and off the pitch.

Possessing the height and jumping ability essential for heading in football, Marlene showcases a good awareness of the game. An all-round good egg, she proves herself as someone you can always rely on in the squad.

**Leah Caleb**
**DOB: 04.04.58**
**Position: Inside Left / Right**

Next to be introduced is Leah, the cheeky 13-year-old scamp, born in Dublin, Ireland, but currently calling Luton home. As the youngest in the squad, Leah, with her long dark hair, bears a striking resemblance to the World Cup mascot 'Xochitl'. Bursting with energy and unbridled enthusiasm, she keeps the older members and chaperones on their toes with her off-pitch exploits.

Leah's football skills draw comparisons to the legendary George Best, as she showcases incredible ball control, rapid pace and a fearlessness beyond her years. A naturally gifted athlete, she attains high standards in various sports she undertakes. Her time in Mexico was nothing short of a life-changing experience. Despite her youth, Leah often displayed surprising sensibility, acting as the glue that held the squad together, earning the protection of her teammates.

Revered as the squad's famous one, Leah handled the scrutiny and attention from adoring fans with incredible maturity. Wherever the squad went, the common question echoed, 'Where's Leah?' Her widespread adoration stems from her undeniable charm and the love she evokes from everyone around her.

**Paula Rayner**
**DOB: 27.10.55**
**Position: Right Wing**

The 15-year-old Paula is often labelled as a 'tinker' by her fellow squad members. Another squad member hailing from Luton, Paula embraces the thrill of living on the wild side and exhibits a penchant for sneaking out of windows to defy curfew or elude the watchful eyes of adults. With her long brown hair featuring a swept fringe, she emerges as a gifted footballer who thrives on the right wing, showcasing incredible speed to skilfully navigate around defenders.

Standing at 1.65m (5ft 5in) tall, Paula may project an innocent and quiet demeanour, but she possesses a knack for thinking outside the box. Balancing a diligent work ethic with a cheeky and mischievous personality, she is a true force on and off the field. A remarkably talented sportswoman, Paula often teamed up with Trudy as her partner in crime during their various escapades.

## Gill Sayell
## DOB: 26.10.56
## Position: Right Wing

Meet Gill, the second youngest in the squad at 14 years old during her time in Mexico, and despite being the smallest at only 1.47m (4ft 10in), she brings a dynamic energy to the team. She has shoulder-length brown hair and naturally thrives as an attacking player, relishing her role on the right side of the pitch. During their adventures off the pitch, she formed strong friendships with Leah and Chris, earning them the playful name 'the Three Amigos'.

Even at a young age, Gill harboured a winning mindset and a relentless drive to improve, akin to the squad's centre forward, Jan. Throughout the World Cup, she blossomed with confidence and navigated with admirable ease the challenge of not knowing anyone in the squad upon arriving at the airport. A fast-paced player with great flair, Gill's quiet nature complements her lovely, gentle personality, harmonizing seamlessly with her competitive spirit in sports. Her dedication to training did not go unnoticed, as manager Harry Batt recognized her potential, marking the beginning of Gill's promising footballing journey.

**Louise Cross**
**DOB: 01.02.54**
**Position: Left Wing**

Hailing from Southampton, Louise undeniably stood out as one of the most talented members of the team. At 17 years old, she exhibits exceptional speed, surpassing many in her age group. Louise's style of play is skilful and unorthodox, a unique approach that she leverages to her advantage, especially when charging down the left wing against defenders. Possessing pinpoint passing accuracy and a left foot shot likened to a rocket, she distinguishes herself in a field where left-footed female players are a rarity.

An attractive girl with shoulder-length light brown hair, Louise garnered many admirers in Mexico. Despite her striking abilities on the pitch, she maintains a shy and reserved character within the squad, preferring to stay on the periphery of group activities. Nevertheless, Louise proved to be a great asset to the team, displaying immense confidence on the football pitch, even if her confidence off it was not as pronounced.

**Yvonne Farr**
**DOB: 31.01.55**
**Position: Wing / Forward**

Meet Yvonne, a Luton native raised in a bustling, large family. Quiet and naturally introverted, she found herself as a newcomer to the squad, arriving at the airport without knowing any other members. At 16 years old in Mexico, Yvonne brings a strong athletics background, boasting victories in hurdles at school competitions. Utilizing her fast pace down the wing, she effortlessly manoeuvres past defenders, expertly leaping over their tackles.

With long brown hair framing a full fringe that she often hides behind, Yvonne embodies the 'girl-next-door' persona. More reserved than her counterparts, she carries a shy demeanour with a lovely, sweet personality. Despite her reserved nature, Yvonne is always a cheerful and all-round delightful individual, bringing a unique charm to the squad.

## Janice (Jan) Barton
## DOB: 18.12.51
## Position: Centre Forward

Last but not least, introducing Jan, a 19-year-old hailing from North London and a devoted supporter of Tottenham Hotspur. With an unwavering focus on her football journey, Jan is always eager to acquire new skills, displaying a strong-willed and determined approach to the game. Despite her petite stature at 1.55m (5ft 1in), Jan, adorned with blonde curls, thinks like a centre forward, constantly strategizing on how to outmanoeuvre defenders and score crucial goals for the team.

Her commitment to success is unparalleled, with a relentless determination to win. While Jan may not exude feistiness off the pitch, once she enters the 'playing zone', she handles herself adeptly against larger opponents. One hundred per cent focused on scoring goals for her side, Jan exhibits an unwavering commitment to the team's objectives and is known for her intense competitiveness.

## The Tales of Trailblazing Women Footballers

*'Complaints having been made as to football being played
by women, the Council feels impelled to express their strong
opinion that the game of football is quite unsuitable for females
and should not be encouraged.'*
1921, FA Council

Records show that women were participating in casual football matches as early as the 15th century. Like their male counterparts, women played within their local communities as a pastime. Over time, teams were formed, and regular matches took place. However, as the sport grew, so did the backlash.

The first recorded match between England and Scotland took place on 7 May 1881, in Edinburgh. The teams then played two additional matches in Glasgow and Manchester, each drawing crowds of around 5,000. These matches were abandoned due to violent protests.

During the First World War, women's football gained popularity, raising the equivalent of millions of pounds for charitable causes. The changing nature of women's work in wartime Britain helped elevate the profile of the game, both as a women's sport and more broadly. Female workers were encouraged to join official workplace sports teams to improve health and productivity, but many also played football during their lunch breaks, forming unsanctioned teams like Bella's Team, the Blyth Spartans and the Carlisle

Munitionettes. Some were even invited to join men's games outside working hours.

After observing women munitions workers playing football from his office window, Alfred Frankland suggested to worker Grace Sibbert that they establish a team to play for charity. Adopting the factory's name, Dick, Kerr Ladies FC became well-known. Between 1917 and 1965, they played 828 games and raised tens of thousands of pounds for charity, a sum equivalent to tens of millions in today's terms.

Dick, Kerr Ladies' match on Boxing Day 1920 against St Helens at Goodison Park set a record attendance of 53,000, with an additional 10,000 fans reportedly locked outside. To put this in perspective, the average attendance for Everton's men's team at Goodison Park that season was just over 38,000.

On 5 December 1921, the FA Council banned women from playing on football pitches owned by Association members.

Despite the matches not interfering with men's games and being initiated to fill the void left by the absence of Football League matches during the First World War, the FA, unhappy with the growing popularity of women's football outside their control, deemed it a threat. These matches were organized to raise funds for charity, with the gate money going entirely to charitable causes, bypassing the FA's authority.

Responding to this, the FA, concerned about the increasing popularity of women's football and the absence of gate money, made decisions that would hinder the progress of women's football for years.

The FA instructed men's clubs to deny women the opportunity to play, thereby overshadowing the achievements of Dick, Kerr Ladies and restricting the advancement of women in football. In effect, the FA had outlawed the sport for women.

Despite the ban, there were pockets of activity for women's football thanks to the Northern Rugby Union who refused to follow the FA's wishes and allowed women to play on their rugby grounds. With no other support, there was little progress and women were consigned to playing on local recreation grounds or pitches for other sports. Businesses such as Marks & Spencer and Woolworths held matches in support of the women's game, but these were few and far between. Women faced criticism for wanting to play football. They were told, 'Football is a man's game.'

And, several decades later and with the ban still in place, this was the story still told to the 14 Lionesses of Mexico when they were growing up in the 1950s and '60s . . .

*'It was the adults saying that I shouldn't be playing football, not the boys. It was something I ignored, and I never allowed it to bother me.'*

Leah

### *Paula Rayner*

*'I was born in Cricklewood, London. I was the fourth child, my three older brothers and I were all very close in age, only five years between the eldest and me, and then Stephen is eleven years younger. As soon as I could walk, I played football with my brothers, but I don't really*

*remember much of my life in London. We moved to Luton when I was*
*about seven or eight years old.'*

Paula's childhood days were marked by a fervent desire to
partake in the boys' football games on the playing fields. However,
the door to this sport remained closed, courtesy of the boys who
deemed her unfit for the game simply because she was a girl.

In a pivotal moment, Paula's brother Gerald stepped forward as
her advocate. Approaching the leader of the boys, he asserted, 'She
can play football, so let her join in.' And with that proclamation,
Paula found herself welcomed into the fold. All thanks go to big
brother. Lunchtimes became a ritual spent on the playing field,
engaged in the lively game of football and no word was said again
about Paula being a female.

The boys, standing in a circle to select teams, initially relegated
Paula to the last pick. Yet her skills swiftly propelled her up the
hierarchy. Fortunate to have open fields in front of her house, Paula
and the boys from the estate would gather for the timeless routine of
'jumpers for goalposts', team selections, and games that only paused
when mothers called them in for tea.

*'My mum used to tell people this story about how I used to have long,*
*blonde hair when I was little and how she used to love to comb and plait*
*it. Then one day when she had gone shopping, I asked my dad to cut the*
*plaits off so I could look like my brothers. When she got home, there they*
*were, the two plaits lying on the kitchen table. I don't remember doing*
*that, but Mum does, and she wasn't very happy.*

*'Growing up in the 1950s and '60s, girls were girls, and boys*
*were boys. My mum did try to encourage me to be more girly,*

*I went to Brownies for a while, and I also have a certificate in ballet, but in the end, Mum was resigned to the fact it was going to be trainers and not ballet pumps with me. I was 13 before I was allowed to have a pair of jeans, and my football boots were always my brothers' hand-me-downs. I got my first new football boots for my 14th birthday.'*

Paula discovered another kindred spirit, Dawn, who lived just a door away and shared her passion for football. Amid the games, there were always negative comments directed at her. The negativity manifested as labelling her as 'weird' for being a girl playing football or insinuations about her sexual orientation. However, she paid little attention to their unkind words.

During those playful afternoons, Paula was nicknamed 'Brucie' by some of her male counterparts, an association with Bruce Rioch, a player for Luton Town during that era. Hoping it was a nod to her playing style rather than a comparison of appearances, Paula continued to grow to love and relish the joy of the game, undeterred by societal expectations and stereotypes.

*'I wasn't allowed to play on the football team at my school. I'll always remember my PE teacher saying, "It's such a shame we can't let you play because you'd be one of my first choices for the team." My brother got selected, so I was always watching the matches after school. I'd run up and down on the sideline cheering the team on.*

*'I then went to an all-girls secondary school, so there was definitely no football played there. I loved taking part in most sports, PE was my favourite subject, and I represented the school in hockey, netball, athletics and tennis, but my football always came first.'*

### Yvonne Farr

*'I am one of seven children, and I am the third eldest. We grew up in Stopsley, Luton. My mum never put any pressure on me to be a "girly girl" and wear a dress. She knew it wasn't for me and accepted the way I was.'*

Yvonne's journey into football was different to Paula's. Her childhood weaves together tales of camaraderie and shared joy on the field, playing sport. The stage was set in the neighbourhood behind her house, where a boy named Paul and her brother Keiron became her constant companions in the game of football. Beyond the confines of school, whenever free time beckoned, the trio would kick a ball around, creating moments that Yvonne cherished.

Being a self-proclaimed tomboy, Yvonne seamlessly integrated herself into the boys' world, finding acceptance and friendship among them. The simplicity of those days was reflected in the shared passion for football, a common ground that transcended gender norms. Notably, Yvonne wasn't alone in her tomboy pursuits; some of her female friends shared the same inclination, forming a tight-knit group that defied what was expected of girls growing up in the 1950s.

Stopsley, then a village with a good sense of community, provided a nurturing environment for these friendships to flourish. With this freedom, Yvonne and her friends delighted in being accepted for who they were. Despite the unconventional nature of their interests – those that were seen to be for boys – Yvonne fondly recollects those days without a trace of abuse or negativity tarnishing the memories. It was a time when the simple pleasures of playing football and the bonds forged in Stopsley painted a picture of a childhood untainted by judgement.

### Louise Cross

*'I was born in Southampton. My mum and dad have five children and I am bang in the middle at number three. I have an older and younger brother and the same with my two sisters. All five of us are good at sport.'*

In the heart of Millbrook, where the green outside Louise's house doubled as a makeshift football pitch, her older brother Richard emerged as a local football talent, proudly donning the jersey of Southampton School Boys. The allure of the game proved irresistible, even to Louise, who, undeterred by the absence of fellow girls, sought to join the ranks of her brother's spirited matches.

There was no coaching for Louise in those early football days. All was self-taught and fuelled by an innate passion. She absorbed the intricacies of the game by closely observing her brothers and their friends. Remarkably, her natural aptitude for football became apparent, earning her brother's acknowledgement with the words, 'You just have a flair for it.'

The transition from the impromptu green fields to the school playground marked Louise as the sole girl in a sea of boys. The initial teases and comments failed to deter her spirit. Instead, she held her ground, swiftly gaining respect as her skill on the ball became undeniable. The taunts dwindled into silence, drowned out by her confident play.

*'My mum wasn't overly keen on me playing football though. In those days, it wasn't as acceptable to have a daughter playing football, only*

*sons. My mum had comments like, "Oh gosh, you've got a tomboy girl!"*
*said to her a lot. Yet they were still supportive. They came back with,*
*"Yeah, that's our daughter Louise playing football and we are proud."'*

Louise's journey was not just about physical prowess; it demanded a mental acuity to read a football match. The ability to anticipate moves, to be that split second ahead of opponents – these were skills she honed without formal coaching. In the absence of such, she became her own teacher, meticulously observing her brothers and translating their moves into her own skillset.

The quest for self-improvement became a driving force for Louise, an innate characteristic that propelled her forward. With the desire to win and her determination to enhance her skills continuously, Louise emerged not only as a player of great talent but as a testament to the power of self-motivation and an unyielding pursuit of excellence.

'Because I had started playing football at a young age with my brothers, I always used to play football in the playground at school with the boys. I was the only girl doing so, and I used to get teased at the start with a few comments thrown at me, but it never bothered me. And soon the comments stopped because I held my own and they couldn't get the ball off me!'

'At school, I was on all the sports teams. In the rounders team, they used to get so fed up because I just used to hit the ball so far and I would be the only one left and they could never get me out!'

'I was good at hockey as well and that helped my football, which in turn helped my hockey. It's a very similar game in terms of tactics and positioning on the pitch.*

*'When I was playing sports, I could be myself. I could be feisty Louise. I'm really competitive and I love to win. I do believe playing sports kept me out of trouble and off the streets too. If I had any worries, I'd go and play football and that kept me sane, especially during times when I had my exams. I'm still like that now. If I need to de-stress, I will go and play walking football. I like to prove to myself that I can still kick a ball just as well as anybody else.'*

### Leah Caleb

*'I was born in Dublin, and I have an older brother and sister. The family came to Luton when I was three years old. I have an Irish passport, but I have spent all my life growing up in England. It's where I've had all my sports experiences. I see myself as "Irish English", which doesn't always work watching sports events! I was truly blessed with my parents. They were supportive and trusting, and understood how important sport was in my life. They understood it made me happy as a child and teenager, which continued into my adulthood.'*

At the tender age of five, propelled by an unexpected introduction – repeated instances of being hit with a football in the playground – Leah decided to bridge the gap between herself and the boys, which led her to kick the ball with newfound enthusiasm. Endowed with natural athleticism, the world of sports unfolded effortlessly for Leah, transforming an inadvertent encounter into a source of pure joy.

The resonance of laughter and fun of playing football in the playground translated seamlessly to post-school adventures in the park. What began as a casual kickabout gradually morphed into spirited, competitive play.

*'I learned my football skills playing with the boys. I was accepted as a girl and often being called a tomboy. To be honest, it was the adults saying that I shouldn't be playing football, not the boys. It was something I ignored, and I never allowed it to bother me. Dad would have preferred me not to be a tomboy running around playing football. My mum would say, "That's what Leah loves to do", and so Dad had to accept it.'*

Leah's recollections paint a picture of simplicity – a time when children, undeterred by societal norms, would spill onto the streets or local parks to engage in the timeless ritual of play. For Leah, the majority of her childhood was spent navigating the football fields with the boys, occasionally pivoting to cricket when summer arrived.

Beyond the joy of the game, there was the universal language that sports speak. In the arena of play, differences disappear, and teamwork prevails. Regardless of whether the opponent is a girl or boy, the essence of sports remains respectful and enjoyable. The playing field becomes a great equalizer, erasing distinctions of culture, ethnicity or gender; it becomes just about the sport.

The profound lesson woven into Leah's childhood narrative is that once you've proven your worth in any sport, be it with a ball, bat or racket, the camaraderie with like-minded individuals knows no boundaries. In the carefree days of youth, differences become inconsequential, and the shared love for the game becomes the unifying force that transcends constraints.

### *Jan Barton*

'*I was born in Islington and have two older brothers. My home was very cramped, it was one of those townhouses with families living up above and below. We all shared an outside toilet. My mum, Edith, worked in a factory. There were no fields to play out on, just city life. As a treat, my mum used to give me money to go to the Pie and Eel shop, which I loved! The mystic of the green liquor . . . oh it's wonderful! Manze Pie and Eel – I think David Beckham still goes on occasion. Our idea of fun when we were kids was going up and down on the tube.*

'*I was a tomboy, and my mother couldn't get me in a dress to save my life. I was always in shorts or jeans or whatever you had in those days. I had no interest in dolls or "girly" things at all. All I wanted to do was play football. My mum despaired as all she wanted was a little girl to dress up as a princess. I had beautiful blonde ringlets right down to my back. Perfect to put ribbons in, and yet I turned out to be the biggest tomboy ever.*

'*We lived in Arsenal territory so everyone in my family supported Arsenal. I started supporting Spurs – not sure how that started, but it was probably to really annoy them. When I was young, Dad drove me to White Hart Lane to watch a Tottenham Hotspur match. I kept nagging and finally he relented. It was against Nottingham Forest. As I got older, I could get on a train and go by myself, which I used to do a lot. My favourite players were Jimmy Neighbour – he was a great little winger – and Jimmy Greaves. I modelled my style of play on Jimmy Greaves. His dribbling ability was sensational.*

'*All the family lived in that area of North London, and it was common to have a knees-up at the King of Denmark pub with my Uncle Fred still singing at 11pm.*

'*During the war, my dad, Bill, was a POW, captured in 1940, and spent the rest of the war in a POW camp. My mum, Edie, was bombed out three times during the Blitz. During the Blitz, she came home three times to her shelled house, but in those days, it says a lot about the community, you just moved in with your neighbour or friend and just got on with it. People don't realize what they went through. It seems like the world has ended if the internet connection goes off now. My parents had their houses blown up. My dad spent the prime of his life (aged 22 to 27 years old) in a German prison camp. When he returned home, he had to work driving coal lorries and all sorts to try and get back into the world of living.*

'*My mum eventually had enough of city life, and we moved to Biggleswade [Bedfordshire] as her sister lived in nearby Sandy. I was about nine years old, and I can still remember breathing clean air and seeing grassy fields for the first time!*'

In the early years of Jan's life, the boys in her world recognized her talent on the football field. With a nod to her skills, they welcomed her into their games, acknowledging that she was every bit as good a player as any of them. The bond with her brother, Ray, separated by only a couple of years, solidified over shared moments of kicking a ball around. The presence of numerous boy cousins provided the perfect companionship for football matches.

'*I was very happy at my secondary school as it had a big playing field. My brother was a good runner and the PE teachers saw that I had the sporty gene too. I played netball at school and was good at the sport.*

*I was centre in the netball team. And we absolutely thrashed the Grammar School girls, which was one up for us. The boys did football of course, but girls weren't allowed to join in there. I was only allowed to play in the playground with them at break. When the boys played matches against the other schools, I used to think, "I'd love to be as good as that!"'*

Fairfield, the park in Biggleswade, became a backdrop for Jan's football heaven. Post-school, armed with just a ball, she ventured to the park alone, honing her skills by kicking the ball against the fence and mastering keepy-ups. She was unaware of the concept of girls' football teams, and no one steered her in that direction. Undeterred, Jan's imagination took flight, envisioning herself scoring goals for the likes of Spurs or England – albeit in the men's team.

Going to watch Biggleswade Town, known affectionately as the 'Waders', became a staple in Jan's routine. Whether alone or occasionally accompanied by her father, they attended matches, engaging in a pre-game and half-time kickaround.

The park emerged as Jan's sanctuary. In the solitude of those moments, a lad named Kevin occasionally joined Jan, sparking a new phase of skill development. He would help Jan practise her left foot composure on the ball and try new ball skills they had seen others do. Being alone in her football pursuits and thoughts didn't deter Jan; rather, it became a source of contentment. Nights blended into one another, especially in the summer, as Jan just loved the simple pleasure of playing, indifferent to the number of friends in her circle. Those moments rendered friendship inconsequential against the backdrop of her cherished park, her sanctuary, and her happy place.

### *Chris Lockwood*

'*I was born in Bolton upon Dearne, South Yorkshire, a place very dear to my heart. My nan and granddad had a farm there, so I had the best childhood ever. The adults never saw the kids all day. I've got two sisters – Susan, me, then Julie – but they didn't like sport at all. My mum didn't either. My dad did a little bit of sport, not that much, however my uncles and my cousins (who were all boys) were football mad. We used to play together all the time in the farmyard, with a bit of cricket thrown in now and again, but most of the time it was football and I loved it!*

'*We didn't even have an actual football growing up. My cousin Tony and I hatched a plan, and we climbed up the drainpipe of a Victorian school nearby, got onto the roof, scooped together all the balls that were stuck there, threw them down, and took them all back to the farm to play with. Sorry kids.*

'*Just before I started infant school, my dad moved to Luton. He couldn't afford to keep farming and Vauxhall Motors were offering good money for jobs on the factory line, so it was a no-brainer. He was in Luton for six months before the rest of the family came down to live with him. My dad was homesick for Yorkshire all the time, so we used to go back up north regularly.*

'*Because our family was always travelling back to the farm, I always felt a strong connection to Yorkshire. I had a northern accent. My first day at school, however, turned into a bit of a drama. The school was*

*only down the road from our house in Luton, and Mum and Dad were*
*so excited for me. They waited at home to see if I'd enjoyed it. They saw*
*me coming down the driveway and walking through the back door.*
*They were waiting for me in the lounge, but instead of me coming into*
*the room to say hello, they heard me go out the back door again. I had*
*got a kitchen knife and was running down the road, chasing the kids*
*who said I came from* Coronation Street. *In my eyes, I was standing*
*up for myself because the kids were saying I was different. (No one was*
*hurt in this incident!) My dad had always told me, "Don't let anybody*
*pick on you. You stand up for yourself."*

'One day, my mum turned to me and said, "Enough is enough!
*You are wearing a dress." I cried all day because I wasn't just a tomboy,*
*I was gay and wasn't feminine in terms of wanting to wear a dress.*
*Looking back, it must have been hard for my mum and dad because*
*I was different, and they had to accept it. They knew that I was never*
*going to be put in the corner and told what to be. Whereas when I played*
*football, nobody judged me. All that mattered was how I played on that*
*pitch. I would always give 100 per cent and work hard for the team.*
*That, for me, was acceptance.'*

Chris's passion for football set her apart from her female peers.
The absence of other girls who shared her love for the sport left her
feeling alienated, prompting a natural gravitation towards the
company of boys. Growing up in Luton, she cultivated friendships
grounded in mutual respect and a shared enthusiasm for football.

The camaraderie with the boys, stemming from her adeptness
on the football field, fostered an environment devoid of animosity.
The selection of team captains, a ritual embedded in the fabric of

their games, saw Chris elevated to the esteemed number one position regularly. There was never a word of exclusion based on her gender; instead, the boys acknowledged her skill and held her in high regard. In the dynamics of team selection, Chris found herself donning the captain's armband, a testament to the nod of acceptance she enjoyed.

Chris's closest ally emerged in the form of a boy named Shane. However, Shane hesitated to visit Chris's home when her father was present. The prospect of encountering Chris's father, let alone engaging in conversation with him, left Shane truly petrified.

*'When I was in junior school, I could play football in the playground, but I wasn't allowed to play for the boys' team. I feel that the teachers were trained to think, "Well that's what the rule is, and we can't do anything about it." When I got to senior school, I wasn't allowed to play football at all. It was a netball school and I hated netball. If I kicked the netball, the PE teacher sent me inside as punishment. I spent nearly every PE lesson in the changing rooms as I couldn't help but kick the netball. Suddenly a barrier between myself and the teachers was there, and it caused problems between us, purely because of the system. We could have worked something out, I am sure, but I rebelled. I fought with them constantly and I shouldn't have done that. I am not that type of person at all. But I needed a shield and so I created a toughness about myself to get through my teens to survive what I was feeling.*

*'I didn't want to pretend to be something different from what I was. I remember getting drunk a few times, even getting aggressive, as a coping mechanism, but it really wasn't who I was. All I wanted to be doing was to be out playing football. My teachers had a tough job with*

me, I didn't want to conform in school. That didn't make me a nasty person, I was a nice person deep down, but my actions got me labelled as a troublemaker.

'I got a black eye in a fight once. One of the teachers called me into their office and said, "Oh, we have got a problem. This can't go on." It was the first act of kindness I remember from a teacher. They asked if everything was OK, and we talked through a few things that were troubling me. I am glad that they still cared even though I got myself in trouble a lot.'

### Lillian Harris

'I come from Silverstone, Northamptonshire, and there was no women's football when I was growing up. I've got a brother and a sister. My dad was killed working on the motorway when I was young. I was only 11 years old when it happened. He would have been so supportive. He played football in the village for the team with my uncles as well. It was a bit of a footballing family. My mum and my nan washed all the football kit. We always had the footballs in our house to keep them pumped up and ready for the village team matches. I grew up with lots of balls all around the house, so I guess I had to be a footballer!'

With Lillian's foray into playing football with the boys, a compelling story unfolds, shaped by her determination and skill. The absence of nasty comments from the boys stemmed from her ability to showcase a prowess that exceeded theirs. Each encounter with the boys became a challenge to elevate her game, an unspoken mandate for girls who sought respect on the field.

Lillian understood the unspoken rule that, when playing against boys, girls needed to surpass expectations to avoid being made fun of. The fear of being dismissed with derogatory comments lingered, and Lillian refused to succumb to the stereotype of being deemed less competent simply because of her gender. Instead, she embraced the opposite narrative; the boys, rather than belittling her, marvelled at her tenacity and skill.

Playing primarily in defence, Lillian's forte was tackling, and she relished the art of the slide tackle. Her approach to the game earned her the nickname 'Chopper', after her namesake, the no-nonsense Chelsea defender, Ron 'Chopper' Harris. It was a testament to her fearless and robust playing style that left an indelible mark on her footballing identity.

*'There was no football at school for the girls, I was only allowed to play that with the boys around where I lived. I played mainly netball at school as I was really nimble and agile. I could jump really well too. Not bad for someone who is 5ft 1in [1.55m]! I love sport. Any sport I could get into, I loved it.'*

### *Gill Sayell*

*'I was born in Aylesbury, and my parents, Bob and Popsy, had seven children. I have four brothers and two sisters, and I come in at number five. We lived on a council housing estate, Southcourt. Everybody knew each other and we were always in and out of each other's houses. It was a nice community. It might not have been an affluent area, it was a working-class area, with most parents working, but there was always support for everyone. We all supported different football teams, which*

*was interesting at times. I supported Chelsea, as a lot of the lads I played with supported them, and Charlie Cooke was my hero.*

*'I was what everyone called a tomboy as I was out with the boys all the time, playing any games that they made up. My two sisters were not sporty at all. All I wanted to do was play football, climb trees, jump off swings, and do any other outdoor activity.*

*'My mum did try and get me in a dress and only succeeded once! My uncle lived in Germany, and on a visit to our house, bought me a lovely dress with frills and lace as a present. My mum made me wear it and I can still remember sitting in the front garden with my face fuming and thinking, "I don't want to be wearing this dress!" I never did wear it again!'*

In the tale of Gill's youth, the Edinburgh playing fields in Aylesbury unfold as a familiar backdrop, situated conveniently near her house. The green pitches were a stage for boys' football matches, and Gill, undeterred by societal expectations, would stride over to the sidelines to immerse herself in the lively spectacles, becoming an ardent cheerleader for the teams.

There was an air of effortless normality surrounding Gill's presence on the football field. The notion of feeling awkward or out of place as the only girl amid boys never crossed her mind. Playing football wasn't just an activity for her; it was a natural extension of herself. The familiarity with the local kids, coupled with the recognition of her football prowess, seamlessly integrated her into the gang. Notable school friends (Jim Brennan, Jimmy Davis and Paul Bettis) often congregated on the green to organize teams and engage in spirited matches.

The camaraderie that flourished on the playing field was underlined by an unspoken acceptance. The boys, far from being deterred by Gill's gender, relished the diversity she brought to their footballing endeavours. To them, Gill wasn't an exception; she was merely another footballer in the mix. When teams were picked for kickabouts, Gill found herself seamlessly integrated, her presence unquestioned. It never occurred to the boys to second-guess her participation; she was valued for her skill and determination.

The legacy of playing with the boys on the green shaped Gill's approach to the game. Her competitive spirit, evident in her commitment to win, was forged on those pitches. Never one to shy away from a tackle, Gill's resilience and tenacity became emblematic of her footballing journey – a journey where gender was incidental, and the shared love for the game eclipsed societal expectations.

*'What I wished for at the time was to be able to play in a team. The boys wanted me to play in the school team with them, but I wasn't allowed. I can remember going on a junior school camp to the Isle of Wight and there was a football competition being held. The lads asked if I could play, and the teachers said, "No, she isn't allowed to play as Gill is a girl." I felt hurt as I knew, and they knew, I was a good player, but those were the rules at that time. I was about nine or ten years old and was one of several pupils from Mandeville School who were selected to go on a residential week to Crystal Palace sports centre. My sports teacher, Miss Warren, knew all about my passion for all sports and in particular football. When we had a gymnastics class, she turned to me and said, "Do you want to go outside and kick the ball around?" I jumped at the chance, and I was just out in the park area, on my own,*

*just kicking the ball, and practising my keepy-ups. That was probably as much encouragement as I had at school for my passion for football, but I was so grateful that my teacher recognized that.'*

Gill found a method to participate in competitive football matches, albeit by assuming the guise of a boy.

*'A new football team in the area was started up by a parent of one of the boys in my school. He became my friend, and he asked me to join him and the rest of the boys. Of course, I said yes! I had short hair at the time, and so the boys in the team called me Billy, and I pretended to be a boy. To be honest, you wouldn't know straight away that I was a girl. We were called the Cougars. We played a few games and then one day, we had a match against Bedgrove Dynamos. I still remember their team's name. The other team then realized I was a girl and put up a huge fuss saying, "We're not playing on. She can't play as she's not allowed. She's a girl." The coach and players were all pointing at me. I never played a football match again at that age, because of that football coach and the team's negativity. I was so sad and disappointed because all I wanted was to be able to play in a team. I was just ten years old.'*

### Jean Breckon

*'I was born in Skipton, Yorkshire, and I'm one of seven children! It goes, boy, boy, girl, girl, boy, boy, girl. I'm the eldest girl. My mum was always saying, "My Jean, she does everything with the boys. Everything." My two older brothers were my main influences. I would see them kicking a ball together, and I would watch them and think, "I can do that." To be honest, it didn't matter what sport it was, football or even cricket, I would play if my brothers were playing it.*

'My dad was a stereotypical Yorkshireman and liked his tea on the table when he got home from work. He didn't want my mum going to work, her job was to look after the kids and keep the house in order.

'Growing up in the 1950s and '60s, society was very gender specific about what boys and girls should be doing. It was very much about the boys going outside, running around and getting muddy, while the girls were meant to stay at home with dolls, learning to sew and cook. It was very stereotypical. I never understood why girls weren't encouraged to run fast or climb trees. We've got the same human bodies and it's healthy to be active, but no, being active and being outdoors is only for boys. Girls were meant to learn to be ladies and sit still. My mum never gave me a doll and I'm very glad she didn't. There were not many girls about, but it didn't bother me. I acted like one of the boys. Even when I started wearing a bra, I used to take it off and throw it in the wash basket, just so I didn't have to be a typical girl.'

Jean remembered her early years in Skipton; the resonant chime of the final school bell marked the commencement of a spirited dash home. Bags were unceremoniously dropped, and the beckoning call of the great outdoors set the stage for a 'symphony' of childhood adventures. The fields surrounding her home evolved into a lively scene where the thud of a football and contagious laughter composed the soundtrack to her formative years.

Peering out from her window, the expansive view revealed a sprawling wood atop the farmer's field – a sanctum that held an almost magical allure for Jean and her friends. When not in school and during the blissful stretches of holidays, they found themselves involved in a realm of games, with football reigning supreme.

The timeless tradition of 'jumpers for goalposts' unfolded beneath the towering trees, etching a scene that encapsulated the essence of all that Jean held dear.

A particular memory, vivid and indelible, etched itself into Jean's consciousness – a zip line strung between two trees, both tempting and tinged with trepidation. Despite her adventurous spirit, a lingering fear of its potential snap under her weight tempered her courage. Nevertheless, the wood retained its status as a haven of boundless possibilities and unbridled joy, always about being cherished playtime.

With the ebb and flow of seasons, the repertoire of activities transformed. In the leisurely days of summer, Jean and her group of friends ventured to reservoirs for invigorating swims, and created memories with the simple joys of football and outdoor play. Through Jean's recollections, the fields of Skipton emerge not just as a playground but as a sign of enduring friendships, echoes of laughter, and an unbridled love for the games that marked her youth.

*'I went to the primary school down the road from where I live now, Greatwood Community Primary School. I wasn't allowed to play football when I was there. Well, I did play football, but if the teachers came out into the playground and caught me, they'd say I couldn't play. The teachers all knew that I was good at football, and I was better than a lot of the lads who played, but it didn't matter to them. They kept saying to me, "You know football is a boy sport. It's not for the girls."'*

### *Trudy McCaffery*

*'I was born in Lincoln. My dad, Edward, was in the RAF, and we travelled all over the world with his work. He was also a football referee (at international level on occasion), but mainly for local football matches. He used to get chased out of the villages on his bike if the supporters thought he made the wrong decision, and their team lost the game.*

*'These were my first memories of football – as soon as I was old enough to walk, I used to go with him when he was refereeing. There was always someone who'd have a little game with me, and Dad and I used to have kickabouts in the back garden regularly too. My mum used to go mad when we wrecked the plants. I've been playing football for as long as I can remember, and it doesn't matter where you live, or where you go on holiday, there are always people to play football with. It brings people together.*

*'I have two sisters. My mum always wanted a boy, but then she said, "With the girls I've got, I don't need boys!" She frequently tried to get me in a dress, and I hated it, so she gave up rather than argue. I've always been a feisty personality. I was lucky because Mum and Dad knew I was a tomboy and accepted that's what they had on their hands. I was never told to get down out of a tree or stop running in the mud, they just let me be me.*

*'I've been a Manchester United fan all my life, though when we used to visit Scotland to see family, my dad took me to see Morton and Celtic play. There was one point in time when I was so fanatical about United, my dad bought me an LP (when United beat Benfica in the European Cup in 1968) for Christmas and I learned that record off by heart. I knew every single word.*

*'In the summer holidays, we'd go to the seaside and stay in a caravan. There would be all the family staying on the same site. It was a lot of fun, and the highlight was always competitive games of football and rounders on that beach, especially when the parents joined in. It was England versus Scotland so the stakes were high!*

*'My dad always laughed about the story when we were on holiday, and we all played crazy golf. I threw my club away as far as I could and was moody because I lost. I just wanted to win everything all the time. I could never see the point of just taking part – in my opinion, you play to win, otherwise, what's the point?!*

*'We used to play on the "backies" too where my nan lived. It was just the alleyway at the rear of all the terraced houses – it was just cinder and gravel with jumpers at each end for goals. We'd play till it was dark then go to the local shop to get sweets and fizzy pop to share.'*

In the era that Trudy fondly recalls, a prevailing sentiment echoed through the communities she inhabited – that of acceptance and inclusivity when it came to girls playing football. Curiously, the resistance to this notion seemed to emanate primarily from those in positions of authority, individuals vested with the power to shape decisions regarding the beautiful game. Beyond this circle of influence, the prevailing philosophy among the general population was refreshingly pragmatic: 'If you're good enough, then you're good enough to play with us.'

Trudy, much like her peers, found herself navigating the football terrain by joining boys' teams or partaking in spirited matches with the local gang. The concept of a 'girls' team' remained elusive, a revelation that would have surprised her younger self. She was unaware of the hidden history of girls playing football in the 1960s, as the narratives and achievements of female players were quietly tucked away.

The norm for Trudy, however, was to seamlessly blend into the world of boys' football. Scabby knees and worn-out shoes stood as badges of honour, tangible proof of her wholehearted commitment to the game. The idea of playing with the boys was not just a preference; it was the only way she knew. In the simplicity of those moments, Trudy found a sense of belonging and joy that far outweighed any of society's expectations or preconceived notions.

*'We lived in Singapore for a while when my dad was posted there, and I asked to play in the boys' football team. The teacher said, "No, because you haven't got football boots and a ball." Which I knew meant, "No, because you are a girl." So, I ran all the way home, got my boots and ball, went back to school, and showed the teacher. He couldn't do anything else other than let me play in the team. Dad thought it was hilarious.*

*'I went to a boarding school in Germany from the ages of 11 to 15 while my dad was posted there. I played all sorts of sports there. I loved it, don't get me wrong, but I missed football and the only time I got to play at that age was when I went home for the school holidays. There was a gang of us who lived on the same road with a green in front of the houses, so it was a perfect place to kick the ball about. All the boys would play there and would knock on my door to ask me to come out and play.'*

### *Jill Stockley*

*'My sister is around five years older than me, and we grew up in Nuneaton, Warwickshire. Backing onto the bottom of the garden of the house I grew up in was a football pitch. I remember there being games on that pitch all the time. All the children from the area who lived around the perimeter of the field would come and play football on this pitch.'*

In the chapters of Jill's childhood, a story unfolds of an enduring love for football. The moment she stepped through the door after school, the gravitational pull of the field behind her house took precedence. It was a meeting point for a lively group of kids, united by their shared passion for football – the beautiful game.

The field was the stadium where the kids played out their dreams, echoing with the sound of feet chasing the ball across the grass. Jill's enthusiasm, however, wasn't limited to the field; her enthusiasm extended to less conventional arenas, including the road and the driveway. It was a dedication to the sport that might have tested the patience of the next-door neighbours, as the rhythmic thud of the ball became the beat of her childhood.

*'My sister and I were always encouraged to play football and to be active, but Mum despaired occasionally. One day she popped her head out of the kitchen window to call us in for tea as she knew we were in the field at the back of the garden, and there I was, straddled at the top of a tree. She knew then she had her hands full with me!*

*'I was four years old when I got my first pair of football boots. Father Christmas left me them and I woke up on Christmas Day with the best present ever. My sister said I slept in those football boots for weeks.'*

In the years of childhood play, one constant remained – football. The bonds forged in the field extended beyond the realm of the game. Jill's closest ally, her best friend Dennis Harding, was a companion whose friendship stood the test of time. The friendship born on the field translated into a lifelong connection. Sports, as Jill acknowledges, has the unique ability to foster enduring relationships weaving a thread that connects individuals across the years.

Dennis respected her not just for her friendship but for her prowess on the football field. In a world where playing football with the boys was a testament to skill and resilience, Dennis held Jill in high esteem. The boys themselves took pride in having Jill as part of their team, affectionately declaring, 'Jill's our girl.' In the midst of childhood memories, the field became not just a playground but a place of friendship, respect and a shared love for the beautiful game.

*'I was lucky in secondary school because the PE teacher knew my dad could get tickets for the Villa games and he was a huge Aston Villa supporter. I wasn't allowed to play football in school, but he would let me kick the ball all day in the gym in return for seeing the next match at Villa Park!'*

### Val Cheshire

*'I am one of five children and have three brothers. That's why I got into football. My sister is the eldest. Middle brother Paul was the one brother who played football all the time and was the best. Our parents used to chuck us out of the house where we lived, the houses near Luton Airport,*

*and we would play football out in the streets. It was no use arguing with Mum and Dad about it, there was never any choice.'*

In the chronicles of Val's youth, the pages turn to a pivotal moment when standing up for oneself became an imperative lesson. The setting was outside the school gates, where the echoes of a heated dispute lingered in the air. The reason for this confrontation could be traced back to a confusing moment in a maths lesson, where Val struggled to grasp the solution to a problem.

A wave of relief washed over her when the teacher eventually unravelled the mystery. However, as she emerged from the school classroom, a boy seized the opportunity to mock her. In response, a confrontation ensued, and Val found herself engaged in a spirited fight with her provocateur. As the fight unfolded, her brothers formed a protective circle, observing the clash and lending their unwavering support.

For Val, this incident was not just a physical altercation; it symbolized the necessity of asserting herself, particularly in the face of challenges posed by the opposite gender. It became a testament to the resilience required to overcome obstacles and carve a space for herself. In the arena of life, especially when dealing with boys, Val learned that self-advocacy and a willingness to push boundaries were crucial ingredients for achieving her aspirations.

*'I started to get sporty at Ashcroft School (now Queen Elizabeth School). I used to love to play netball and hockey even though we hardly ever had proper PE teachers. The art teacher took netball, sometimes a biology teacher (who I'm sure was in her eighties) would take a class as well. I never forgave her because she arranged for me to have an*

*interview for a job on the same day as the school house sports
tournaments, and I was the captain of my school house! I didn't get
the job – and to be honest, I could never have worked at such a place as
Vauxhall Motors, but my dad made me go.*

*'I was a good girl at school – I knew I'd have to be, or I'd have been
in trouble at home. I've always been lacking in a bit of confidence to be
honest, perhaps from teachers not pushing me or giving me enough
encouragement at school. But you can't go back in time and do things
differently.'*

### Marlene Collins

*'I was always sporty growing up, I guess you could call me a typical
tomboy as most girls were labelled then if they were active. My mum
despaired at times and told me repeatedly that she never could put me
in a white dress, or anything light-coloured, as I was always running
around in fields, and I used to end up with dirt, mud and grass all
over me.'*

Marlene didn't grow up playing with the boys on the fields but
had a natural sporting ability and a one-match inspiration from her
elder sister, Pauline. She had a stint as a secretary at Whitbread
Breweries, a connection that serendipitously led them to Stratford-
upon-Avon. During a visit to a nearby biscuit factory, Pauline was
invited to play in an organized women's football match. The sight
of Pauline on the pitch, navigating the game with skill and
determination, ignited a spark within Marlene. A pure desire to
partake in the beautiful game burgeoned; an aspiration she hadn't
realized was possible for girls in that era.

The revelation that girls played football was a breakthrough moment for Marlene, a devoted supporter of Luton Town FC. Her family didn't get a television until she was 10 or 11, limiting her exposure to football matches in her formative years. Despite this, the seed of passion for the sport had been planted, waiting to blossom in later years.

Interestingly, the football match in Stratford-upon-Avon marked a singular instance of Pauline's foray into the sport. She was more of a netball player, but her natural athleticism paled in comparison to Marlene's. The younger sibling emerged as the embodiment of fierce competitiveness, approaching every sporting match with a relentless drive for victory. For Pauline, sports served more as a social hobby, a means to while away the time.

During her sporting pursuits, Marlene found herself drawn to the Girl Guides, relishing the sense of community and purpose it provided. However, a tinge of guilt now colours her recollections of summer camps. In the halls, if a ball materialized, Marlene would revel in spontaneous games, often challenging her friend Christine to bouts of 'who could keep the ball the longest'. It was a game where Marlene's prowess dominated, leaving her friend at the mercy of her competitive spirit. Looking back, Marlene hopes that Christine has forgiven those fervent displays of athleticism, painted against the backdrop of their shared Girl Guide memories.

*'When I was at school, I used to play hockey and netball a lot and was in the school teams. I didn't know of any teams outside of school though. In the playground, I would see the boys play football; of course, the girls were not allowed to get involved. I then went to Hitchin Road*

*Girls School in Luton, so there was definitely no football happening there!'*

### Carol Wilson

'I was born and bred in Newcastle. Me dad, Raymond, was from Gateshead, and he used to play for Gateshead Football Club. As soon as I was toddling along, I was kicking a football! We lived in a downstairs flat with a huge, long passageway, and I used to shuffle the ball up and down. When I got a bit older, I used to take the ball out into the backyard and play there all the time.

'There's only one time I can remember me mam asking me to wear a dress. It was just before Christmas; I was about five and I had asked for a "bogey". Mam wouldn't give me a bogey – it's a longboard with wheels off a pram attached, and a rope around the board. The kids used to push you down the back lanes on a bogey – no brakes on these things! We could have got killed because we used to fly across the crossroads at the bottom of the lane. To be fair, there weren't many cars around at that time, just mainly council trucks digging in the roads, but these bogeys used to go so fast!

'But even after lots of pleading, Mam still wouldn't buy me a bogey. I switched tactics and asked her to buy me a pram. Instantly, she said, "Oh of course you can have a pram! Why don't you have this one?" and pointed to a pretty, girly pram. It had big wheels, and that was no good to me, knowing what I was going to do to the pram, dismantling it and turning it into a bogey. Eventually, we chose a pram with the perfect wheels.

'In all fairness, I didn't dismantle the pram, I got the bloke up the road to instead. He asked, "Are you sure your mam said yes lass?" And I said, "Yes of course!" My gosh, I didn't really know what I was doing was so wrong. Me mam was so upset when she found out I had turned that pram into the fastest bogey I could. Me dad laughed!

'Me dad and I were close. Really close. He worked for a company called Newcastle Tea Company and they had a Sunday League team. Dad used to play in a park that had loads of football pitches, and he used to take me along in the pram and I had to stay in there until half-time. Then I was allowed to kick a ball on the grass. It was a different experience for me, I remember it still today. From that moment on, whenever we went out as a family, we took the ball, so I was always playing, whether it was in the park or on the beach.

'There was a park called Leazes Park, not far from where we used to live. Me dad and I used to go there a lot to kick a ball about, and Leazes Park backs on to St James' Park, Newcastle United's football ground. We didn't have any money as a family. We were skint in them days, really skint. I remember one day when it was snowing. I was only about five or six years old, and the snow came up to about halfway up me waist. Newcastle United had a big, corrugated iron fence around it back then, not like it is now. Me dad and I stood at the side of the fence, and we used to hear this roar! It was like a huge jumbo jet flying over us, it was so loud! Me dad turned to me and said, "Ah they've just scored! That's everybody clapping, shouting and jumping about!" I remember then thinking, "Oh, I wish I was inside there. I wish I was inside." And I thought, "One day I'm going to get to go in there." I will always remember standing there with me dad taking in all the excitement that was over the wall.

*'Even when I was on my own, I used to kick a ball against the back lane fast and try and get it back and see how many times I could get it back and forwards. The boys didn't want to play with me at first. Not at all. When they saw me kicking a ball though, they thought, "Hang on a minute, that girl can play!" I got the invite. At first, it was only me and two other boys, but then other kids would join in. No other girls though.'*

While the FA Council and medical practitioners were arguing about the inappropriateness of girls and women kicking a ball when boys and men were championed to do so, girls had no choice but to play with the local lads in their area. These boys had been told that girls don't play football, yet this didn't stop some girls from trying and proving their worth to them.

Footballing skills were honed at home with brothers, dads or cousins, and then it was time to shine with the lads in the community. For the girls, they had to show they could be one of the boys.

The boys approved. The girls could match their footballing ability, and some of the girls were better.

Playing football with their friends where the girls could shine was their passion. All the girls had a natural sporting ability and athleticism, yet when they were at school, football was off limits and the teachers were rigid in their approach to the girls' footballing talent. It was a resounding 'no' to kicking a ball, the only balls the girls were allowed to play with were the ones in netball or hockey. A girl was allowed to throw a ball or hit a ball with a stick, but no way were girls allowed to kick a ball.

Football was apparently unsuitable for the female body.

# Chapter 2
# Mastering the Beautiful Game

---

Unfortunately, women's football in several of Europe's major countries faced similar challenges to those in England during the same period. As the sport began to flourish across the continent, European associations, like the Football Association in England, felt threatened by the rise of the women's game. Consequently, many imposed bans on women playing football.

Germany had a long history of women playing football, dating back to the 18th century. The first clubs formed in the 1920s after the First World War endured for nearly three decades before the German Football Association banned women from the sport in 1955. Though discussions about establishing a women's football association occurred in the 1960s, they never materialized. It wasn't until 30 October 1970, that the German Football Association allowed women to play again, albeit with significant restrictions. They could only play in warm weather, football boots with studs were banned, and games were limited to 70 minutes. A league was formed in 1971, and the first championship took place in 1974, won by TuS Wörrstadt.

In France, an independent women's football federation, led by pioneering figure Alice Milliat, established a proper league in 1918. Despite this progress, a ban was instituted in 1932, and the sport wasn't revived until 1975 when the French Football Federation provided funds to restart the league, allowing amateur and semi-professional teams to compete again.

In Spain, women were forbidden from playing football between 1930 and 1975. The Spanish Football Federation didn't recognize women's football as a sport until the early 1980s, and a national league wasn't created until 1988.

In Italy, the National Olympic Committee prevented women from participating in tournaments and matches until the formation of the Italian Women's Football Federation in 1968 and the creation of an Italian Championship. The Italian federation quickly became one of the strongest in Europe as clubs embraced the sport in search of professional football opportunities.

Even in football-loving Brazil, during the Vargas regime and the military dictatorship, playing football became a criminal offence for women and girls.

The success of England's national football team at the 1966 FIFA World Cup ignited a surge of interest in football among women in England. With the tournament broadcast worldwide and fuelled by the empowerment of women rejecting male-imposed restrictions, the latter half of the 1960s witnessed a global expansion of the women's game.

It was now time for the girls to find teams to play in, in order to develop their game more. For some, it was easier than for others.

## Finding their feet

Chris's introduction to girls' football was at the age of 13. It all began when a fellow school student approached her, revealing the existence of a new girls' football team on the estate. Intrigued, Chris decided to explore this opportunity. However, upon arriving at the training session, she couldn't help but feel a bit disheartened when she saw the lack of skill of the other players. Nevertheless, recognizing their enthusiasm, undeterred Chris and the team ventured to join a league.

To contribute in the best way possible, Chris found herself assigned to the goalkeeper position. This decision was made to keep the score as low as possible given her apparent prowess in that role. She hated being a goalkeeper, but Chris selflessly embraced the position for the sake of the team.

Louise was introduced to the game at the age of 11. Encouraged by her father, she eagerly joined a newly formed team called Tottonians. Excitement surged through her as she became the youngest, yet standout, player on the team. Louise's style of play was described as unorthodox, showcasing her natural talent for dribbling, shooting and making precise crosses. With no formal coaching, the team relied on self-discovery to improve their skills, fostering a unique learning environment.

After a year, Louise was scouted to play for Patstone United, sponsored by a local sports shop. Training at The Dell occasionally, the home ground for Southampton FC men, added a special touch to the experience. Despite being considerably younger than her teammates, Louise remained focused on her love for football rather than forming friendships. She wore her hair short, many believed, to resemble a boy, but Louise laughed at this, saying it was a personal choice for convenience rather than an attempt to be perceived as male and sneak into boys' teams to play football!

Home matches for Patstone United took place on Southampton Common, an environment riddled with challenges such as long grass, potholes, dog waste, below-par nets and a dilapidated changing room. 'That's what you just had to put up with,' Louise says. 'We were girls, and no provisions were made for us. We were told we were lucky we even had a fixture.'

Gill's brother had started dating a girl who lived in a town called Thame and knew how much Gill loved football. Gill, being 12 years old at this time, was still desperate to play competitive football, and the girlfriend told Gill, 'There's a women's football team in Thame', which was 16km (10 miles) from Aylesbury. She introduced Gill and her dad to the manager and soon Gill was straight into a training session. Seeing Gill's talent immediately, the manager signed Gill on the spot and put her into the reserve side. Gill said, 'An all-girls football team! I didn't even know any other girls who played football, let alone in a team!' Finally, Gill could play a football match, without someone saying, 'You can't because you're a girl.'

*'For the first time, I felt I belonged somewhere.'*
Gill

Gill played for the reserve side of Thame Wanderers as they were the younger girls. She won 'Player of the Year' in her first season, and then she was selected for the first team the following season. The girls in this team were all ages, with an average age of 20 years old, and Gill was still only 12 at the time! It didn't deter her as she stood out on the pitch, mainly from playing with the boys and knowing how to tackle. She was incredibly focused and always played to win.

All the girls at Thame loved football and all felt accepted for being a girl who loved to play the game. They were a team, and Gill felt great to be part of something.

It was a big step up from playing with the boys on the green, but with Gill's determination, she proved that she was good enough to be there. Thame were a very good team, one of the top teams in the country. They had girls join from Oxford and surrounding areas and even managed to have a player/coach from Oxford United to train them. This was all voluntary, but he saw that the girls were serious about their football.

Thame played matches on the local recreation ground, as at this time of course women's football was banned from playing on any FA-affiliated pitches. There were no changing facilities for the girls to use, so they used to change in the scout hut down the road, and then walk back to the pitch. As it was a local recreation pitch it got used a lot by many boys'/men's teams, and as the girls played on a Sunday afternoon, and were the last to play (as they were not allowed to book the pitch or play before the boys or men), it was often a bit of a marsh by the time Thame Ladies got their chance.

One of the girls used to submit a match report for the local newspaper, *The Thame Gazette*, with the results and who scored. As Gill was a winger, she scored regularly, and her name was often in the paper. She was getting noticed.

Lillian's journey into women's football began with a chance encounter – an advert in the *Northampton Chronicle and Echo* seeking ladies interested in joining a team. A friend informed Lillian about the opportunity. Seizing the moment, Lillian dialled the number in the paper, only to be met with the query, 'Can you play Sunday?' It was a Thursday, leaving her with minimal time to prepare. When she enquired about the playing location (and told it was Brixworth), she realized her lack of familiarity with the place and had to rely on her uncle to drive her to Northampton, where she would be picked up by one of her new teammates.

At the age of 19, Lillian, whose previous football experience involved casual kickabouts with boys, found herself questioning whether someone would brief her on the rules before taking the field. But her uncertainties surrounding the game didn't diminish her enthusiasm. Coincidentally, when her future husband, John, initially met her, he had no inkling of her football prowess. However, upon discovering her talent, he took pride in having a girlfriend with remarkable football skills, often boasting about it to his friends.

★

Marlene's initiation into women's football unfolded through the corridors of the International Supermarket on Waller Street, Luton. Having left school at the age of 15 during an era when such early exits were permissible, she caught wind of a colleague's desire to establish a ladies football team. Intrigued by the prospect, Marlene attended the training sessions, although the initial enthusiasm from the girls eventually faded.

At 18, Marlene transitioned from her position at International Supermarket to become a telephonist at the Post Office. Unbeknown to her, the realms of Luton Ladies, Chiltern Valley Ladies and other local women's football teams were thriving, centred around the playing fields on Ashcroft Road.

Jean Bentley, a telephone supervisor at the Post Office, is the woman credited with the formation of the 'Luton Daytels'. The name reflected their shared occupation as Post Office telephonists, defined by incessant phone answering during the day – 'Day Tel(ephonists)'. Another key figure was Pat Dunn, deeply involved in football and trailblazing as one of the country's earliest female referees. Pat's journey to attain the necessary training and navigate through FA-related challenges was fraught with arguments, but her determination prevailed. (Notably, she joined the later Mexico trip as a chaperone, trainer and first-aider.)

Despite Marlene's later reticence in expressing her feelings from her football playing days, the experience held profound significance for her. The joy of taking the pitch alongside fellow female enthusiasts, coupled with her natural talent and interest in the sport, propelled her into the role of captain for the Daytels. Drawing on her netball experience, Marlene swiftly grasped positional dynamics on the football field. Many teammates were novices, but the camaraderie and sense of belonging eclipsed any skill differentials.

While the FA ban and the political constraints on girls using FA pitches posed challenges, Marlene and her team persevered, arranging matches and making the best of available pitches. Her journey in women's football burgeoned, propelled by the guidance of a supportive supervisor, Jean.

Yvonne's first love wasn't football, but athletics, and she excelled in hurdles. Despite being deeply entrenched in track and field, an impromptu football match between boys and girls after a school meet changed the trajectory of her sporting pursuits. The intensity of that particular match sparked a newfound interest in football, leading Yvonne to discover the 'Yellow Scorpions', a team based in Stopsley, Luton, when she was around 14 or 15 years old.

Transitioning from athletics to football, Yvonne's shift was fired by a desire to play a sport she had unexpectedly grown passionate about. The knowledge about the Yellow Scorpions likely came through word of mouth, with the team's manager, Mr Toyer, residing conveniently in the same row of houses as Yvonne. Intrigued and accompanied by friends, Yvonne attended one of their training sessions.

Naturally gravitating towards the wing position due to her track and field background, Yvonne's athleticism shone through. Her quick starts, honed through years of hurdles, seamlessly translated into football, making her an asset on the pitch. With innate football skills cultivated from childhood games in her neighbourhood, Yvonne showcased both her ability to tackle and evade opponents with finesse. The Yellow Scorpions, a diverse mix of abilities, provided a blend of seriousness and casual play that occasionally frustrated Yvonne given her competitive nature.

Despite this, Yvonne found comfort in her team and continued playing for the Yellow Scorpions for a year or two. Reflecting on her football journey, she acknowledged that a more outgoing personality might have propelled her to consider joining a team like the Daytels. However, contentment within her familiar team and a reluctance to disrupt that dynamic deterred her from pursuing opportunities with more competitive teams like Chiltern Valley.

For Yvonne, it was more than football. Many of the Lost Lionesses talk about 'finding their place and being able to be the person they want to be'. Yvonne, for the first time, found a sport that matched her personality. Even being the third eldest of seven children, Yvonne claims that no one would know she was in the room; she would be the one in the corner, sitting there listening to everyone else, trying to hide.

During a big athletics competition for the school, with many other schools competing, Yvonne was truly petrified and found the whole experience extremely daunting. The next athletics competition she was due to compete in, one of the sports teachers came around the house to find Yvonne, because she had begged her mum to let her stay off school as she didn't want to go. Yvonne was overcome with anxiety and nerves. She gave up athletics after that moment, knowing she never wanted to go through that ordeal again. The lack of confidence was affecting her, and she wasn't ever going to enjoy doing that. Yvonne did not like to be out on her own as the centre of attention.

However, with football, there wasn't so much pressure and attention on just herself, the focus was on the team. That made a big difference to Yvonne and her self-esteem.

Jill's introduction to organized football came unexpectedly during a day at the cricket with her father, who ran a youth cricket side. At around 11 years old, while casually kicking a ball around with a group of boys, someone took notice and approached her father with a suggestion. The person recommended that Jill explore joining a girls' team in Nuneaton, specifically 'Sterling Metals', named after a local factory – a common naming convention for women's football teams associated with factories during that time.

The team initially thrived but faced a setback when the factory decided against supporting the women's team. Undeterred, the group relocated to Attleborough Cricket Ground, which housed a football pitch. Renaming themselves 'Nuneaton Wanderers', they embarked on a footballing journey that extended beyond local leagues. Tournaments across the country became a regular feature, including international trips to France and Belgium during Easter breaks. The team's resourcefulness allowed them to stay in empty boarding schools for affordability and turning the long coach travels into enjoyable adventures. Jill's older sister also joined the team.

The Nuneaton area boasted a vibrant footballing scene, with the

Nuneaton League and other women's leagues in Warwickshire contributing to a robust setup. Jill recalls approximately eight teams participating in the Nuneaton League. Despite the prevailing ban on girls and women on FA-accredited pitches, exceptions occurred, allowing Jill and her teammates to experience playing on proper pitches.

Jill's footballing feats extended beyond local competitions, reaching the women's FA Cup later rounds. These matches were played on local men's team pitches but also at esteemed stadiums such as at The Dell, Southampton men's home ground, showing the desire to play the highest level of women's football at the time on FA-accredited pitches. Nuneaton Wanderers became a stepping stone for Jill's progression, leading her to represent Warwickshire and eventually the Midlands in regional competitions. The thriving football community in her area provided Jill with invaluable experiences, shaping her love for the game during her formative years.

In 1967, Arthur Hobbs, a carpenter hailing from Kent, demonstrated foresight by organizing a tournament in Deal, a coastal town situated between Dover and Ramsgate. The inaugural tournament saw the participation of eight teams, a number that swiftly expanded to 32 teams the following year. Hobbs, aware of a handful of clubs, including the formidable Manchester Corinthians and Fodens from the North of England, brought them together. As the tournament gained momentum, so did the concept of establishing a governing body.

After the 1969 tournament, there were 47 teams taking part – a sign that the popularity of women's football was on the rise.

Arthur Hobbs' tournament in Deal for girls' football highlights the importance of having a male voice in women's sports. The top positions in sports were held by men in the 1960s so they had all the power and influence over important decisions. Having men supporting and fighting for the girls' inclusion gave their quest for support and more opportunities more gravitas. These men were fathers of daughters, and brothers of girls, who could see the injustice and the gender inequality in football, where there was talent and passion.

Trudy's revelation about women's football unfolded during a family evening watching *Opportunity Knocks* on TV in the UK after their return from her father's RAF posting to Germany. As the programme concluded, host Hughie Green made an announcement that caught Trudy's attention. He mentioned the charity ladies' football matches scheduled in Deal in 1969, urging viewers to attend and support the event.

Trudy's enthusiasm surged, and she bombarded her father with requests to go. 'I shouted at my dad, "What was that? Dad, can we go? Can we go? Please?" After relentless pleading, he finally relented, agreeing to take the family to the event in Kent. Upon arrival, Trudy was captivated by the sight of various teams, including some from Scotland, participating in the matches. However, what left the most profound impression on her were the countless women and girls engaged in football, all wearing proper football kits – and no male players at all. The presence of supposedly well-known teams that she was unaware of added to her astonishment. It was an unexpected revelation for Trudy, who had no prior knowledge of such events.

Overwhelmed by the experience, Trudy turned to her father and declared her newfound aspiration. She insisted, 'I want to do this. This is what I want to do. Why can't I do this? How do we find out? Where can I play?' Determined to pursue her passion, Trudy, accompanied by her father, traversed the different pitches, meticulously collecting contact details from various teams. The subsequent process involved the toil of writing letters to teams, requesting trials, and the agonizing wait for replies – a far cry from the immediacy of today's emails. Trudy admired the skill and dedication of the women she observed on the field, aspiring to join their ranks and become a part of the captivating world of women's football.

There is a stark contrast between the present and the past when it comes to girls' football and the opportunities on offer. With the accessibility of women's football on television and numerous club options for those who have played in their gardens with their families, contemporary girls benefit from this extensive exposure and many options to pursue the sport.

This is in sharp contrast with the experiences of the Lost Lionesses, where such pathways and opportunities were non-existent. Despite some living close to the sports and social club where the teams practised, they were completely unaware of any women's football occurring!

And because of the lack of these opportunities most girls required the helping hands of their fathers and brothers to start them on the first rungs of the footballing ladder.

## Paternal influences

Carol had a close bond with her father. He worked for the Newcastle Tea Company, which had a Sunday League team. Encouraged by him, Carol participated in various sports at school. One day, she received a remarkable opportunity – an invitation to a week-long sports camp in Scotland with England coaches. Though she hesitated due to financial constraints, her father's support made it possible. Carol, feeling guilty about the financial burden, initially kept the invitation a secret. But eventually her father found out and, determined to ensure his daughter didn't miss out, worked extra hours to cover the expenses.

Likewise, Trudy fondly remembered her father's unwavering support for her football passion. Her dad, seemingly impervious to the negative attitudes surrounding female footballers, carried a resilient, positive perspective. In retrospect, Trudy recognized that he had a penchant for championing the underdog in any situation.

Her father's love for football became a shared bond between them, and they often played the sport together. For him, the simple joy of engaging in the game with his daughter overshadowed societal expectations and stereotypes. In Trudy's recollections, their connection through football remained a testament to her father's open-mindedness and the genuine joy they found in pursuing a shared passion.

'Dad always said to me, "Don't ever let anybody tell you that girls will never be as good as boys in football. You will be as good, but it will be in a different way." He had the same view as Harry Batt in that the girls' game will be more thrilling to watch, because they'll have to be more technical and quicker, therefore more entertaining. And it's true, women can't expect to compete with men. And women shouldn't want to. It's like comparing apples and pears. My dad was a massive supporter of girls playing football. Massive. He believed in it.'

And it wasn't just Trudy's father who supported his daughter in her footballing endeavours. Louise's dad took her to her first football match at The Dell to watch Southampton aged eight years old. She turned to her dad and said, 'I can do that. It doesn't look too hard.' With that revelation, her dad supported her to be as good as the Southampton footballers she saw that day and even used to drive the coach for the girls' team to take them to tournaments like the one in Deal.

Jill's father, Albert Stockley, was a dedicated sports enthusiast who served as the chairman of the Aston Villa Supporters' Club and worked as a Football Talent Scout for the Midlands club. Growing up, Jill accompanied her father on numerous journeys across the country to watch football matches and scout potential players. She embraced a multi-sport background, actively participating in netball, hockey and swimming competitions under her father's supportive gaze.

In the fields of Nuneaton, Jill honed her skills against bigger boys, guided by her father's mantra, 'Remember, the bigger they are, the harder they fall.' This philosophy shaped her playing style, as she evolved into a defensive player with a keen awareness of the dynamics on the pitch. Survival on those fields demanded constant vigilance, cultivating a natural defensive prowess in Jill, albeit with a touch of tenacity that she humorously referred to as being a 'bit of a dirty player'.

The challenges on those makeshift pitches prepared Jill for encounters with rough-playing teams. Bruises and black eyes became badges of honour from matches where physicality often overshadowed finesse. While some girls faced misogyny in football, Jill found herself fortunate to have her father's unwavering support. Her family, however, struggled with the expectations of society. Jill's uncle and grandfather expressed reservations about Jill's footballing, suggesting ballet or dancing would be better choices over football for a young girl.

Jill's selection for the 1970 Women's World Cup in Italy met with opposition from her uncle, who deemed football unsuitable for girls. Even her grandfather contemplated sending her to boarding school to divert her attention from the game. Despite family objections, Jill's parents, especially her father, weathered the criticism and stood by her side. Reflecting on her journey, Jill expressed deep gratitude for her parents' resilience and their decision to let her embark on those remarkable footballing adventures.

*'My dad was my biggest supporter, and I am so grateful that a man was encouraging about women's sport at that time. He was proud of me. He would say, "This is my daughter. She plays football." He would let me be me. He would say, "You've got to be the best. If you're going to play, be the best."'*

Meanwhile, over in Aylesbury, Gill fondly recollected the abundance of playmates she had for football, thanks to her sport-loving brothers – Steve, a fervent football enthusiast, and Dave, who leaned towards boxing but also shared a love for the beautiful game. Even Tim, the youngest sibling at four years her junior, eagerly joined in. Gill's residence was a hub of activity, with Tim's friends routinely knocking on their door, specifically enquiring about Gill's availability for a game.

Gill's father, a seasoned footballer who once captained Wing football club, imparted his love of the sport to the family. Gill's parents, embodying a spirit of unwavering support, lent their encouragement and assistance consistently.

For Gill, Sunday meant football training and matches, with her father taking on the role of chauffeur for this football-centric family. Given the family's substantial size, their commitment to each child's sporting endeavours presented a considerable undertaking. Yet, their parents embraced the challenge with pride, fostering a norm where family life seamlessly intertwined with football. The entire household revolved around the beautiful game, shaping a lifestyle centred on shared sporting passions.

In Luton, Marlene remembers there were a few men, some of the engineers from work, who used to come and support the Daytels' matches. Overall, the men were supportive of women's football, especially the boyfriends, husbands, male coaches and managers. They saw how much it meant to the women and were with them all the way, all trying to get the women's game moving.

When it came to male influence at home, Paula's mother was a single parent so her three older brothers were the inspiration.

At 14 years old, Paula experienced her first international football match – an age many would consider quite tender. However, she doesn't describe herself as a typical 'young' teenager. Life had thrust significant responsibilities upon her shoulders from a young age due to family circumstances. Paula, 11 years older than her baby brother Stephen, often found herself in the role of a caretaker mother because her mum, Nora, had to return to work shortly after Stephen's birth, given the limited maternity leave available during those times.

Paula's daily routine involved preparing her younger brother for the day – ensuring he had his bottle, placing him in the pram, and pushing him to her auntie's house before heading to school. At just 12 years old, Paula juggled these responsibilities, evolving into a young 'mini mum' and shouldering housework chores after school. Raised in a single-parent household, Paula's maturity and resilience surpassed her years.

During her youth, Paula didn't fully grasp the challenges her mother faced in raising five children alone. Instead, she adopted a pragmatic 'just get on with it' attitude, a trait inherited from her mother. By the age of 14, Paula exhibited remarkable maturity, determination and resilience – a testament to the lessons learned from her mother.

Although Paula sensed that her mum might not have been entirely enthusiastic about her playing football, Nora never directly expressed any opposition. Curiously, whenever there was a newspaper article featuring Paula's football exploits, her mum would proudly share it with her friends at work. An uncle later revealed that Paula's grandmother in Ireland took great pride in her football achievements, suggesting that Paula's mum must have boasted about her accomplishments to the family across the seas.

> *'My mother always said, "I have four sons, but it's my daughter who is the footballer!"'*
> Paula

### Facing adversity

There were inevitably some men who couldn't keep their opinions to themselves when they saw a group of girls and women playing a sport they felt was just for them. Even with the sexist abuse being shouted at them, and no sports bras for the female anatomy when playing the game, the girls carried on, determined not to let this stop them.

There was no abuse at an early age for Trudy. However, she remembered the abuse starting as she got older, once she'd gone through puberty. That's when Trudy remembers the comments starting as if this was a sign for it to be allowed – a girl blossoming into a woman means it is 'acceptable' for men to shout about a girl's body. Trudy, when running with the ball, would have shouts of, 'Oh she's got the wobbles on!' as there were no breast supports in those days, no specific kit at all for women.

In the quest to play football, girls faced persistent barriers erected by the FA. Their rationale, often absurd, revolved around the notion that girls and women were ill-suited to the sport due to presumed anatomical vulnerabilities. It seemed as if the FA still had concerns that playing football – or specifically being hit by a football – would inhibit a woman's ability to conceive – a view put forward by medical experts, influencing the 1921 FA Council ban. It's a well-known joke with professional female footballers that the authorities made up of men thought 'women's ovaries might fall out' if they were to play the sport.

Acknowledging the inherent physiological differences between male and female bodies, the challenges were palpable. Wearing white shorts during matches presented a discomforting problem for female players, particularly during menstruation. With only half-time providing a brief respite, some players had no option but to hastily retreat during matches. In an era devoid of the convenient menstrual products available today, and lacking innovations like internal pant lining in shorts, female footballers had to put up with the limitations imposed by the unforgiving nature of their circumstances.

Adding to the adversity, the absence of sports bras exacerbated the challenges faced by female players. When matches unfolded on the local common the experience was tainted by the unsettling presence of onlookers, because modest audiences of 20 to 30 spectators often gathered. Male passers-by, often oblivious to the gravity of their actions, resorted to shouting derogatory comments around the pitch. The verbal abuse hurled at the female players reached levels of sheer vulgarity, exposing the harsh realities women endured in their pursuit of playing the sport they loved.

Louise often heard insults like: 'You're a lesbian!'; 'Why are you playing football? You're a girl, girls can't play football!'; 'What do you think you're doing? Hahaha, you're absolute dog s★★t'; 'Let's see those tits bounce!'

She navigated the comments with resilience and determination, enduring a barrage of verbal abuse brimming with disdain. Positioned on the left wing, she stood defiantly by the sideline, subjected to a relentless stream of derogatory comments from grown men. The urge to respond with swearing, even uttering a few 'Bog offs', proved futile as the laughter echoed around her. This distressing experience unfolded during her formative years, from the ages of 11 to 14, as she faced the harsh reality that these individuals found it acceptable to subject a young girl to such abuse.

In the face of this, Louise found solace in the resolve to prove her detractors wrong, using their unjust scorn as a catalyst to elevate her game. However, Louise still felt perplexed as to why grown men would target a young girl in such a manner. There was an overarching sense of opposition to women's involvement in football, a sentiment that Louise and her fellow female players sought to challenge. Their desire was not to overshadow the men's game but to assert their right to play as women. Despite their plea for recognition, the authorities seemed willing to overlook their plight, accepting the mistreatment they endured.

*'One way of shutting up the men shouting abuse to me was to go in for a great tackle, get up, dribble around three players, and then shoot and score in the top corner. So, I did that. I used to ask my dad, "Why don't men like us?" and Dad just said, "It's simply because you're a woman. They don't like it because you can play as well as they can."'*

# Chapter 3
# Harry Batt

---

Harry Batt was born on the 7th day of the 7th month, in 1907. 07.07.07 the lucky 7s. In biblical terms, the number 777 is deemed to be God's triumph over the Devil's number 666. In spiritual terms, it can signify a message of 'stay strong and continue to move forward on your journey – even through changes and obstacles.' Both are apt in Harry's life.

Harry wasn't the biggest man in stature, at just 1.65m (5ft 5in), but what he didn't have in height, he made up for in character. He loved being the centre of attention and was a natural extrovert. Harry was one of life's showmen, a professional entertainer in fact, and was always playing that role. Harry was a talented singer – a tenor – and he likened himself to the great opera singers. Often on the bus, travelling to matches with the girls, he would give renditions of his favourite songs. His voice was incredible, and he wasn't afraid of singing any time and any place.

Harry's wife, June, was a lot younger than Harry and they met on the entertainment scene. June was a contortionist and together they used to perform all over the country as 'June Alberto and the Singing Stevedore!' in the early 1950s. June gave up her entertainment career to have a family with Harry, and they had three boys, the youngest being Keith, born in 1961. June was Harry's rock, his support, his steadiness next to his exuberance.

Even though Harry was a flamboyant character, perhaps even eccentric in many ways, he was very strong-minded. He was forthright with his views and didn't like injustice. He never liked any wrongdoing, and he hated suffering of any kind. As a veteran of the Spanish Civil War (he served as part of the International Brigade), he was always on the side of the underdog.

There's no doubt that Harry was a visionary, a dreamer and he had ideas about the future. He was always looking for a niche, that thing that could make him money, or stand out from the crowd. He had that entrepreneurial mindset and when he had an idea, he was determined to see it through.

From his time in the Spanish Civil War, Harry picked up Spanish, German, French and even Urdu. Yet in his later years, he was working as a bus driver in Luton. He wrote a weekly column in the local Luton newspaper documenting his thoughts and what he saw while he drove the bus on his route.

In 1966 England won the men's World Cup and the whole country was celebrating wildly. After the final, Harry had a concept, a women's football concept. England's Bobby Moore lifted the Jules Rimet trophy, and Harry said out loud, 'Why is there no women's football?' Keith, still very young at the time, remembers this question being asked amid the celebrations in the front room, and it was like a light bulb switching on for Harry. He wouldn't let go of the idea of women's football and said,

*'It's going to be as big as the men's game, it's going to be as*
*big because there's going to be a women's Arsenal or there's*
*going to be a women's Manchester United one day.*
*This is going to happen.'*
Harry Batt

An English Ladies' Football Association (ELFA) was established in the immediate aftermath of the ban in 1921 with predictions of a membership of 'fifty or sixty women's clubs' and a competition consisting of five divisions. However, this was short-lived and only a few teams such as Manchester Corinthians survived, playing matches abroad due to the lack of other teams and support for pitches.

As society began to change during the 1960s, women started to campaign more for their social rights and with this came sport. Women's football in England saw significant growth. While the exact number of teams can vary according to accounts, several notable women's teams emerged during that time. Some of the leading teams in Leicestershire were British Railway, Emgals, Leicester City Supporters and Rainbow Dazzlers.

Women's amateur football leagues began to surface but were very dependent on location and support from local men's clubs and willing volunteers. The exact number of women's teams and leagues is unknown.

Harry wanted his idea to become a reality, so Harry and June decided to form a team. Harry started out building a team called 'Luton Ladies' but later Harry decided to break away, and in 1967 Chiltern Valley Ladies was born.

## A new dawn

In 1969, FIFA, the world governing body of football, announced that control of the women's game should be the concern of the national associations. Worldwide, that announcement did not spur much change, if any, because in many places the sport was effectively still banned for females. The FA, however, established the Women's Football Association (WFA) that year, in an attempt to start to organize the women's game due to the demand to recognize women's rights in society. It was proposed that the participants of the 1969 Deal tournament would form the nucleus and an initial meeting took place in November 1969 with representation by 38 of the 51 clubs affiliated and a Steering Committee was formed to draw up a constitution.

The following people were also elected to the committee alongside Harry Batt: Patricia Dunn (the pioneering female referee), Arthur Hobbs (orchestrator of the Deal tournament) and Patricia Gregory. At just 19 years old, Gregory became a pioneering activist for women's football, and was among the first women to challenge media and officials on why girls and women were banned from playing. Undeterred by the FA's ruling, she and her improvised football team, named White Ribbon, travelled across the country, seeking matches against youth men's teams. They advertised in a football magazine to find opponents, which caught the attention of Arthur Hobbs. Following their meeting, Hobbs and Gregory decided to establish the South-East of England League. Between 1967 and 1969, they collaboratively set up numerous leagues.

Later in 1969, the FA rescinded the ruling of 1921 with the FA confirming:

1. *That the Council's Resolution of 1921 be rescinded.*
2. *That women's football teams may be allowed to use grounds under the jurisdiction of The Football Association and registered referees may be permitted to officiate at matches between women's teams.*
3. *That the appropriate Rules of The Football Association be amended accordingly.*

The newly formed WFA was invited to observe women's football in Czechoslovakia that year. Harry, June and Keith, along with the newly formed WFA, went on the long coach journey to Eastern Europe.

In the early hours of the morning, at 5am precisely, the journey encountered an unexpected halt at the border to enter the Communist bloc. Troops intercepted their bus, brandishing weapons, and subjected the passengers to an unsettling ordeal. Keith, still a child at that time, found himself bewildered, unaware of the events unfolding. The soldiers ordered everyone off the bus, forming a line along its side, as they meticulously searched the vehicle for a prolonged three hours. Eventually, with nothing incriminating discovered, except an abundance of football kits, the passengers were allowed to resume their journey.

The Czechoslovakian Army and the Iron Curtain weren't the only issues out there though . . .

There was no hotel, more of a complex that resembled a prison campus. No one was allowed anywhere on their own and all movements were restricted.

If the circumstances weren't testing enough, Keith recalls friction developing among the English visitors. During the journey, a conflict surfaced between the WFA officials and Harry. The details remained elusive, but what became evident was that his father fell out of favour. As a family, they found themselves ostracized in Czechoslovakia, as a palpable shift in attitudes isolated them from certain individuals. Keith vividly recalls the exchange of harsh words, marking the inception of a noticeable divide within the group.

After returning from the trip, and even though tensions were running high between the WFA committee members, Harry seemed to be spurred on by the women's football he saw there. He returned home to Luton with more enthusiasm and passion for Chiltern Valley Ladies and was determined to build an unstoppable team. This they did. Chiltern Valley Ladies won over and over again.

A game was organized against Arthur Hobbs's team (made up of his selected players from across the country). Hobbs was at this time the president of the WFA. By half-time, it was 5-0 to Chiltern

Valley. The second half started and even though a completely different team came onto the pitch (players from other teams that Arthur had sourced for this match), it didn't make any difference. It ended up a thrashing – 14-0. June diplomatically said to Harry, 'This is not going to make us friends.'

And June was right. This match and the scoreline infuriated Hobbs. But the big victory against the president of the WFA did wonders for Harry's ego and gave him even more passion and enthusiasm for the team.

Harry always took pride in his appearance. Photographs of Harry show him smartly dressed in a suit with his glasses, never in a tracksuit, even when he was managing the football team. He loved the fact that he was able to create a football environment for the girls and allow them to shine, but he took his role as a manager seriously, making sure he was well-presented in case a business opportunity came about.

While Harry was the frontman of Chiltern Valley, June was the background support. She was very much involved with the decision-making and supporting everything Harry did. A far cry from her entertainment days, June was a remarkable woman, known for her unwavering adoration and commitment to being Harry's wife. She was often described as matronly and motherly and exuded a caring nature to the girls on the football team, prepared the refreshments and travel arrangements, and was the first-aider if needed. But even with this nurturing nature, June possessed a stern side that emerged when necessary, ensuring all things were in order, and that included the girls. She was highly practical and organized, and seemed ready for any challenge that was put in her way. June exhibited incredible attention to detail and with her dedication to women's football, it made her an indispensable pillar of strength for her family and the women's football community.

Back home in Luton, a constant symphony of clacking keys emanated from Harry's typewriter, a tool that never seemed to rest. This typewriter was the connection through which Harry tirelessly networked, generating a continuous stream of reports and letters. The keys bore the unmistakable marks of wear, a testament to the relentless cadence of Harry's fingers striking them. Each evening, Harry would settle in, fingers flying over the keys, contributing articles for the local paper in Luton and composing a multitude of letters rallying support for his vision of women's football.

There's a vivid recollection from Keith, of Harry approaching his boss, a financial plea in hand, seeking a loan from his wages. The purpose? To procure a football kit for the girls he was coaching and managing. His preference for green and white manifested in a mishmash of scraped-together pieces, none perfectly coordinated but gathered together with earnest efforts.

The financial struggle continued, prompting the family, alongside others, to embark on a multitude of ventures – sponsored walks, jumble sales and any conceivable means – to raise funds for the team. The stark reality was that there was no support forthcoming from the FA or WFA. However, within the community, a groundswell of support burgeoned. Every family embraced the cause, contributing their share to the collective endeavour. The community at large eagerly jumped on board, exemplifying a spirit of solidarity. There was no discord or reproach; instead, everyone echoed a chorus of, 'I want to help! What can I do? How can I support?'

There was this incredible attitude about women's football and support for the girls who played. Families of daughters, neighbours and friends, all within the context of the rising equality of women in society, meant that men didn't understand why there were not more opportunities for girls wanting to play the sport. It seemed that the FA and the authorities missed chances to come into the communities to experience this, watch the girls play, and listen to them as well as their coaches. If they had, then maybe they would have had a completely different outlook and a more positive approach to girls and women playing the game.

As the weekend dawned, a familiar routine awaited Keith, his responsibilities etched into the rhythm of those days. Ensuring the kits were ready, the oranges sliced and the water bottles full, became his regular tasks. Despite his tender age, Keith embraced his role with a sense of purpose, understanding that Chiltern Valley Ladies was the focal point in his household. The two older Batt brothers remained uninvolved, an observation that left Keith convinced they were overlooking something significant. In his eyes, their lack of interest translated into a missed opportunity, as the exciting world of Chiltern Valley Ladies unfolded around them.

## Going international

But Harry had a dream greater than Chiltern Valley Ladies. He wanted to lead a women's England team on the world stage. There would be ongoing debate about whether this team was unofficial or endorsed by the authorities. However, the seeds of this project were first sown in 1969 and it's all down to a group of visionaries.

Conceived by a consortium of Italian businessmen, the Fédération Internationale Européenne de Football Féminine (FIEFF) was founded, among them Dr Marco Rambaudi, a connoisseur of furniture and the proprietor of the esteemed Real Torino women's football club. At the helm stood president Dr Lucci, a legal luminary. The genesis of FIEFF marked an era when Italy, boasting a thriving women's football league established in 1968, sought to showcase its athletic prowess.

In a pivotal move to inaugurate its endeavours, FIEFF extended an invitation to Harry Batt to assemble an independent English team, adding an exciting dynamic to the FIEFF European Cup hosted in Italy that year. The inaugural cup competition featured a quartet of distinguished teams: England, France, Denmark and the host nation, Italy. With Italy particularly eager to flaunt the triumphs of its burgeoning women's football league, the stage was set for a spirited competition showcasing women's football on the European stage.

Harry started scouting for the best players to take to Italy for 'Coppa Europa'. Most were recruited from the existing Chiltern Valley team, but only two of the Lost Lionesses made the squad.

Paula Rayner was one of those players. Already a Chiltern Valley

Ladies footballer, her football talents remained a guarded secret at school until the pivotal moment when she decided to reveal her passion. She showed the headteacher the invitation to participate in a European tournament in Italy with Harry as a manager in 1969, prompting the need for time off school in early November. It was a significant event, with Paula wearing the new football boots she received for her 14th birthday a week previously for the occasion.

However, the acknowledgement of her football achievements at school was noticeably absent. Instead of celebration, Paula found herself in trouble for the missed school days, a stark contrast to the recognition she believed would have accompanied success in sports like hockey or netball. The reticence to showcase girls' football achievements was palpable, a sentiment that lingered even as Paula represented England.

The competition's banner, titled 'International European Cup for Girls Football Teams', serves as a reminder of Paula's participation. Reflecting on the matches held more than 50 years ago, Paula admits the details have blurred with time. Still, she vividly recalls the proper football stadiums and the impeccably flat pitches – the flattest she had ever encountered.

The memories of the tournament unfold like a series of snapshots. The first game, set in Valle d'Aosta, was punctuated by the early morning serenade of cowbells as the animals descended from the mountains. Despite the enchanting backdrop, England lost 4-3 against Denmark.

The subsequent match in Turin brought a change of scenery but also a different soundscape. Paula's hotel room, positioned at the level of a highway flyover, traded cowbells for the ceaseless hum of traffic. The game against France unfolded in Juventus's revered home stadium, resulting in a triumphant 2-0 victory for England and securing the third-place spot. Meanwhile, Italy emerged victorious in the final against Denmark with a score of 3-1. The tournament, a mosaic of experiences and emotions, etched a lasting imprint on Paula's memory.

After these championships were played, French journalist Michel Castaing wondered about the ability of women to play football. He wrote in *Le Monde* on 5 November:

*'Football is a male team sport . . . representing man in all that is most virile and athletic that is open to the people.*

*'There were around 60 of them in Aosta and Novara on Saturday, Turin on Sunday, swapping their silk stockings for woollen ones. A team of beautiful warriors no doubt tired of washing the kit for their brother, boyfriend, or husband, of trailing around after them at soccer stadiums every week or having to watch it on television on Sunday afternoons, but most of all wanted to show that women were indeed capable of kicking a ball of this kind. And much to our surprise we are prepared to admit they actually managed it.'*

Following the triumph of the 'Coppa Europa' in 1969, a resounding success both in terms of acclaim and financial gain, the Italians, in defiant rebellion against FIFA, joined forces with sponsors Martini & Rossi to envision hosting additional tournaments. The next ambitious venture took shape in the form of an eight-team 'Coppa Mondial' for the following year, 1970.

The turnout for the Coppa Europa surpassed the expectations of both the press and organizers, prompting them to contemplate an even grander tournament. In December of that year, a newly formed women's football federation committee convened to strategize for a global spectacle.

In its pursuit of a more extensive reach, FIEFF transformed into the International Federation of Feminine Football (FIFF), seeking active participation from the South American region. This change marked a significant step towards the intent to expand women's football commercially on an international scale.

Italy's professional women's football league were paying players on a part-time basis and importing foreign footballers from other European countries to raise the profile of the league. Recruited players came from Denmark, Scotland, England (but none of the Lionesses), Ireland and Spain. Times were changing . . .

## Coppa Mondial, Italy 1970

Under the sponsorship of Martini & Rossi, renowned producers of the popular fortified wine of the 1970s, Torino-based FIFF orchestrated an independent event that operated outside FIFA's remit. This tournament, featuring eight invited teams – West Germany, Denmark, Mexico, Austria, Switzerland, England, Czechoslovakia and Italy – bore the distinctive mark of the inaugural women's World Cup.

Despite facing setbacks with Czechoslovakia's withdrawal due to visa complications and Brazil's invitation being rescinded due to legal restrictions for girls' participation in football in certain regions, the competition was a groundbreaking event. The teams, though, comprised of club teams, reflected the emerging state of women's football with national governing bodies in some nations.

Spanning across major stadiums in Genoa, Bologna, Milan, Bari, Salerno and Naples, the tournament reached its climax with the third-place playoff and final held in Turin. All teams vied for the coveted 'Martini & Rossi Cup' in what is now regarded as the pioneering Women's World Cup, a milestone despite the evolving structures of national football governing bodies.

Harry had asked England's star players Sue Lopez and Dot Cassell, Sue had been one of the players playing professionally in the Italian League that year for Roma, to play in the tournament. Both were star players in the Southampton Ladies team, seen as the best in England at the time, and winners of the 1971 FA Cup.

Amid the excitement of the inaugural 'unofficial' World Cup in Italy, orchestrated by FIFF, Harry once again tapped Paula to join the team for this prestigious event. The anticipation hung thick in the air as Paula prepared to join her teammates. However, the group's intended completeness was marred by the absence of Lopez and Cassell who failed to materialize.

A cloud of uncertainty enveloped their non-arrival, prompting Paula to enquire into the cause of the no-show. The prevailing narrative suggested that the Southampton Ladies players had been dissuaded from joining the expedition by the WFA. However, the players themselves countered this with a different explanation, citing travel difficulties as the reason that had prevented their timely arrival. The divergent stories added a mysterious layer to the journey, casting a shadow of doubt over the circumstances surrounding their absence.

The exact make-up of the squad for the Coppa Mondial seems to be lost to the mists of time, but in relation to the Lost Lionesses' participation only Paula, Jill, Louise and Val made the trip.

England faced West Germany in their first match. Both teams trained at Genoa's impressive stadium on the day before the game, with the managers of each team accusing each other of spying on the other's training. Both managers were feeling the pressure as both England and West Germany teams were classed as 'unofficial' participants in the Coppa Mondial by their national associations. Both had been threatened with consequences for participating in the competition.

Playing in front of 3,000 fans, England quickly seized control of the match. Jill Stockley knocked in a penalty on 25 minutes, and Louise Cross's goal on the half-hour mark contributed to England's commanding 4-0 half-time lead. It finished 5-1 – England crushing their rivals in the Stadio Luigi Ferraris in Genoa, in a scoreline matched by the England men's team in 2001.

The match was reported in the West German newspaper *Abendzeitung*, with journalist Veit Mölder focusing on the players' looks. He wrote about the English girls' 'tree-trunk calves', and ignoring the scoreline, seedily branded the German teens 'die schönere Elf' (the beautiful eleven).

However, the England girls' jubilation was tempered by a 2-0 loss to Denmark in the semi-finals in Milan.

Amid the competition, players found themselves in the spotlight of scouts. Harry, the visionary coach, approached Paula's mother with the news that a team was eager to sign her daughter. Yet, the reality of Paula being only 14 and still in school posed a hurdle. Unbeknown to Paula, her brother later revealed that the manager of the Italian team had visited their house, attempting to persuade Paula's mother to allow her to join the Italian side. Reflecting on the missed opportunity, Paula muses that she was born too soon, recognizing the significant advancements in women's football that Italy boasted – spanning support, leagues, facilities and professionalism.

Louise's selection for the team had unfolded when Harry travelled from Luton to Southampton to witness her talents on the pitch, having heard high praise of the left-winger's skills at Patstone United. Having convinced her family to overcome financial constraints for passport expenses, Louise embarked on the Italian adventure.

Post-tournament, an enticing offer materialized – a two-year contract from an Italian team, complete with a weekly wage of £60 (about £780 in today's money). Eager to pursue this opportunity professionally, Louise was met with parental reluctance. At 16, she had to relinquish the dream of playing professional football in Italy, leaving her pondering the alternate trajectory her career might have taken.

Jill was 16 at the time when the world of women's football beckoned her to the inaugural international tournament in Italy. The sheer magnitude of playing in the Juventus stadium and ascending the steps into the iconic San Siro in Milan remains an

astonishing reality she is still astounded by even today. The
pinching sensation persists, grounding her in the undeniable truth
that it was indeed her, and it wasn't all a dream.

In the realm of shared experiences, Jill found herself rooming
with two exceptional players, Louise and Paula. As she fondly
reflects, Paula added a touch of mischief to their camaraderie,
earning her the endearing label of a 'tinker'. Jill introduced an
element of playful banter and chuckles as she recounts the
humorous revelation that Paula, in her own words, 'doesn't
remember anything' about their time in Italy. A recent reunion
prompted Jill to playfully confront Paula with the claim that she
once clandestinely exited the hotel window to rendezvous with a
footballer. Laughter ensued, with Jill admitting to her unwitting
role as Paula's accomplice in covering for her during such
escapades.

The final was between Denmark, represented by the Danish
club Boldklubben Femina, and the host nation Italy. The Danes
had their team kit go mysteriously 'missing' and so the team had
to go to a local sports shop and purchase a replica AC Milan kit
to wear. There were 24,000 ticket sales for the final, but
attendance reports claim more than 40,000 fans were inside the
stadium.

The Italian business consortium FIFF had made a lot of
money with the tournament, but by hosting this event and making
a good profit, they had now got the attention of FIFA and not in
a good way. It was apparent and noticed by the other countries
that the draw was rigged so Italy would make the final and play

against Denmark, who were the best European nation at the time. Initially, these two teams were due to meet in the semi-final, so that was discarded and a redraw took place with the desired outcome.

Despite the kit issues, Denmark won the final 2-0 and returned home as champions. Faxe Brewery was keen to sponsor the team after their success, but the Danish Football Association still wouldn't recognize Boldklubben Femina's win and tried their best to diminish their achievements.

Undeterred and with new contacts in European football as well as the good relationship with Martini & Rossi, Harry kept on the pressure with the FA to support his women's football vision.

### Fighting for recognition

Trudy recalls her father, Edward, engaging in multiple confrontations with the FA alongside Harry, a recurring event in their shared efforts. On one particular occasion the duo found themselves banned from a meeting due to their robust expression of dissent. Edward, driven by a strong sense of fairness, was known to voice his opinions assertively and call out injustices. The Chiltern Valley family held a special place in his heart, earning admiration from those who witnessed his dedication alongside Harry.

To Trudy, Harry was a unique individual, a true one-off. Yet, she acknowledges that this very uniqueness became a source of contention with authorities. She fondly recalls Harry, standing tall on the team bus, belting out the song 'Granada' at the top of his lungs. His singing voice, she emphasizes, was nothing short of fabulous. Harry's irrepressible spirit, boundless enthusiasm and infectious energy defied containment. He was a force of nature, and that, perhaps, posed a challenge for those in positions of authority.

There was a clear clash between Harry's dynamic personality and the conservative approach of the authorities in the country. The bureaucratic insistence on paperwork and a specific procedural approach stood in stark contrast to Harry's style. For him, it wasn't about conforming to rigid structures; it was about embracing vision, recognizing potential and actualizing those visions with a sense of urgency. Harry was inclined to charge forward at full speed, eager to make things happen in a way that clashed with the more reserved and measured approach of the authorities.

Despite his constant irritation with the FA, Harry was careful to shield the girls from the stresses he faced. Harry, a visionary advocate for women's sports, managed to keep much of the FA-related turmoil at bay for the benefit of the team. Jill believed that Harry's forward-thinking perspective gave the FA a sense of jealousy that added to the tensions between them. According to her, Harry's intelligence and unwavering motivation allowed him to seize opportunities and navigate the complexities of advancing women's sports in an era that might not have been fully ready for such progressive initiatives.

Still, the the WFA and the FA were slow to progress with the development of women's football. Harry was getting more and more frustrated as it seemed that all his hard work networking and involvement in the international tournaments were to no avail. His enthusiastic and inspirational words from Italy were falling on deaf ears.

When Keith talks about his father, Harry emerges as a remarkably adept manager and leader, excelling in his role. There were moments when Harry, burdened by the weight of his frustrations and the pressures he faced, would share his thoughts, the strain palpable in his voice. Despite this, Harry remained steadfast in preventing his personal struggles from permeating the team dynamics. He maintained an upbeat demeanour during meetings. He had exceptional communication skills and the ability to infuse rooms with positivity. Harry, devoid of preconceptions about individuals, possessed the charisma to effortlessly take command of any space. His massive personality served as a catalyst, drawing exuberance and energy from those around him.

However, such a dynamic character could irk those in authoritative positions. Harry's penchant for taking over rooms, even when it wasn't his designated role, likely clashed with the more formal expectations of officials. Keith imagined how the rigid and bureaucratic nature of certain authorities might have struggled to accommodate Harry's high spirits, leading them to dislike him. Despite this, Keith insists that Harry wasn't inherently a bad person.

Central to Harry's ethos was a profound belief in gender equality. He firmly asserted that women possessed the capability to excel in any field just as men did, and, in many instances, they might even surpass their male counterparts. Harry's visionary perspective on gender equality, while progressive, likely fuelled further tension with those who resisted change within the established order.

Later that year, feeling the frustrations that women faced in society at that time, Harry sat at his typewriter and wrote:

*The show must go on.*

# Chapter 4
# Forming the Chiltern Valley Squad

———

Harry was still on his mission to get the best girls to play at Chiltern Valley. Val was one of the first Chiltern Valley Ladies members and went to Italy for the Coppa Europa in 1969, as well as the Coppa Mondial with Paula, Louise and Jill.

Val's entry into 'proper football' came through responding to an advertisement in the Luton newspaper about Harry's new team in 1969. The first few matches were challenging, and the team was thoroughly thrashed. Determined to improve, Val enlisted sporty friends and encouraged others on the team to do the same. Within a year, their recruitment efforts bore fruit, and their fortunes reversed as they began dominating matches.

Finding local opponents proved difficult, with only a team from Leighton Buzzard providing regular competition. The team had to traverse the country for matches, participating in Northampton leagues, five-a-side tournaments, and even the London League. The logistics of travel varied, from minibus journeys for longer distances to carpooling when feasible. Val often found herself driving her Mini, leading a convoy of cars through foggy conditions at the bottom of Dunstable Downs every Sunday night during winter, a challenging experience.

One notable encounter took them to the countryside of Northamptonshire, where they faced hostility from locals in a village match. Val's intense response to a foul nearly led to her sending off, prompting her father to run onto the pitch in an attempt to calm her down. 'I turned to this girl and said: "If you do that once more, I'll do it back to you harder!"' recalled Val. 'Well she did it to someone and I had to tell the referee to do their job and send her off! My dad saw the anger in my face and shouted, "Val! Calm down!"' Despite the challenges, Val's determination to play her best remained unyielding.

Surprising the spectators, the guys who emerged from the pub on Sundays to watch assumed that women playing football would be a more genteel affair. However, they soon realized that the intensity and competitiveness mirrored that of Sunday League football in the men's division. 'If someone hacks one of the players, then that player gets hacked back exactly in the same way!'

*'You know, just because we've got boobies, we're not just standing around wanting to look pretty.'*
Val

Meanwhile, the dad of Paula's friend Dawn had heard about Harry's team and wondered whether she would be interested in joining. Paula was only 12 at the time. While initially hesitant, her mother allowed her to attend with Dawn. From the very start, Paula felt a sense of belonging and comfort, a feeling she hadn't experienced before. 'When I played with the team at Chiltern Valley, it was like I fitted in for the first time.'

Living on the opposite side of town from Crawley Green Sports and Social Club, where Chiltern Valley Ladies played, posed logistical challenges. Despite Dawn eventually stopping, Paula continued her playing, committing to taking two buses to practices and matches, funded by her earnings from a morning paper round and a Saturday job at Woolworths.

Sunday matches meant returning home to a reheated Sunday roast. As time went on, Paula eventually mustered the courage to ask her mother not to save a dinner for her as by the time she got home, it was usually very dry and not the tastiest. Playing on park pitches with rudimentary facilities, such as small changing huts without showers, characterized her football experience. Team talks took place on the pitch sidelines, half-time refreshments were limited to a quarter of an orange, and first aid involved a 'magic' sponge in a cold bucket of water.

Despite these challenges, Paula cherished being part of a team and the identity that provided. An exception to their usual venues was a charity match at Great Yarmouth Town FC in 1969, where celebrity Bruce Forsyth kicked off the game, creating an amusing moment for the publicity photographs. 'Bruce had to lie across our legs for some reason,' recalls Paula.

Paula's dedication to the team reached a memorable point when, aged 17, she played a cup match with a chipped bone in her elbow. Her arm was in plaster due to the severity of her injury but that didn't stop Paula. 'I told Mum I was just going to watch the girls play the match, but I had every intention to play.' With a daring spirit that might not be allowed today, Paula tossed her football boots out of the window to evade her mum seeing, and headed off to play.

There was already a good team spirit within the squad, and owing to their experiences abroad, Chiltern Valley was attracting other players. The team were all ages, but a young Leah turned up to training one day.

Leah was only 11 when her mother, having learned about the team from a colleague, arranged for her and Gill, a fellow player, to travel together to Crawley Green Sports and Social Club in Luton. At the time, Leah's natural talent for football drew comparisons to the legendary George Best, her idol. As a dedicated and aspiring young player, Leah spent countless hours practising dribbling, keepy-ups, and emulating skills she observed from boys. 'I'd kick the football over the washing line in the back garden, then control it on the way down, and practise new skills I had seen from the boys.'

Inspired by Best's remarkable balance and skill, Leah's style on the pitch mirrored her hero. Although she sometimes attempted to beat opponents more than once, her teammates advised her to focus on scoring goals, prompting Leah to find a balance between individual skills and teamwork. 'I accept the criticism from the girls! Sometimes I did like to beat everyone on the pitch!'

Excelling in both the inside right and inside left positions, Leah showcased her versatility as an attacking player, often donning the number 8 or number 10 shirt.

Her enthusiasm extended to five-a-side football, where Leah thrived and frequently emerged victorious in tournaments with the team. Despite her slender build, Leah's wiry and agile physique, coupled with natural fitness acquired from various school sports, rendered her tireless on the field. Her perpetual energy became a defining trait, enabling her to sustain high levels of performance.

Chiltern Valley Ladies received favourable coverage in the local Luton newspaper, thanks to Harry writing positive articles highlighting the team's achievements and giving commendations for their exceptional play against formidable odds. Leah's name regularly appeared in the paper as a recognized goalscorer, further solidifying her presence and contributions to the team's success.

**Spreading the word**

With the regularly posted match reports in the local paper, word of mouth got out to those who lived a bit further afield.

Janice wrote a heartfelt letter to Harry Batt, expressing her eagerness to join the team. Although Luton, where the team was based, was 25km (15 miles) away from her, the positive response from Harry, welcoming her to the team, filled her with delight. The warm welcome she received from the other girls at Chiltern Valley gave her an immediate source of belonging.

Training sessions, held once or twice a week, provided Janice and her teammates with opportunities to hone their skills. Securing fixtures was a challenge due to the scarcity of girls' teams and obtaining playing fields often meant dealing with less-than-ideal conditions – cleaning up dog faeces being a recurring task. The team, known for cleaning up pitches literally and figuratively, faced occasional unwelcome comments during matches, but most of the time they played in relative solitude.

Despite initial nerves as a newcomer, Janice felt embraced by the Chiltern Valley family. Admiring the exceptional skills of players like Leah, she found herself on a par with the talented roster. The shared passion for football bonded the team and created a close-knit, family atmosphere. For Janice, playing football with Chiltern Valley was a preferable alternative to nights out at bars and discos. 'My mum and dad were so happy I had found somewhere to play football and be happy.'

Positioned as a striker, Janice's speed on the pitch allowed her to outmanoeuvre opposing defenders, contributing significantly to the team's goal tally. Revelling in the glory of scoring goals, Janice appreciated the success of Chiltern Valley, where Harry's leadership fostered effective teamwork. Her parents witnessed Janice's integration into a team that became more than just players – it became a strong unit brought together by a love for the beautiful game.

> *'We were a group of girls all faced with the same problem.*
> *We loved to play football but weren't ALLOWED*
> *to play football.'*
> Jan

As well as the regular players coming to Chiltern Valley, every weekend Harry would scout for more players to build the squad and make it stronger. Chris was one such player.

Word of mouth (or perhaps keen observation) led Harry to approach Chris after a match, extending an invitation to join the team. The team Chris was currently playing for, understandably, wasn't thrilled about losing the one player who could perform at a commendable standard. Harry, however, convinced the manager that Chris needed to take her talents to the next level, playing alongside more skilled teammates.

Her inaugural appearance for Chiltern Valley occurred in a summer five-a-side tournament in 1970, introducing Chris to a new, wondrous world of female football. Until then, her sports idols had been the men of the professional league, but witnessing the skill and dedication of the Chiltern Valley players marked a transformative moment in her life.

In the tournament, Chris found herself back in the goalkeeping role, a position she typically enjoyed only during penalty situations. She must have performed well, as she secured her first medal in her debut tournament with the team. The pounding of her heart echoed the intensity of the experience, pushing Chris to surpass her own expectations and prove her worth. It was a drive reminiscent of that she had displayed when playing with the boys – an unyielding determination to demonstrate her capabilities on the field. 'I had to excel to fit in with the team and thankfully I did that. I wanted to show the girls I was worthy, just like I used to when I played with the boys back home.'

Some players were recruited to the team following a nerve-racking trial set by Harry. One such player was Trudy. Having been picked, overwhelmed with pride, she couldn't contain her excitement and eagerly shared the news with everyone she knew. The act of paying her subs and receiving the team kit felt like a monumental achievement, celebrated with the enthusiasm one might expect from a call-up to the England squad.

Being part of Chiltern Valley became a source of belonging for Trudy, a place where she felt she truly fitted in. It provided a sense of purpose and a team unit that differed from her experiences playing with boys. Among fellow girls who shared her passion for football, Trudy discovered a community that resonated with her. 'I felt that I had finally found where I belonged. I was part of something special. Instead of playing with the boys, I was now with other girls who were serious about football like me.'

Her journey on the field started as a goalkeeper, echoing the sentiment of current Lioness Rachel Daly, who once stated, 'I don't care where on the pitch I play, just as long as I'm in the team.' Trudy embraced a similar mindset, willing to contribute wherever necessary to secure her place in the team. Eventually settling into the number 4 shirt, she found a position that suited her well. Forming a formidable defensive partnership with Big Jean, Trudy significantly contributed to the team's success, with few opposing teams managing to score against them.

*'There is a place for me. There is a place for girls with feisty personalities, strong physical ability, and who want to win.*

*There IS somewhere I can fit in. And that's what it is all about.*
*Finding that place to not feel like a freak.'*
Trudy

Situated 19km (12 miles) away from Crawley Green Sports and Social Club is an RAF base in Henlow. After speaking with Edward McCaffery, Trudy's father who also helped train the team, Harry went to watch some of the football training there as he had heard about two women, Carol and Jean, that could be huge assets for the squad. Knowing there was an international tournament in Sicily approaching, in June 1971, and with more pressure from the FA on players not to play in the tournaments unsanctioned by FIFA and for Harry Batt, Harry was constantly searching for new talent and players who were perhaps under the radar and not affiliated with any team.

Carol wanted to join the Royal Navy, fuelled by a desire to follow in her mother's footsteps as a Wren. Initially drawn to the idea of becoming a PE teacher, she encountered a significant obstacle – her struggle with exams, a challenge that left her frozen with anxiety. The dream of pursuing a PE teacher course at Loughborough seemed unattainable.

Undeterred, Carol shifted her focus to a different role within the Navy. Enlisting in November 1967, she discovered that the Navy wasn't accepting new intakes until June, leading her to mention joining the RAF instead. As fate would have it, a chance encounter with a sergeant from the RAF altered the course of her plans.

Engaging in a conversation about her life, the sergeant delved into Carol's memories and experiences. The unexpected turn of events led to an intelligence test that focused on unconventional problem-solving rather than traditional exam-style questions. Despite initial panic, Carol persevered through the two-hour test. To her surprise, the sergeant revealed a proposition: 'How do you fancy being a PE instructor? The only thing is you probably won't be able to get in until June.'

Ecstatic about the prospect of fulfilling her dream, Carol embraced the opportunity, even if it meant waiting for the main training. Before formal training commenced, she undertook a learning period under the guidance of another Physical Training Instructor (PTI), observing and absorbing the intricacies of the role she was about to undertake at RAF Henlow.

Jean's journey into the Royal Air Force began with a moment of frustration at her job in a transport cafe after finishing school. Tired of the monotony, she decided on a whim that she would enlist with whichever armed forces caravan arrived next – be it the Army, Navy or Air Force. As fate would have it, the next group to pull in was from the Royal Air Force.

Completing all the necessary paperwork, Jean committed herself to the enlistment process. This departure from her roots in Skipton, where options for young women seemed limited, presented a welcome change from the prospect of working in a mill, a fate she was eager to avoid.

In the world of women's football, Jean was aware of Doncaster Belles, a team based over 100km (60 miles) away. However, the challenges of frequent travel to Doncaster made it an impractical choice for her. The limited accessibility of women's football teams in Yorkshire added another layer to Jean's decision-making process.

*'When I joined the RAF, that was the first time I got to play football properly. I was 18 years old. I instantly loved it. I felt at home on that football pitch.'*

Jean

The initiative of Trudy and her father to expand the Chiltern Valley team led her to a kickabout at her dad's workplace in RAF Henlow, where she encountered Jean. Approaching her during the informal game, Trudy pitched the idea of Jean joining their football team. With enthusiasm, Trudy's dad provided Jean with all the necessary information about Chiltern Valley, and to Trudy's delight, Jean decided to join.

During that period, Trudy's dad took on the role of training them, a challenging task given his commitments at work and home. Unable to be present as often as he desired, Carol stepped in to lead the training sessions. As a PTI, Carol brought a new level of intensity to the training regime, pushing the team to their limits. Trudy vividly recalls one particularly gruelling session that concluded with her being physically sick.

During Jean's first training session, she quickly felt a sense of belonging as she played alongside the other girls. One player who particularly caught her eye was the talented Leah, whose dribbling skills mirrored those seen on television. Impressed by the atmosphere and the team's playing style, Jean found herself aligning with the defensive role, a natural fit given her height of nearly 1.83m (6ft).

As a defender, Jean's commitment to the game often left her with bruises scattered across her body. She contemplated the efficacy of shin pads, dismissing them as ineffective against the array of bruises that adorned her legs after each match.

*'If you're a girl and you've gone through similar to what I've gone through, not being able to play a sport you love because it's deemed only for boys, and then suddenly, you find a group of similar like-minded girls who have been through the same, it felt like I was coming home. Almost euphoric.'*

Jean

Carol reflected on the origins of her journey into football, a tale that unfolded on the pitches of RAF Henlow. It all began when she found herself engaged in a spirited game of five-a-side, and she was getting stuck into the match. Little did she know that Harry was silently observing the match on the adjacent pitch.

Carol noticed Harry's gaze fixed on her game for a good 10 minutes before he redirected his attention to the other pitch. Days later, a phone call interrupted the routine of her day, offering a tantalizing proposition – an invitation to trial at Chiltern Valley. Eagerly, she made her way to Crawley Green, where Harry extended the invitation to join the team. With excitement bubbling within her, she responded, 'Oh, great. Yes please! Proper football!'

The first encounter with Chiltern Valley and its spirited female players felt like a homecoming for Carol. Amid the camaraderie and shared passion, she discovered a sense of belonging that had eluded her on the boys' football field. Playing with them, she had often felt like an outsider, a girl navigating a traditionally male space. However, on the hallowed grounds of Crawley Green Sports and Social Club, those concerns melted away. For the first time, she could simply relax and revel in the joy of the game.

The team was starting to come together. Harry and June had brought in Leah, whose attacking dribbling skills shone brightly; Jan, known for her goalscoring and focus; and the dedicated Jean and Carol, stalwarts in defence. They also added Paula, whose speed on the wing was unmatched, and the spirited and passionate Val and Trudy. Each game they played deepened their connection, forming a close-knit football family. Then, an unexpected opportunity came their way – a trip to Sicily with the team. Determined to strengthen the squad for the upcoming World Cup Qualifiers, Harry scoured England for new talent.

## World Cup Qualifiers, Sicily 1971

This was the tournament in June, organized by FIFF yet again, to decide which teams were going to compete in Mexico in August, later that year. With two new defenders in Carol and Jean, Harry was confident with the players he had, though he knew it was going to be tough. With all the politics behind the scenes with FIFA, there was still pressure from the national associations not to sanction any teams entering.

Harry had shielded his team from the intricate web of politics that often entangled the sport. While the seasoned players, with their experienced gaze, might have discerned the potential repercussions, the younger members of the team remained blissfully ignorant.

And so, the squad was selected. All expenses were paid for by Martini & Rossi yet again.

Jean's journey into the realm of international football began with a simple yet thrilling proposition from Harry. One day, he approached her with an offer that echoed with excitement, saying, 'We're going to send the team to Sicily, and are you interested in coming?' The prospect was undeniably enticing, but practicalities needed addressing.

With the enthusiasm still fresh in her mind, Jean navigated the bureaucracy of her life in the Royal Air Force. She approached her boss, seeking permission to embark on this footballing adventure. His response, while not an unequivocal yes, carried a promise – 'Well, we will give you a week, and then you can use a week of your leave.'

### Recollections of Sicily

The journey to Sicily was a whirlwind of train rides and awe-inspiring landscapes of the Alps. The expedition unfolded with a coach ride to the ferry, where they embarked on an overnight train adventure, traversing France before winding through Italy. The three-day train journey to the island left a lingering sensation of perpetual motion, and even as Chris viewed the surroundings, the echo of train wheels over tracks persisted.

On the sleeper train one day, a temporary abode, a guard entered the cabin with a duvet, an offering of comfort during the night. However, when he returned to retrieve it the next morning, Chris, not known for her morning cheerfulness, promptly told him to 'sod off'. It was too early for any duvet exchanges; sleep held too precious a place in her heart.

Upon reaching Palermo under the veil of darkness, the stark contrast between the opulence of the hotel and the poverty of the surrounding area struck Chris. Despite the tournament's location, the hardships of the region were palpable. A later return to Sicily revealed its true beauty, but at the time, the shadows of poverty lingered in her recollections.

As an aside, some weeks later Chris was offered an unexpected opportunity. Mirroring the offers made to Paula and Louise following the 1970 World Cup, Harry and June visited Chris's house to discuss a proposal from an Italian professional league team. They wanted to sign her as a goalkeeper, offering not only a significant weekly wage of around £100 but also covering the cost of her trips home twice a year. However, the decision rested on Chris, who, despite the enticing offer, grappled with uncertainties. At just 15 years old, she faced the dilemma of pursuing football professionally or prioritizing her education. Ultimately, her parents made the call, citing the importance of exams. Chris, hesitant about going alone and uncertain about her position as a goalkeeper, agreed with her parents and chose to stay in England. Reflecting later, she couldn't help but ponder the allure of the lucrative offer she had foregone, recognizing that £100 a week (roughly £2,000 in today's money) was a substantial sum at the time . . . 'That was good money back then. Damn.'

But back to Sicily . . . Janice holds fond memories of the enthralling qualifying tournament for Mexico, which unfolded on the sun-soaked pitches of Sicily. The event again bore the stamp of Martini & Rossi, the generous sponsor that provided everything the girls needed, from kits to support, making the trip an unforgettable experience. Their accommodation in a splendid Sicilian hotel, complete with a pool and proximity to the beach, added an extra layer of luxury to the adventure. The picturesque view and idyllic weather marked not just a football tournament but Janice's first time abroad, a journey that required her father to make a trip to Peterborough to secure her passport.

On the field, memories lingered of a tenacious encounter with the Austrian centre-half, whose frustration manifested in a push that sent Janice flying. Despite the blatant foul, the referee remained passive, allowing the incident to pass without intervention. 'She fouled me badly because I beat her to the ball every time! She was so frustrated and took her anger out on me.'

Away from the pitch, the escapades of some teammates added a touch of mischief to the Sicilian nights. Janice, the self-proclaimed good girl, resisted the allure of nocturnal adventures, never venturing out to clubs or partaking in drinks. Such naivety was characteristic of the team in those days, but Janice took pride in her steadfastness. However, tales of Trudy's daring outings, including an exit through the hotel window, added a playful twist to their shared memories.

A side trip to Mount Etna offered a welcome break, and beyond the scenic landscapes, it provided a taste of what it felt like to be treated as a male footballer. Harry's extensive contacts within women's football stood in stark contrast to the reluctance of the Football Association to collaborate with him.

Amid the exhilarating matches and scenic excursions, Janice remained blissfully unaware of the tournament's political intricacies. The stadiums and pitches were a blur in her memory, overshadowed by the sheer joy of playing football in a foreign land.

For the talented Leah, Italy, with its semi-professional women's football league, was an unexpected revelation, overshadowing the fact that success in this competition meant qualification for the World Cup in Mexico – a detail which, incredibly, was never disclosed to the team.

The team's lodgings formed a triangular pattern across Sicily – Trapani, Catania (near Mount Etna), and Syracuse – each offering a unique experience for the players. The crystal-clear turquoise of the Mediterranean Sea marked Leah's first encounter with its beauty, a stark departure from their familiar surroundings in England.

For Leah, it was not just about playing football; it was an introduction to the concept of crowds watching her in action. The revelation of a semi-professional women's football league in Italy, although she was deemed too young at 13 to be approached by a team, left a lasting impression. The matches played on diverse pitches included one on a gravel-like surface.

Lillian also struggled with the rough pitches and one incident left her with a significant injury on her right leg. The playing surface, more gravel than grass, wasn't conducive to her infamous 'Chopper Harris' slide tackle against an opponent, stripping away layers of skin and the wound refused to heal.

Concerned for her well-being, Harry insisted that Lillian seek medical attention. The doctor's diagnosis mandated antibiotic injections, not just on either side of the wound but, strangely, one in her bottom as well. As the other girls headed off for a leisurely swim, Lillian found herself waiting for the arrival of the person tasked with administering her injections.

To her surprise, the 'nurse' turned out to be none other than a male barber. This unconventional choice was compounded by a language barrier – he spoke no English, and Lillian was unfamiliar with Italian. In Sicily, it seemed, barbers were not only skilled in hairdressing but also in administering injections. The unexpected scenario unfolded with the barber giving Lillian the required injections, including the memorable one on her backside.

Amid the football fervour, the Sicilian nights offered a moment of escape. On one occasion, the team stealthily slipped out of the hotel in the evening, finding their way to a disco. Lillian, captivated by the music and the rhythm, threw herself into the dance floor revelry. 'I loved being at the disco! I was giving it all on the dance floor!'

Trudy's Sicilian journey unfolded against the backdrop of her devoted boyfriend back home. It was he who had gifted her a pair of coveted Adidas football boots, a thoughtful gesture initially intended in place of a ring. His mother's pragmatic advice – 'If Trudy wants football boots, then buy football boots.' Proudly sporting the expensive boots, Trudy secretly used her mother's Nivea cream to maintain their softness, diligently massaging it into the leather each night.

Playing football in Sicily presented a kaleidoscope of experiences for Trudy, revealing the diverse personalities and playing styles of international teams. The German players exuded a sense of superiority, an attitude that fuelled the English team's determination to defeat them. The Danish team, on the other hand, played with finesse and exuded a cool demeanour, while the Argentinians were relentless in their pursuit of victory. The prevailing sentiment, however, was that the English team was viewed as the underdog, reflecting the varying degrees of development in women's football across countries, including disparities in funding.

At the time Trudy didn't fully comprehend the significance of the tournament; her focus was solely on the joy of playing football.

Sicily, with its mesmerizing landscapes, captivated her, and she entertained the idea of staying there professionally. Surprisingly, offers to pay her £30 or £40 a week (£600–770 in today's money) opened her eyes to the possibility of playing football on a more substantial scale, a prospect she hadn't considered. However, parental insistence on returning for school exams curtailed this potential venture, leaving Trudy disappointed but with a sense of responsibility. 'My mum's perspective was that when all this "football nonsense" was out of my system, I was going to need a proper job! I was gutted.'

Amid the serious undertones, Trudy did confess to a bit of mischief during the trip. Encouraged by Paula, she found herself in the company of AC Milan or Juventus players one night, leading to an eventful evening out. Unfortunately they got stuck while trying to re-enter the hotel and had to face the consequences of a severe telling off from Harry and June. 'I have to confess I wasn't one of the good girls on that trip . . . in my defence, I was led astray by Paula!'

Paula declined to comment, but she did have a surprise on her return home. A telegram awaited her after school, bearing the words, 'I've come over to see you! I'm staying at a hotel in Leagrave!' It was from Gino, her pen pal from Sicily. For the 15-year-old Paula, this news was met with excitement, a sentiment not entirely shared by her mother. Despite reservations, arrangements were made for a chaperoned outing with Paula's older brother Peter, and his girlfriend. Over a meal, Peter tactfully reminded Gino of Paula's schoolgirl status. This seems to have done the trick and Gino's interest in Paula waned after his return, and the correspondence between them faded away.

### *Mexico bound?*

On the pitch the football tournament itself brought both triumph and challenge. Victory against Austria 3-0 propelled the team towards World Cup qualification. Progressing to the semi-finals was a notable achievement, but facing the Italian team, who played semi-professionally in a league that showcased the evolution of women's football in their country, posed a formidable challenge. Chris, the goalkeeper, had to summon two or three exceptional saves to counterbalance an earlier mistake. 'At times, I felt like I was facing a firing squad!' she said. But it was to no avail as they lost 7-0.

That loss to Italy meant that it was unclear whether the girls had done enough. The qualifiers in Sicily, intended to determine which teams would play in the tournament in Mexico, turned into a fiasco, with only five of the thirteen expected teams participating. Luxembourg, Switzerland and Spain pulled out after unsuccessful hosting bids. Sweden, Belgium, Czechoslovakia and West Germany also withdrew. This led to a winner-takes-all match between France and the Netherlands, with neither side knowing the stakes. To save face, FIFF used earlier friendlies to decide qualifications and eliminations without anyone knowing. Consequently, Denmark qualified for Mexico thanks to a 4-0 win over Sweden in a friendly.

However, Harry delivered the news from FIFF that they had

secured a spot in the upcoming World Cup. Yet, he tempered the celebration with a hint of doubt, expressing concerns about the financial hurdles that might hinder their journey.

Unaware of the intricate workings behind the scenes, Carol and her teammates remained in the dark about the diligent efforts put forth by Harry and June. It wasn't until later that she grasped the extent of their tireless endeavours. The duo, it seemed, had toiled day and night, navigating the complexities and challenges to ensure that the team could embark on the remarkable journey to Mexico.

For a lot of the Lost Lionesses, it was their first trip abroad and the first time that they got a sense of the Italian professionalism. For Harry, it meant more networking and more connections.

Keith didn't travel to Sicily but was told a story about his dad having a meeting while the tournament was going on. It involved a startling encounter, an unexpected meeting between Harry and a Sicilian gentleman. Clad in a dark suit with a mane of dark hair, the Sicilian man engaged in a lengthy conversation with Harry at a table. The gravity of the situation escalated when, shockingly, the dark-suited man produced a knife.

In a surreal turn of events, the Sicilian man cut his own hand. With a strange camaraderie, the man then handed the knife to Harry, who reciprocated the gesture. The two men proceeded to shake hands in a bizarre initiation that left Keith's family stunned. It later transpired that the enigmatic Sicilian was affiliated with the Mafia.

This ominous encounter took an unexpected turn when the

Sicilian informed Harry, 'You know, you are family, whatever you need . . . If you ever need us, we're here for you.' From that moment onward, the Mafia's support was unwavering, transforming Keith's family into virtual superstars and celebrities wherever they were in Sicily. This handshake had forged an alliance that would resonate throughout their journey, shaping the dynamics of their experience on the island and beyond.

# Chapter 5
## 'Las Chicas de Carnaby Street'

Mexico had already hosted the 1968 Olympic Games and the men's 1970 World Cup and was keen to carry on hosting more sporting events.

The 1970 men's World Cup was won by Brazil with the magnificent Pelé playing a starring role. When Mexico was announced by FIFF as the host for the 1971 Coppa Mondial (or Copa del Mundo as it would be called in Mexico), FIFA immediately sprang into action. It sent warnings to all the national associations that they had not been approved or sanctioned by them in any way, and any national association sending a team would be penalized by FIFA for doing so.

FIFA's press release read:

*'If you consult a list of representatives of women's football across the various countries you will immediately realize that they are unknown in footballing circles in their own countries and instead are managers and agents of companies with advertising capacity who are merely trying to make money by exploiting football played by women as a show.'*

FIFA contacted the Mexican FA and said there would be consequences for hosting Copa del Mundo. If the Mexican FA wished to continue its good relationship with FIFA, then they were not permitted to stage any of the matches on Mexican FA-affiliated grounds. If they did give FIFF access to these stadiums, there would be consequences for Mexican football.

The Mexican FA did not want to be in the bad books of FIFA and agreed. The information was passed on to FIFF, but when an obstacle is put in front of entrepreneurial minds, especially those of FIFF, solutions appear.

At the time, two stadiums in Mexico were not owned by the Mexican FA. One was Guadalajara's Jalisco Stadium, and the other was the mighty Azteca Stadium in Mexico City. Both were owned by media giants Televisa. Televisa had complete control and could do whatever they wanted, and that included hosting a Women's World Cup.

Televisa may come out of this looking like they were supporters of gender equality at this time, but linking with FIFF, this was about business, pure and simple. There may also have been an element of wanting to deliberately rub the authorities up the wrong way, too.

And Mexico's biggest media company could make sure this event was a success and fill the stadiums, because it had its own TV channels, newspapers, radio stations and magazines. So during the two months before the tournament, Televisa promoted the Copa del Mondo everywhere. It was on every front page, and on every radio station, and posters of Xochitl, the mascot, were appearing on every street. It was the ticket to have. Martini & Rossi signed up as the major sponsor.

There was still criticism over the event and the standard misogynistic remarks. Brazilian health experts were claiming that females playing football were at risk of becoming homosexual, while Mexican officials were outspoken about their concern that playing the sport would cause 'masculinization of the female body'.

But the tournament was going ahead.

## British Independents

The Football Association once more did not endorse any team representing England, but Harry wasn't to be put off yet again. This time, a tournament in Latin America was an opportunity too good to miss.

Keith shed light on a contentious chapter in the journey to the Mexico World Cup, highlighting the FA's staunch opposition. Their disapproval was categorical – 'You cannot take an England team out to Mexico.' The FA's rationale rested on the tournament's lack of sanctioning through FIFA or any recognized football governing body. Going against the official channels was not something that was customary, and without proper accreditation, the tournament faced strong resistance.

Undeterred by the FA's rigid stance, Harry was resolute. He saw an opportunity too significant to bypass. Naming the team 'British Independents' instead of 'England' was a subtle shift that allowed them to sidestep the FA's pride-driven objections, while still seizing the chance to participate in the prestigious tournament.

Harry's commitment to assembling a team for Mexico became an all-consuming quest. Weekends intended for family relaxation morphed into cross-country journeys, with Harry tirelessly scouting women's football matches. On the sidelines, he meticulously took notes, identifying potential players to approach after the games. The squad from Sicily was too small to take to the World Cup and Harry was still hoping some of the older and more experienced women footballers playing at that time would say yes to an opportunity to play in Mexico, undeterred by the warnings of the FA or unsupportive managers at work. Conversations with both managers and players ensued as he gauged their interest in representing the newly christened 'British Independents' in Latin America. While some declined the invitation for various reasons, Harry's persistence paid off, and he successfully pieced together a squad determined to make its mark on the international stage.

## Squad selection

When Harry broached the subject of Mexico with Trudy's parents, her father, in a teasing manner, asked if she had any interest in going. Trudy's enthusiastic response was immediate and unequivocal, but the scepticism she anticipated from others and the lack of belief in her potential journey made her keep the news to herself. It seemed unnecessary to expend effort persuading others when she felt confident in her decision.

Jan confided in Trudy about the potential sacrifice she was contemplating – leaving her job to join the team in Mexico. While it was a shock, it underscored the challenges women faced in sports, encountering resistance and opposition, even from their workplaces. The reality that some couldn't seize the opportunity due to the lack of support or understanding loomed over the team.

Additionally, the repercussions from the FA cast a shadow. There was a fear among players of potential bans upon their return to England, but the younger members like Trudy were blissfully unaware of these political intricacies. Trudy's father, who likely understood the potential consequences, nevertheless encouraged her to pursue the opportunity. His initial plan to accompany the team to Mexico had to be abandoned due to work constraints.

Harry's relentless pursuit of sponsorship became an obsession. Despite facing numerous rejections, he persisted in his efforts. Eventually, his tenacity bore fruit, securing a team uniform featuring a distinctive checked blazer and white skirts from Jon Bryan's in Luton, the first time they had a team parade uniform. While Trudy found the outfit less than appealing, she acknowledged that it brought a sense of unity and identity to the team, looking professional for the first time in photographs. However, her personal preference, as well as that of most of the girls, were the green tracksuits – also new for the tournament. Comfort beat smart.

Harry had got a team together, mainly made up of the players that went to Sicily apart from a few. One of the players missing from Sicily was Bobbie Wing, the goalkeeper, unable to go as her work wouldn't allow her the time off, so Lillian stepped into that position. While Chris demonstrated versatility by excelling in various positions, including goalkeeping, the fact that she was a mere 15 years old added a layer of concern to the situation. Entrusting such a significant responsibility to someone of that age was a weighty decision, so Lillian got the nod.

The team had a dilemma and contemplated the option of swapping goalkeepers based on the opponent. During discussions with Chris, Lillian couldn't help but think, 'She's a bit crazy.' Yet, a touch of madness might be a prerequisite for goalkeepers. Lillian, with her own brand of eccentricity described as a 'crazy 5-foot-tall ping pong ball', understood the unique mindset goalkeepers needed. Fearlessness, boldness and bravery were essential attributes for the last line of defence, the player tasked with thwarting every goal attempt. In the world of goalkeeping, a bit of craziness was not just tolerated, but perhaps even celebrated as a necessary ingredient for success.

Val's experience was different from most of the other girls. Balancing her responsibilities as an office manager at Whitbread, she found unexpected support from her employers. But the decision to head to Mexico came with a certain level of uncertainty, as funding considerations loomed large. When the call came, signalling the green light for the trip, she was swiftly handed her uniform for the opening ceremony, and the whirlwind preparations commenced.

Jean's situation was similar. Uncertain about obtaining permission from the RAF, she found herself pleasantly surprised by the supportive stance of her bosses. The prospect of positive publicity seemed to outweigh any reservations, and with their blessing, Jean's path to Mexico began to materialize.

Harry had asked other players, some of whom had played in his teams in 1969 and 1970 and others he had seen in tournaments. But they had all said no for various reasons: work commitments, studying and maybe some were nervous of the possible ban from the FA if they said yes.

After one of her games with the Daytels, the team manager, Jean, approached Marlene with unexpected news. The words relayed by Jean lingered in Marlene's memory: 'Harry Batt has asked if you'd be interested in going to Mexico to play in the Women's World Cup.' The impact of those words left Marlene utterly gobsmacked.

The sheer incredulity of the proposition was huge, and Marlene struggled with the surreal nature of the offer. The idea that Harry Batt, known for scouting players to bolster the squad, had set his sights on her was both astonishing and validating, not having played in an international tournament before.

There was an article about Marlene's selection in the local press with a photograph of her. Underneath the photo, reading more like a beauty contestant profile, the caption read:

*'The girl with golden boots. Luton telephonist Marlene Collins is really a girl with golden boots. And now she's been picked to play for Britain in the women's football World Cup. But football isn't the*

*only thing in Marlene's life. She's keen on amateur dramatics and knitting.'*

In the build-up to the Mexican expedition, Jill – who was set to celebrate her 17th birthday in Mexico – became a local star. The press documented her journey throughout and there was a collective sense of pride in Nuneaton.

In mid-July Gill found herself playing a charity match for Thame Ladies in Aylesbury against Fodens, a formidable opponent. The stakes were high, with the match heavily advertised to draw a sizeable crowd and raise funds for a good cause. The event even boasted the presence of Ron Atkinson, then captain of Oxford United, who ceremonially kicked off the game.

The encounter carried a hint of rivalry, caused by a narrow defeat to Fodens in a previous clash. However, this time, Thame Ladies emerged victorious with a 5-3 scoreline. Little did Gill know that Harry Batt was in attendance, scouting for players to join his squad for the Mexican adventure.

Post-match, Gill's casual encounter with Harry altered the trajectory of her football career. Her father, seizing the opportunity, introduced her to Harry with a game-changing proposition, 'Gill, this is Harry Batt. He's asking if you would like to join his team and play in the World Cup in Mexico?' At a mere 14 years old, Gill faced an extraordinary opportunity. Her father, cautious yet supportive, sought more details before consenting to her participation.

In her mind, Gill had already committed to this remarkable adventure. While three other Thame Ladies players were also approached by Harry, logistical constraints prevented their inclusion. Gill's school schedule, coinciding with the tournament during the August school holidays, made her the ideal candidate.

Following limited interactions with the rest of the squad and a couple of training sessions at Crawley Green Sports and Social Club in Luton, Gill was on the plane. The haste with which decisions were made, paperwork completed and permissions granted, reflected the whirlwind nature of her selection. Flying halfway across the world at 14 years old with strangers became an unexpected reality.

The process of obtaining a passport added to the craziness. With just weeks before departure, Gill's father took a day off work to drive her to Peterborough to secure the essential travel document. Her passport, still treasured to this day, records her height as 1.47m (4ft 10in).

News of Gill's selection reverberated through the local Aylesbury press, earning her the name 'World Cup Gilly' on the front page – a nod to the mascot of the 1966 men's World Cup, 'World Cup Willie'.

Leah was even younger than Gill at a tender 13 years of age. She fully admits that had others taken up Harry's offer she probably wouldn't have made the squad. 'It was a case of the right time, right place for me and I don't think it matters that I may have not been the first choice to go.'

Leah's enthusiasm contrasted with Yvonne's stance. When Harry turned up at her home and asked her and her mother whether Yvonne might take the trip to Mexico, she was nervous: 'I don't want to go, Mum! I can't go! I don't know anyone!' In response, her resolute mother insisted, 'You're going. You're not turning this opportunity down.' Eventually, conceding to her mother's encouragement, Yvonne relented and joined Harry's Mexico-bound gang.

The team dynamics Harry sought for the squad encompassed a mix of players, and Yvonne's shy but driven nature seemed to fill a void in the ensemble – a characteristic she dubbed as being an 'introverted gazelle'.

The passport office in Peterborough must have wondered what was causing such a rise in demand as Yvonne followed Gill in a rush to secure documentation ahead of departure. Yvonne's involvement was finalized at the eleventh hour and she does not feature in the original team photo. Juggling work responsibilities with the imminent football venture, Yvonne informed her colleagues at Jon Bryan's ladies fashion shop in Luton, 'Oh, by the way, I'm off to Mexico to play football in the Women's World Cup!' The managers, recognizing the significance of her participation, not only supported her but assured her of a job upon her return.

However, it seems that not every workplace was so encouraging about the girls being picked for the tournament.

When Jan received the news that she had been chosen to represent her country in Mexico, she was employed at the TSB bank, a job she valued highly despite the modest wage. She was filled with excitement at the opportunity ahead, but there was a catch. None of her work colleagues knew about her passion for football. When she mustered the courage to inform her boss about the life-changing news, he simply dismissed it with, 'Well, you can't go because of your job!'

Undeterred, Jan staunchly replied, 'I can't miss an opportunity like this!' Unfortunately, the bank remained steadfast, so she made a difficult, but swift decision. Faced with the ultimatum of 'job or no job,' Jan never hesitated . . . she was Mexico bound.

Marlene didn't have to sacrifice her job for the trip. The chief supervisor understood the significance of the opportunity and granted her precious permission and time off to represent her country. However, because the FA refused to sanction the team, Marlene had to sacrifice her wages for six weeks. The Post Office did not want to be associated with going against the FA. As a compromise, Marlene would have a job to return to but unfortunately it wouldn't be paid leave. Marlene's selection caused a buzz around her colleagues. Learning about the financial challenge she faced, they rallied together to support her. They organized a collection that raised £110 (about £1,400 in today's money), providing Marlene with some much-needed spending money. Touched by their generosity, she has held onto all the good luck cards they gave her, cherishing the tokens of their encouragement and support. The collective effort from her colleagues meant the world to Marlene. There was a sense that even though the FA weren't on board with the Mexico tournament, everyone else was.

For many in the squad, being away from their jobs meant losing money. Those who were employed at the time found themselves relying on the goodwill of understanding bosses who would grant them the time off to pursue their passion for football.

At that time, Lillian held the position of a shoe machinist in Northampton. When she approached her line manager with the news of her selection for the Mexico trip, the initial response was silence. Eventually, the foreman of the factory, unaware of the significance of the opportunity, uttered a simple, 'Right. OK then.' Lillian had to navigate the bureaucracy to secure official approval for the time off. In the end, she managed to obtain permission for a couple of weeks, although her absence extended to a month. Grateful for the support from her workplace, Lillian even found herself featured in the factory magazine, sharing news of her exciting journey with her colleagues.

Carol's no-nonsense attitude, natural ability to earn the girls' respect, organizational skills honed in the RAF, and excellent fitness made her the first choice for Harry Batt's squad. Her appointment as captain was a natural progression.

As the prospect of Mexico loomed on the horizon, Carol, armed with geographical knowledge and insights into the challenges faced by England's men in the 1970 World Cup, felt a weighty responsibility settle on her shoulders. With a keen awareness of the altitude and climate awaiting them, she knew she needed to whip the team into peak fitness for the conditions they would encounter, particularly with Mexico City's altitude. Assuming the roles of trainer and captain, Carol sensed a certain distance from her teammates, perhaps heightened by the suddenness of her promotion to these positions. Against the backdrop of a captaincy transition, she pushed them to train rigorously. 'I did feel a huge responsibility on my shoulders. I felt a bit apart from the girls but there wasn't much I could do about it. The girls needed pulling into shape and that was it.'

As the departure date for Mexico drew near, Harry gathered the team to share a crucial piece of information. 'We can't be called *England*,' he emphasized, 'because we're not recognized by the FA. As I've entered us independently, we will be called "British Independents."' The team, unfazed by this news, remained committed to the journey. However, upon reaching Mexico, they discovered that the officials had designated them as England or 'Inglaterra', a title that contradicted the intended distinction from the FA.

Paula's mind raced. Unaware of the politics influencing the choice of the team's name, and aged only 15, she saw no reason to delve into such details and believed it was tied to Leah's birthplace in Ireland. Jean and Jill also admitted to their lack of awareness regarding the significance of being dubbed 'British Independents' by Harry initially, and later adopting the name 'Inglaterra' during their Mexican adventure. There was a blissful ignorance about the political undercurrents in play.

## Ready for the off

It was the eve of departure and the girls arranged to stay over in Luton, all sleeping in the houses of those who lived there, ready to leave for the airport early in the morning. However, there was a significant distraction . . . Luton Town FC was hosting a friendly against Manchester United at their Kenilworth Road stadium.

While conventional wisdom would suggest resting up before embarking on a long and tiring flight to another continent, the Lost Lionesses were cut from a different cloth.

The eve of the Mexico trip should have been a time for relaxation and preparation, but for Leah, a devoted fan of George Best, there was no chance of that. The opportunity of seeing her hero play for Manchester United was too enticing to resist. Alongside her companions, Chris and Trudy, Leah decided to attend the game.

The trio soaked in the atmosphere of a crowded Kenilworth Road. Manchester United ran out 2-0 winners, but the vibrant energy of the fans left an indelible impression on the teenagers, who headed home straight after the match, mindful of the early departure.

Returning to Chris's house, the adrenaline and excitement from the football match and the upcoming trip to Mexico made sleep elusive. They opted for a game of Tiddlywinks instead. The game extended for a considerable time until sleep finally caught up with them. The next day, during the coach ride to the airport, Trudy hesitantly remarked, 'I didn't know you had a birthmark on your leg, Leah.' Puzzled, Leah glanced down at her attire – white tights complementing their fashionable walking-out suits with a white nylon shirt and crimplene skirt – and to her surprise, a brown Tiddlywinks disc was nestled in her tights.

As it happened Trudy, Chris and Leah weren't the only members of the squad at the game that night. Jill and Paula also couldn't resist the allure of witnessing George Best in action.

Val was apprehensive about boarding the plane. She had an underlying fear of flying that she chose not to disclose to her mother, who would have been disappointed if she declined the opportunity. However, a couple of days before the flight, her anxiety reached breaking point, prompting a desperate call to her brother.

In that crucial conversation, Val confessed her reluctance to go through with the trip. Her brother, sensing the magnitude of the opportunity, reassured her with unwavering insistence that it was a chance of a lifetime she couldn't pass up. Thus, Val found herself at the airport with her brother's encouragement still fresh in her mind.

As the plane taxied down the runway, Val began to shake, her fingers tightly gripping the armrests during take-off. A visit to the toilet offered a moment of respite, as she realized the similarities between flying and train travel, and managed to ease her anxiety slightly. However, the traumatic ordeal left an indelible mark, leading Val to swear off flying altogether. 'Well I couldn't bloody afford it anyway!' Her limited travel experiences had mostly confined her to Norfolk.

Leah embarked on her maiden airplane journey with a mix of anticipation and trepidation. The flight marked a significant first for her. As the group later reminisced about the experience, Gill claimed to have been shown an 'upstairs', a detail that no one else seemed to recall. The ensuing banter and teasing playfully suggested that Gill might have been on an entirely different flight.

That wasn't true but Gill did occupy a seat separate from the rest. Seated next to a couple, her natural shyness held her back from initiating conversation, and she opted to remain quietly absorbed in her thoughts. The aircraft, an early model of the Pan Am Jumbo 747, carried an air of grandeur.

During the flight, one of the stewardesses noticed Gill's reserved demeanour and extended an invitation: 'Do you want to come and have a look upstairs?' Delighted at the unexpected opportunity, Gill gladly accepted. As she ascended, she discovered a sophisticated setting, presumably first class, complete with a cocktail bar and lounge. The chance to explore this elevated realm added an unexpected touch of luxury . . . Gill did go 'upstairs' on the plane.

There was a seven-hour stopover in New York during their journey to Mexico. As the girls meandered through the airport lounge, a curious American lady approached them, asking if they were a choir. Amused by the misconception, Leah clarified that they were, in fact, a group of football players heading to Mexico, not a choir. Jan, in particular, engaged in conversation with the lady, who turned out to be a professor at a New York university.

Jan shared her story with the professor, explaining how she had to relinquish her job at the bank to pursue this opportunity. The professor, visibly irked by Jan's boss's attitude, made a sincere offer: 'After the football, come back to New York, and I will get you a job here!' In her distinctive New York accent, she urged Jan to contact her after the tournament. The specifics of the job were momentarily inconsequential; what mattered was the genuine offer of support and understanding, symbolized by the professor handing Jan her business card.

Jan, reflecting on the experience, admitted the youthful naivety of her and her teammates, not fully grasping the magnitude of their upcoming journey across the globe to play football. Martini & Rossi, the sponsor, generously covered all expenses once again, from flights to tracksuits and hotel accommodation, making the adventure possible for each team member.

The second leg of the journey to Mexico was in a less glamorous aircraft. The ageing plane prompted Leah to peer out of the window at one point, only to witness the wings flapping. A moment of uncertainty gripped. 'Is that right?'

## Arrival in Mexico

As the plane descended onto the runway at close to midnight, the powerful hum of its engines signalled the triumphant end of a thrilling journey, and a huge relief for Val. The anticipation from the girls inside the cabin was unmistakable, as the young footballing passengers eagerly prepared for the moment they could step onto solid ground. The cabin crew announced the opening of the aircraft doors and as they swung open, the warm breeze of a new destination beckoned. Stepping onto the mobile staircase, the passengers were met with a dazzling sight below. A swarm of TV cameras and hundreds of photographers stood to attention, their lenses poised to capture every moment of this grand arrival. Amid the flashes and shouts from the photographers, Chris mused, 'There must be someone famous on this plane.'

Confused, the team scanned their surroundings, expecting a celebrity. To their astonishment, they realized that the press was there for them!

For Leah, the true enormity of the experience sank in shortly afterwards. As the youngest member of the team and possessing an Irish passport, she had the daunting prospect of navigating the 'Visa and Passport Control' alone.

By the time they reached Mexico, exhaustion was evident after the long journey. Previously accustomed to the support of friends and family as the primary audience for their football outings, the arrival at the airport raised questions about the multitude of people eager to see them. Photographers and fans alike greeted them, leaving the team in a state of disbelief. In the confusion, the collective thought struck them: 'There's no way that all these people turning up are here for us.' Harry, with an optimistic outlook, remarked: 'If this is the level of interest now, this bodes well for the rest of the tournament.' They were utterly blown away by the scale of attention and anticipation surrounding their presence in Mexico.

The team was ushered into a bus decked out with 'Inglaterra'. The 'British Independents' name had been ignored by the organizers, and all were taken to the five-star rated Plaza Hotel. Everywhere the team went in the bus, there was a police escort to accompany it. Two police motorbikes on either side and a police car behind as security to the total bemusement of the women. If only their friends and family could see them at this exact moment.

The Plaza Hotel was the one in which the England team had stayed the year before for the men's World Cup. It was a sign that the women were held in high regard for this tournament and treated on a level playing field with the men.

Jan recounted the warm welcome at the hotel, with hundreds of fans gathering outside to greet them. The hotel staff greeted them with a 'Welcome England' banner upon their arrival and flowers and chocolates labelled 'To the England Ladies!' awaited them in the reception area, a gesture that left the team in awe. Leah, still processing the surreal nature of the constant camera flashes, was taken aback to discover that they would be playing in the Azteca Stadium. In the excitement, a few members, including Leah and Lillian, were whisked away for a TV interview. Despite their weariness, and the late hour, they were swiftly ushered into a television studio. The barrage of questions from the interviewers proved challenging for Lillian, who, fatigued and eager to rest, found herself struggling to keep up. In a moment of whimsy or perhaps sleep-induced confusion, she blurted out, 'I'm getting married next year. I'm going to get married to John!' Whether her response made any sense in relation to the question remained uncertain, but it was the best her tired and jet-lagged brain could muster.

Trudy couldn't contain her surprise upon learning from the Hotel Plaza staff that she had been assigned the room in which Bobby Charlton had stayed during the men's World Cup the year before. Meanwhile, Leah, impressed by her own room, decided to pen a detailed letter to her parents, meticulously describing every aspect of her accommodation. Oddly, the focus remained solely on the hotel room, with no mention of the flight, football, visits or the country itself – she was captivated by the lavishness of her living space, documenting the sofa, desk and wardrobes.

Outside the hotel, a tempting burger bar caught Trudy's attention. The fresh burgers, infused with various dips and spices, proved irresistible, and a visit became a nightly indulgence despite her having already eaten dinner.

In the team dynamic, June assumed a matronly role, with Val and Marlene, the only players over 20 years old, keeping the younger players under their watchful eye. Rooms were paired, with an older player rooming with a younger one. Trudy gravitated towards Chris and Paula, immersing herself in the experience, seizing every opportunity to explore new places and meet new people.

Leah roomed with Yvonne, feeling sorry for her roommate having to share a space with a 13-year-old. Forming a bond with Chris and Gill, Leah and her pals playfully dubbed themselves the 'Three Amigos'. During the whirlwind, Leah found moments of reflection, writing letters home to her parents, creating cherished memories for her and her family. Despite this her time in Mexico was marked by an absence of homesickness. Immersed in the local culture, she eagerly embraced the experiences, joining in card games with her teammates at the hotel. She found genuine joy in getting to know the Mexican people.

Jean found herself rooming with Chris, although Chris's mischievous nature led her to spend most of her time with Leah and

Gill. Jean's personality, self-described as a 'good girl', stood in stark contrast to Chris's adventurous spirit.

It was time to adjust to the time difference, the heat and the altitude, as well as fitting in the endless interview requests.

The training was at 7:30am to escape the heat. Even at these sessions, 300–400 children would turn up to watch the English girls practise, to get photos and autographs.

At breakfast, the team faced a daily ritual of taking salt tablets. Initially sceptical about their necessity, Jean quickly realized their importance as soon as she stepped into the scorching heat. The intensity of the sun in Mexico surpassed anything she had experienced before, leading to soaked T-shirts and the need to maintain hydration levels. 'I've never been anywhere where it has been that hot. I hated the heat. It's not for me. Even in England, we don't get it that hot. It might hit 76 degrees Fahrenheit up north but that's the best it gets!'

There was a well-structured routine established by Harry and June, encompassing aspects like eating, sleeping, team talks and strategic planning. Carol, responsible for the fitness regime, pushed the team through a series of intense training exercises, including slaloms, jumps and circuit training. The demanding workouts left them drenched in sweat. Trudy's mother – aware of the soaring temperatures – had made a well-intentioned but misguided gesture of gifting her daughter paper knickers. Intended to ease the laundry burden, the ill-fated paper knickers succumbed to the intense Mexican heat during training, disintegrating into shreds that clung to Trudy's skin. 'All I ended up with was a bit of elastic around my hips and bits of paper on my legs that I had to peel off! . . . brilliant idea.'

There were limited options for entertainment post-training as the girls were restricted from venturing into the town, so the scorching weather often drove them to the nearby Cuban Club for a refreshing swim. Despite this, Lillian and a couple of teammates sneaked off during their time away. She likened the experience to being in an adventure movie, with the excitement of being part of a team and the thrill of being away from home.

Jill, on the other hand, admitted to being solely focused on the football aspect. Young and somewhat naive, she missed out on some of the fun experiences her teammates engaged in. Football was her primary concern, and she remained oblivious to other potential diversions.

Wherever they went there was an incredible warmth and kindness extended by the Mexican people during the team's time in the country. The locals embraced them with open hearts, regardless of age or gender. The love for football in Mexico elevated the experience to another level, intensifying the connection between the English players and the passionate Mexican fans.

Despite not fully grasping the magnitude of the tournament they were about to play in, the English team appreciated every moment in Mexico. The atmosphere was consistently warm and friendly, with everyone they encountered expressing genuine excitement at meeting them. They had the surreal experience of signing autographs, a task they never expected to undertake. However, the fans' love for the players was true, and requests for photos and autographs were met with enthusiasm, creating a sense of gratitude and appreciation among the players.

The contrast between the celebratory atmosphere in Mexico and the more reserved environment back home left a lasting impression on Leah. The Mexican nation's vibrant embrace of women's football, the tournament and their culture, stood in contrast to what felt like a more stifled and authoritarian approach in England. The experience allowed Leah to fully express herself joyfully and enthusiastically, a stark departure from the constraints she perceived in her home country. 'In Mexico, I could truly be myself. A happy, enthusiastic Leah playing football.'

Everywhere they went, joy accompanied them. The constant presence of mariachi bands, jokingly referred to as their perpetual followers, brought vibrant music that infused every moment with dancing, singing and an overall sense of happiness.

Jan, echoing Leah's sentiments, acknowledged the special place the Mexican people held for the English team. Crowds gathered outside the hotel, with ordinary people eager to catch a glimpse and interact with the players. The endearing nickname, 'Las Chicas de Carnaby Street', highlighted the distinctive bond formed between the English players and the welcoming Mexican community.

Carol recounted the pre-tournament whirlwind of interviews, one in particular that turned out to be more significant than she anticipated. Positioned as the captain, she sat patiently in a chair, awaiting her turn. To her surprise, what she assumed would be a small newspaper column transformed into a half-page spread complete with a photo.

Val, adopting a somewhat cynical perspective, noted that the Mexican press sometimes orchestrated events for mere photo opportunities, especially involving the younger players. While initially finding it challenging, she grew to understand the importance of these activities for the promotion of women's football. She playfully referred to herself as 'Granny Val'.

Many of the staged group activities were designed to showcase their feminine side. From playing with toys in a shop to enjoying swings in the park, and even posing in bikinis at the swimming pool, the team was subjected to various photo sessions. Despite the potential for exploitation, Leah emphasized that they genuinely had fun and never felt objectified. London's fashion-forward status during that era, featuring miniskirts and hot pants, further played into the narrative.

Jill, recalling an article where she was photographed in a bikini, expressed frustration at the unnecessary inclusion of her body measurements in the caption. She highlighted a segment of the Mexican press aiming for a 'sexy' portrayal of the Women's World Cup, which, in reality, didn't align with the genuine experiences of the team.

Paula had a less-than-fashionable episode with her hair in the scorching Mexican heat. Irritated by her long fringe falling across her face, she impulsively chopped a chunk off, resulting in a less-than-ideal outcome. It wasn't helped by the fact she mistakenly sewed her badge on the opposite side for the team photo, leading to a redo of the stitching process.

The strangeness of the situation brought about a camaraderie within the team and a deep respect for each other. There were moments of excitement, especially in and around the hotel, but the watchful eyes of Harry and June ensured their overall good behaviour. Post-training rituals often led them to the Cuban Club swimming pool, where relaxation and spontaneous football matches became inevitable. Playful antics in the pool, with Leah often perched on Captain Carol's or Big Jean's shoulders, helped with the team's bonding.

As an aside, several decades later a Mexican footballer reached out to Leah, expressing gratitude for a past incident. Following a group match between their teams, Leah had come to the rescue when the Mexican player was pushed into the water by her teammates, unaware that she couldn't swim. Leah, being a reasonable swimmer, swiftly intervened and pulled her to safety. The message from the Mexican player served as a heartwarming acknowledgement of Leah's act of kindness.

Afternoons were dedicated to social outings, allowing the 'British' team to explore different facets of the city. The Mexicans, brimming with pride for their country, eagerly shared their culture and landmarks with the visiting players.

People followed them everywhere. Jean still has photos with various individuals, including the hotel manager's son, who happened to be a doctor. She even has a shot of herself holding a baby in one photograph, despite having no connection to the child. During the craziness of the tournament, the entire team found themselves caught up in the whirlwind, blissfully unaware of the pandemonium unfolding around them.

However, the nerves were beginning to show for some.

Yvonne found herself grappling with homesickness. In the solitude of her room, and with Leah out with her amigos, emotions overwhelmed her and led to a momentary breakdown. In an impulsive act, she emptied out every wardrobe, drawer and desk, scattering her clothes, shoes and personal items across the floor and bed. She cried a torrent of tears, but, true to her nature, swiftly regained composure. With resilience, she meticulously tidied up, neatly restoring everything to its place before Leah returned to the room. Yvonne's emotional release remained her private affair, undetected by her roommate.

For Yvonne, a member of a close-knit family, the homesickness was amplified by her limited experiences away from home. The immersive nature of the tournament, coupled with the realization of the considerable distance from England, intensified her emotions. In that half-hour of solitude, she struggled with the enormity of the situation. The inability to make a simple phone call home (as Yvonne's mother didn't have a phone) added to the challenge, leaving her only with the options of sending postcards or writing letters. 'Looking back, I think Mexico was the making of me,' she said.

The British Embassy held a reception for the team featuring diplomats from various nations. As the team captain, Carol felt a responsibility to ensure the girls behaved, especially considering the presence of alcohol there. Engaged in conversation with the British military attaché, she held a glass of wine, discreetly planning to avoid drinking it. Amid the diplomatic affair, her watchful eyes darted around the room, wary of Leah's spontaneous antics, and Chris's playful nature, which often led to them winding up the captain, a suspicion that proved correct when she spotted Leah under the table at one point in the evening.

It was at the event that Leah had her first encounter with guacamole – she wasn't impressed. As Louise scanned the unfamiliar offerings at the banquet she was intrigued by a dish entirely new to her – the taco. Unacquainted with this Mexican delight, she hesitated before attempting a bite. To her disappointment, the taste did not resonate with her palate. Holding the taco in hand, Louise aimlessly wandered for a while, unsure what to do. Eventually, she found a place for the Mexican dish – a nearby bin.

The hidden history of England's women's national football team participating in this tournament derives from the fact that it is not considered official by FIFA or any of the national governing bodies of the competing nations, even though there was an official reception at the British Embassy to celebrate a team in the tournament representing England.

Jaime de Haro, who was president of the organizing committee, was quoted in a *New York Times* article dated 27 June 1971 saying, 'We are going to focus on the femininity.' It was a decision which he saw as 'a natural one' since 'soccer and women are two of the main passions of most men around the globe!' He continued to state that the players will have access to beauty salons in the dressing rooms so they can 'be interviewed and go to public ceremonies wearing false eyelashes, lipstick and a pretty hairstyle' before adding that the players' shorts would be as sexy as possible.

An exhibition game was arranged before the official tournament kicked off. This unique match featured teams composed of celebrities and models, all gathered for a magazine photoshoot. The promotional images from this event portrayed these glamorous women in provocative poses, strategically incorporating footballs into the scenes. The goalposts themselves were adorned in pink and white, reflecting a marketing approach attempting to sexualize the female football event.

However, just days before the tournament was due to start, the comments from Jaime de Haro and the nature of the exhibition game were looking out of place. It was becoming obvious that the Copa del Mundo was not going to be 'a mixture of sport and a beauty contest', but a serious football contest.

Leah pondered whether the provocative images influenced people's expectations when attending the subsequent matches. However, as she delved into the tournament programme and various sporting magazines and newspapers covering the event, it was clear that the focus remained squarely on football. Despite the initial marketing strategy, the Mexico '71 experience, particularly for a 13-year-old like Leah, unfolded without any inappropriate incidents. The tournament's essence was a celebration of women's football.

Archive photographs and videos show that the kit donned by the players during matches was anything but form-fitting and enticing. The shorts sported by Pelé in 1970 were considerably smaller than the ones seen in the 1971 tournament.

Leah found herself unwittingly stepping into the role of a local celebrity during Mexico '71, thanks to an unexpected resemblance to the official mascot, 'Xochitl'. The warrior princess, named after a flower, shared certain visual characteristics with Leah – a young girl with dark hair, although Leah's was styled in a ponytail rather than Xochitl's characteristic bunches.

The attention Leah garnered was particularly pronounced due to her age and striking resemblance to the mascot. Even at the tender age of 13, Leah became the recipient of significant attention, with boys in the crowds often holding roses and enthusiastically urging others to pass them on to her.

Keith fondly recalled a remarkable instance where two boys travelled from the outskirts of Mexico City solely to greet Leah. Recognizing her as a superstar with her long dark hair, the boys engaged in a conversation with her while Harry accompanied them.

## The tournament gets underway

The final six teams were: France, Italy, Denmark, Argentina, Mexico and England. Brazil had been asked to compete as winners of the men's World Cup the year before, and the immense popularity of football in the country made Brazil an obvious choice, but due to it still being illegal in some areas for girls to play, the invitation was rescinded. Another South American team was needed and so Argentina rallied a team together and replaced Brazil.

The organizers were keen to maximize profits and did everything in their power to ensure that the host country Mexico would meet the 1970 champions Denmark in the final. The draw for the groups was rumoured once again to be rigged. The groups were announced:

**Group 1 (to be played Mexico City, Azteca Stadium)**
Mexico / Argentina / England

**Group 2 (to be played Guadalajara, Jalisco Stadium)**
France / Italy / Denmark

On 15 August, 80,000 fans packed into the Azteca Stadium to watch the opening ceremony, featuring parades, military choirs, national anthems, speeches from FIFF, and a Mexican party. The stadium was one big carnival.

The promoters kept the tickets at reasonable prices – 30 to 80 pesos – to attract more fans. There were merchandise stalls too, with T-shirts, pin badges, bags, pendants and dolls, all featuring the mascot Xochitl and the participating nations.

Jan and Leah strolled towards the grand opening ceremony, adorned in their pristine uniforms – those white skirts, white blouses and a vibrant red, white and blue checked blazer from Jon Bryan's in Luton. Despite looking sharp, there was an underlying sentiment of disdain, the girls all yearning to be in their tracksuits yet again.

As they stepped into the spotlight, the girls raised their sombreros to acknowledge the crowd. The strains of the bands filled the air, prompting Leah and Jan to break into spontaneous dance. The atmosphere resembled a lively carnival, bursting with vibrant music and a kaleidoscope of colours.

During the festivities, Carol, being the captain, proudly held the flag as they embarked on a lap around the stadium. The crowd erupted in shouts and songs, creating a cacophony of noise that seemed out of this world. The passionate fans unmistakably labelled them as 'Inglaterra', proudly representing England in the upcoming tournament. Despite any reservations, Leah couldn't help but feel a swell of pride at the prospect of being a representative of her homeland.

### Mexico vs Argentina
### Sunday 15 August 1971, Azteca Stadium
### Attendance: 80,000 (est)

The Mexican team, also known as 'La Verde', won the opening match of the tournament, 3-1. A goal from Argentina was disallowed which the Argentine players disputed. Soon there were claims of bias from the officials. Hardly a surprise after the antics of FIFF in the previous tournament.

The defeat left a bad taste in the mouth of the Argentines. Some players were convinced that they had been given unfair treatment, believing the disallowed goal to be proof that, as the host country, Mexico *had* to make it through to the final.

All matches in Mexico City were played at the weekend to maximize ticket sales. With six days to prepare after the opening ceremony, it was time for the English girls to show what they were capable of.

### Argentina vs England
### Saturday 21 August 1971, Azteca Stadium
### Attendance: 30,000 (est)

As Leah peered out of the coach window on the journey from the hotel to the stadium, she saw a police escort guiding them through the bustling city. The coach descended into the stadium grounds through a tunnel, and she was overcome by the noise of the crowd and the intense heat that greeted her as she stepped out.

In the dressing room situated beneath the pitch, Lillian and her teammates were enveloped in a mysterious noise. It gradually intensified, and it finally dawned on them that it was the roar of the crowd. And as they emerged onto the grand stage of the Azteca Stadium a mix of overwhelming and exhilarating emotions swept through them. The roar of the crowd hit them like a deafening wave.

Not everyone was overwhelmed. In fact, Val couldn't help but express disbelief at the relatively modest attendance of 30,000 spectators. However, it was nevertheless a huge number of spectators for a group of girls who were more used to playing in front of just a handful of people. 'I do remember I was very disappointed with the state of the pitch at the Azteca Stadium. Sorry, it was worse than a park. That's my impression of it. Hitchin Town pitch was three times better.' The pitch was so dry and hard that Gill changed from nylon studs to rubber for better traction.

The adrenaline was pumping, and the girls kicked off their World Cup campaign. The media claimed the English were the favourites, but after the loss to Mexico, Argentina needed a win to be sure to stay in the tournament.

Paula took on the role of a forward, stationed out on the right wing during the intense matches. Opponents attempted to tackle her, but her speed and skill often allowed her to elegantly manoeuvre the ball past them. The games were not without their rough moments, marked by dirty play and a heightened physicality that included some unexpected elbowing, an element the British girls were not accustomed to.

It wasn't a good start for England as Argentina took the lead after seven minutes. However, 15-year-old forward Paula restored parity, not that she remembers . . . Despite the intensity, Paula's memory of scoring against Argentina remains elusive. She is, however, among the rare few Britons who have scored in the iconic Azteca Stadium, achieving the feat with a header in the 13th minute. Leah's shot had rebounded off the crossbar, and Paula, in a moment she couldn't recall, headed it into the goal, equalizing the score at 1-1.

A newspaper article chronicled the moment, featuring a photo capturing the team's lone goal. Leah had hoped for an assist, but technically, it wasn't justified. Paula was on the right wing and Leah played inside right – and they maintained a strong connection, having been teammates at Chiltern Valley.

Many of the girls remember Lillian's performance for her exceptional bravery as goalkeeper. Despite her modest height of 1.56m (5ft 1in), her acrobatics and adept shot-stopping abilities played a crucial role in keeping the team in contention throughout the matches. Lillian's resilience inspired the team, and they needed resilience. The tackles from the Argentina players got worse. The play was getting rough.

In the realm of English football, Paula associated tackles with a certain cleanliness and sportsmanship that avoided deliberate nastiness. However, the match against Argentina unfolded as an entirely different story. It seemed that in this clash, anything and everything was fair game. The Argentine women, characterized by their physicality, played a robust game and shirts were constantly subjected to tugging, especially around the neck.

Marlene, recalling her stint on the field during the first match against Argentina, revealed the challenges she faced in an unfamiliar position. Normally a left half for Daytels, she was deployed as a left back for this crucial game – a decision that didn't sit well with her. Her playing time was abruptly cut short as she exited the field at half-time. A failed attempt to jump for the ball resulted in an unexpected fall, with her legs giving way beneath her. Reaching shoulder height, and landing the wrong way round, the impact left her with dizziness and discomfort. Determined to soldier on, she played until half-time, hoping to assess the extent of the damage. But once the severity of the situation became apparent, Harry promptly substituted her. It was the end of her tournament.

At half-time it was 3-1 to Argentina. In the second half, Val made sure her presence was known but was shown a yellow card for doing so. 'The players were very physical, so if you can't get the ball, you get the player, right? Well, I showed her the English slide tackle anyhow!' Despite not being the fastest player, Val's forte lay in her exceptional passing skills. Her defensive plays often involved retrieving the ball from opposing attackers and elegantly passing it to Leah on the left side, who, with her George Best skills, was ever ready to take on the opposition.

With Val on a yellow card, the brutal tackles flew in from the Argentina players. The referee was seemingly oblivious to the rough play, while Harry Batt was chain-smoking and shouting instructions from the sideline. But there was more drama to come . . .

In the midst of the scorching heat, Jan found herself caught off guard by the intensity of the weather. When the referee blew the whistle following a decision on the field, Jan seized the opportunity to hurry to the side of the pitch to remove her shin pads, hoping for a brief respite from the sweltering conditions. However, what was intended as a quick adjustment turned into chaos. As Jan left the pitch, she was suddenly shown a red card. Harry erupted in frustration at the decision, unaware of a crucial rule that required players to seek the referee's permission before leaving the field. This rule had never been communicated to the team. Despite the entire team explaining that Jan had left the pitch solely to remove her shin pads, the referee remained obstinate, repeatedly asserting, 'You left the pitch!' The pleas fell on deaf ears.

It took the intervention of another official, who acted as a mediator and helped translate the issue, to break the impasse. Finally relenting, the referee acknowledged the misunderstanding, allowing Jan back onto the field.

Argentina won the match 4-1 with all four goals coming from Elba Selva, a penalty in the second half adding to her first half hat-trick.

The scorching heat and high altitude added to the challenge for the English players, casting doubt on the team's endurance for the full 90 minutes. Despite the tough conditions, they persevered, completing the entire match in 32°C (90°F) heat.

It was a crushing disappointment for the team. Reflecting on it, Gill understood that they hadn't fully grasped the South American style of play. Accustomed to success with her club team, the defeat was a bitter pill to swallow for someone who despised losing. The collective morale took a hit, with a sense of self-doubt creeping in. Despite the team's belief in their capabilities, the match didn't unfold as anticipated. Gill attributed part of the challenge to Harry's limited time in which to fine-tune tactics and prepare the team adequately for the physicality of South American football. Despite the setback, Gill stressed the team gave everything.

In the aftermath of the Argentina match, the dressing room resembled a scene of post-battle recovery. Injuries were rampant, with Carol nursing a foot ailment, Lillian grappling with a shoulder issue, Val requiring oxygen to overcome altitude sickness, and Marlene receiving the disheartening news from the doctors that her football tournament had come to an abrupt end.

Harry told reporters: 'We tried to play clean English football, but things didn't go to plan . . . The girls were hacked to pieces. It was absolutely diabolical. They came after our blood.'

The match finished at 6pm, but there was no time to be disappointed as the girls had their second match, against Mexico at 12pm the next day.

### Mexico vs England
### Sunday 22 August 1971, Azteca Stadium
### Attendance: 90,000 (est)

An electrifying atmosphere enveloped the stadium. The thunderous roar of the crowd echoed in the players' ears. What was astonishing to them was the crowd weren't just mere spectators; they were cheering for the women on the field. In that moment, women footballers were not only acknowledged but celebrated.

Despite the fact they were playing Mexico, there was still an intense excitement surrounding the team. People eagerly gathered outside the hotel, waiting for the girls to emerge. The enthusiasm of the crowd was nothing short of phenomenal. Carol, caught in the midst of it all, couldn't help but feel that this was a pivotal moment for women's football. Even if the full impact might not be felt immediately, the signs of progress were evident. Harry had envisioned it, and as Carol stood at the end of the tunnel, the screams of the fans intensified her belief in the burgeoning future of women's football.

The stadium, with a reported attendance of 90,000, boasted the largest audience for an England women's football match. The gravity of the moment nearly overwhelmed Carol, and her legs threatened to betray her as they trembled uncontrollably. She silently grappled with her anxieties, urging herself not to succumb to the nerves. The responsibility of leading her team out was immense, with the knowledge that her fellow players likely shared similar feelings.

Once she stepped onto the grass, crossing the athletics track around the pitch, she found her composure. The once-deafening noise became a distant hum, akin to white noise, as her focus shifted to the ball and the pride of representing her country.

The assault on the team's eardrums as they emerged from the tunnel resembled a mega-carnival, with drums beating, horns blaring, and the crowd's continuous screams creating an unrelenting symphony of support. The contrast between this overwhelming response and their usual experiences at Crawley Green Sports ground was stark. 'The sound of the crowd, the banging of the drums, and the intense midday heat as we walked out onto the Azteca pitch, has stayed with me for the last 52 years,' says Trudy.

However, it was another bad start for the English team. Mexico took the lead within three minutes. Alicia 'La Pele' Vargas scored, and the crowd went wild. Even with many banners of 'Inglaterra' in the stadium, and the English girls' popularity, it wasn't enough to keep the Mexicans from wildly supporting their own players.

England got stuck in and played better than the day before and had Lillian, again in goal, to thank for keeping the scoreline down. Despite this, they went into half-time losing 3-0.

Lillian observed the notable differences in the playing style of the Mexican team compared to the Argentines. The Mexicans, though smaller in stature, possessed remarkable speed. From her vantage point in goal, Lillian could discern their swift advances down the pitch, putting the English defenders under considerable pressure. There were instances when three attackers bore down on her, requiring her to make a swift decision on whether to hold her ground or venture out towards the ball. Opting for the latter strategy on several occasions, she managed to disrupt the flow and thwart potential threats. Her bold decision-making and quick reflexes resulted in some remarkable saves, effectively keeping England in the game. Keith, Harry's son, was amazed at Lillian's acrobatics at specific moments. She entered a zone when stepping onto the pitch, a state of focus that seemingly turned this diminutive woman into an acrobatic cat. A photograph capturing her mid-dive served as evidence of her remarkable efforts. Lillian speculated that perhaps her age played a role, preserving a certain innocence and a 'go out and play' attitude.

The Mexicans were less physical than the Argentina players, but the midday heat, the altitude and the fact the English team was playing two matches in less than 24 hours was taking its toll on the girls and their fitness. Yvonne was next to fall . . .

She found herself in uncharted territory during the tournament – her first time wearing shin pads, a mandatory requirement. However, this debut encounter with shin pads took an unexpected turn, resulting in a fracture. She was left unable to put weight on her foot. Despite her efforts to play on, Yvonne found herself in a situation where she couldn't contribute effectively, hopping around and signalling to her teammates not to pass to her. With no other substitutes left to use, Yvonne had to continue the match the best she could.

Jean, tasked with directing the ball down the wing, received a hard tackle but, upon Harry's advice, stayed down to draw the referee's attention to the aggressive nature of the Latin American players. The concern for the younger and smaller players on the team, such as 13-year-old Leah and the petite Gill, prompted Harry's protective stance. When an injury occurred, the appearance of the 'magic sponge' and water seemed inadequate.

Louise, despite enduring cramps in the second half against Mexico, thrived in the atmosphere of the stadium, in awe of the sheer number of spectators. The adrenaline rush and nerves made her queasy, but the prospect of playing in front of 90,000 fans outweighed any discomfort.

During the match Harry was heard to say, 'Our girls are getting butchered!' The intensity and physicality of the game justified

Harry's cautious approach, choosing to field Leah only as a substitute and protect her the best he could. The opposing team, with a markedly different footballing style, employed a more robust and calculated approach to the game. Despite the English team's competitive spirit and the occasional display of strong tackles, they found themselves struggling with the challenge of adapting to the opposing style while also contending with numerous injuries sustained in the previous match. This dual setback hindered their ability to showcase their creativity on the field, leaving them yearning for more time to acclimatize and assert their own distinctive approach to the game.

The full-time whistle was blown, and it was 4-0 to Mexico.

Harry was furious and complained to reporters and the organizers. 'It's too much for the girls to play two games in less than 24 hours. You don't even see this in men's football.'

Despite the scoreline, Carol found a peculiar sense of pride in that match against Mexico. To her, it stood out as their strongest performance because every player gave their absolute best, pouring their hearts into the match. Carol felt that the team played at full capacity; Mexico were simply the superior team.

Again, there were many injuries after the match, notably Carol and Yvonne.

Yvonne, feeling the weight of her injury, made her way to the dressing room where the medical staff assessed her leg and foot. Initially, they thought all was well, considering the team's history of injuries. Opting to return to the hotel for a more thorough evaluation, Yvonne managed to get to her room in the lift. Later in the evening, as she went for dinner, she encountered her injured teammates preparing to board a bus bound for the hospital. Harry, noting Yvonne's struggle, advised her to join them. This decision proved crucial, as her leg ended up encased in a heavy plaster cast. The most frustrating aspect of her situation was her restriction from the swimming pool, where she could only watch others enjoy while seated on the side.

In a parallel tale of determination, Carol had suffered a small bone fracture in her foot during the Argentina match. Despite the excruciating pain, missing the upcoming Mexico game was inconceivable for her. It wasn't about heroism; it was about being on that pitch. Post the Mexico match, she finally succumbed to the necessary plaster cast and a similar watching brief at the pool.

The girls were hugely disappointed. With a 4-1 and a 4-0 defeat in the group matches, this meant England were out of the tournament and Mexico and Argentina would progress to the semi-finals.

The weight of disappointment hung heavy on the team. The impact wasn't solely confined to the results; it was the sting of defeat in the grandeur of Mexico's largest stadium, with 30,000 spectators against Argentina and a staggering 90,000 against Mexico.

Jean, accustomed to the dominant victories of Chiltern Valley Ladies, found the defeats to Argentina and Mexico particularly hard to digest. In their local league, they were accustomed to overwhelming victories with scorelines reaching 8 or 9-0.

Losing 4-1 in the first match was a stark departure and caused a profound sense of hurt. Unaccustomed to being on the receiving end of defeat, the team collectively aimed to improve in the second game, pouring in relentless effort. Each member gave 100 per cent, dismissing the notion that they were there merely for the sake of participation. The team had set out with a clear objective – to win – and the misconception that they were in it for the fun irked Jean.

Despite the unfavourable outcomes, there was a collective determination to hold their heads high. The team's competitive spirit, while contributing to the emotional toll of the losses, also served as a testament to their passion for the game and the desire for success on the international stage.

Meanwhile, in Guadalajara . . .

## Group 2 Round-Up
### Games played at the Estadio Jalisco, Guadalajara

The Group 2 matches were staged 500km (310 miles) away from Mexico City. Denmark, champions in 1970, got their campaign underway with a winning start, defeating France 3-0.

Three days later, needing a result to stay in the World Cup, France narrowly lost to Italy, 1-0. France were out of the tournament. The match was feisty, and a photograph taken during the game shows Italy's Elena Schiavo delivering a right hook to France's Jocelyne Henry.

The following day, Denmark and Italy played out a 1-1 draw,

meaning that Denmark and Italy both went through, Denmark as winners of the group.

And so to the semi-finals . . .

## SEMI-FINAL 1 – DENMARK VS ARGENTINA
### Saturday 28 August 1971 – Azteca Stadium

On the way from the hotel to training, the Argentine bus collided with a van, resulting in injuries to eight players. Fortunately, none of them suffered broken bones, but Elba Selva, the top scorer, couldn't participate in the semi-final against Denmark due to injuries to both her legs. Three other players were unavailable for that crucial match as well. The Argentine team, nicknamed 'Albicelestes' (the 'White and Sky Blues'), had already faced numerous challenges before the tournament, including financial constraints, a lack of studs for boots, an absence of medical staff and a coach, and even their team jerseys disintegrated during washing.

Argentina did not play well considering, and Denmark emerged victorious with a 5-0 scoreline.

## SEMI-FINAL 2 – MEXICO VS ITALY
### Sunday 29 August 1971 – Azteca Stadium

The Mexico vs Italy semi-final unfolded with a series of comical refereeing errors that left the Italian 'Squadra Azzurra' team incensed. Allegations from the Italians claimed that, on the eve of the match, Mexican fans created a disruptive ruckus outside their hotel, disturbing their night's sleep. Although there was no conclusive evidence linking the disruptive fans to tournament organizers, suspicions lingered.

The situation took a turn for the worse during the match when the referee controversially disallowed two seemingly valid goals for the Italians. Mexico narrowly secured a 2-1 victory, earning them a spot in the final against Denmark. This was helped by the referee blowing the full-time whistle in the 80th minute, 10 minutes early. Despite protests, unbelievably the result stood.

The game itself had enough standalone drama to warrant its own television show. Archival footage showcases a high-quality, fiercely competitive match as the stakes were exceptionally high. It culminated in a mass brawl between the players.

In Chris's opinion, the dynamics between the teams in the tournament revealed their competitiveness. The Mexico and Argentina teams seemed to harbour some animosity between them, and the Italian team projected an air of unapproachability, confident in their anticipated victory. However, their bubble of confidence burst when they were surprisingly knocked out in the semi-final against Mexico. The controversial match caused great shock and disappointment throughout the squad and Chris even caught wind of a rumour suggesting that, in the aftermath of their unexpected exit, the Italian team had vented their frustration by smashing up the dressing room.

The strains of the Mexican farewell song 'Las Golondrinas' echoed through the hotel as the English team prepared to bid adieu to the tournament. Having faced defeat in their group matches against Argentina and Mexico, their journey seemed to be concluding on a sombre note. As they gathered their belongings to depart, the hotel staff, visibly emotional, came to see them off, shedding tears.

But at the last hour, there was some good news. Harry was called to the offices of the organizers where Martini & Rossi, having been impressed with the girls' behaviour and friendly attitude, offered to pay for the team to stay in Mexico and play a 5th/6th playoff match against France. The organizers seemed to appreciate the team's connection with the Mexican public, recognizing their impact and interest.

So the team unpacked their bags and promptly decided to celebrate with another party. The unexpected extension elicited tears of happiness from everyone, including the staff. The three Mexican musicians from the Mariachi band continued to trail the English team.

The news transformed the team's mood. They felt like they were part of the 'party of their lives', having forged numerous friendships during their stay. While the details of how families were notified of the players' extended stay in Mexico remained unclear, the team embraced the opportunity.

Despite the challenge of fielding a complete team due to injuries, the match against France presented another opportunity to play in the remarkable Azteca Stadium and pursue a victory.

Harry Batt, surrounded by members of the Chiltern Valley Ladies, 1971.

Pat Dunn (centre) coaching a training session with the England women's football team, 1971.

On the rooftop of the Plaza Hotel where the team stayed in Mexico.

Harry Batt (centre right) dancing with the team at the hotel.

Team photo in the empty Azteca Stadium, Mexico City, before the Women's World Cup tournament, 1971. Harry Batt is seen on the right next to Pat Dunn; June and Keith Batt are on the left.

Some of the team out sightseeing with their interpreter, Nelly.
This photo was taken on top of a pyramid.

Leah Caleb, the youngest in the squad at just 13 years old, wearing the official 1971 Women's World Cup T-shirt featuring the mascot Xochitl.

Fans surround the team bus arriving at a training session in Mexico City.

*Above* Paula Rayner scores England's only goal against Argentina, 21 August, 1971.

*Left* Lilian performs heroics in goal against Mexico.

*Above* Tere Agullar scores her second goal for Mexico. Mexico ran out 4–0 winners. This was the England team's second game in 24 hours and resulted in eight of the team being treated in hospital.

*Left* Carol Wilson (left) and Yvonne Farr on their return from Mexico, each with their leg in plaster. Carol has a broken bone in her foot and Yvonne has a broken leg.

The team at Heathrow Airport on their return from Mexico. Left to right: Harry Batt (Manager), Gill Sayell (obscured), Leah Caleb, Jean Breckon, Paula Rayner, Carol Wilson, Chris Lockwood, Janice Barton, Yvonne Farr, Keith Batt (team mascot), Jill Stockley, Trudy McCaffery, Lilian Harris, Louise Cross, Marlene Collins, Val Cheshire, June Batt (Assistant Manager) and Pat Dunn (Coach).

'Don't laugh – one day there may be a female Arsenal' is one of the few reports on the team's return from Mexico, seen in the *Beds and Herts Saturday Telegraph*, 18 September 1971.

The Lost Lionesses on their way to France with UEFA who invited them as special guests to the FIFA Women's World Cup semi-final, July 2019.

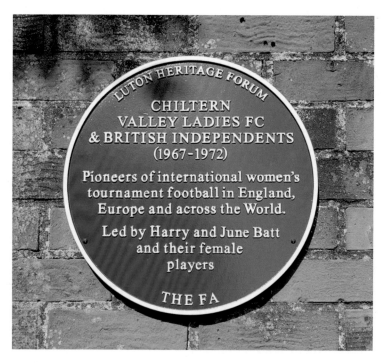

The FA and Luton Heritage Society unveiled a blue plaque at Crawley Green Recreation Ground, the old home of Chiltern Valley Ladies, 16 September 2023.

## 5th / 6th PLAYOFF – FRANCE VS ENGLAND
### Saturday 28 August 1971 – Azteca Stadium

Due to injuries sustained in the group matches, extra players from the Mexico squad were recruited to represent 'Inglaterra' against France.

For once, England got off to a good start, taking the lead on two occasions – both goals coming from Jan.

The sting of disappointment lingered in the aftermath of losing the group matches, and Trudy noted Jan's visible frustration. In Trudy's eyes, Jan's anger seemed to manifest in her curls, becoming even curlier. However, the French team bore the brunt of Jan's pent-up energy in the subsequent match. She unleashed her fury on the field, executing what Trudy deemed one of the best goals in the tournament. With remarkable finesse, she dribbled the ball past three opponents one by one, swiftly moved around the goalkeeper, and struck the ball into the back of the net.

While the details of the second goal are vague, the first one stands out vividly for Jan.

*'I collected the ball on the halfway line. I beat one player and then another. The last defender tried to tackle me, but I dribbled the ball around her, just as the keeper came out to attempt to block me, and there on the angle and I just poked it past her into the open goal. Left foot as well. I never used my left foot ever. I thought, "Oh my God, I've scored a goal!"'*

'It doesn't come any better than that,' she reflected.

There are only six English people to have ever scored in the

Azteca Stadium. Derek Kevan in a friendly match vs Mexico 1959, Paula Raynor vs Argentina (World Cup 1971), Jan Barton vs France (2) (World Cup 1971), Kerry Dixon vs Mexico (Copa Ciudad de Mexico 1985), Peter Beardsley vs Paraguay (FIFA World Cup 1986), and Gary Lineker vs Paraguay (2) and vs Argentina (1) (FIFA World Cup 1986). And in those rankings, with two goals Jan Barton is second only behind Gary Lineker.

However, the joy was short-lived as France emerged victorious with a 3-2 scoreline. There was a bittersweet feeling of seeing Jan's two individual goals being overshadowed by another defeat.

'Inglaterra' finished the tournament in 6th place.

## COPA DEL MUNDO FINAL – DENMARK VS MEXICO
### Sunday 5 September 1971 – Azteca Stadium
### Attendance: 110,000 (est)

The Mexican team had seen the promotions and the fans and realized that there was a lot of money being made, but none of it was going to them. Together, united as a team, they requested 1,000,000 pesos (approximately $US320,000) to be shared among the squad of 16, along with the coach, fitness trainer and doctor.

This request inevitably sparked a standoff with the tournament organizing committee and its president, Jaime de Haro. The local press accused the players of seeking money, despite their amateur status. Responding to the criticism, Alicia Vargas stated, 'Of course, we are amateurs, but we are the ones playing. If they don't want to pay us, then the tickets and matches should be free!'

The Mexican team's threat of not playing the final had little impact, as De Haro was prepared to assemble another Mexico team, or one comprised of players from other participating nations instead of cancelling the final. Eventually, the players relented, as Vargas explained. 'In the end, we decided to play the match for the spectators' sake as it wasn't their fault that this situation has come about.'

The final became the most attended women's football match so far, earning the Copa del Mundo a special place in history.

Denmark emerged victorious with a 3-0 win, defending their world title from the previous year in Italy. Notable individual performances included a hat-trick from 15-year-old Susanne Augustesen. The trophy, known as the 'Winged Goddess' or 'Angel de Oro', provided by Martini & Rossi, was made of gold and depicted an angel wearing a Greek crown with a football at its feet.

For Harry's team, the Mexican experience had been a rollercoaster of emotions. Despite the highs of the experience, the lingering disappointment stemmed from the football results – losses to Argentina, Mexico and France. The pain was palpable, as every member of the team harboured a burning desire to win. The notion of merely enjoying a trip to Latin America and making up the numbers was far from their mindset. They were a fiercely competitive team, proud to don the England shirt. However, tactical adaptability eluded them in the face of a different style of football. The challenge was compounded by the schedule, playing both their group matches within 24 hours. It was a steep learning curve, a unique footballing experience on a grand stage vastly different from their previous encounters. Their Latin and South American opponents, acclimatized to the heat and altitude, held a distinct advantage.

But what was clear was the warmth of the Mexican people.

The five-week stay in Mexico, with supportive work managers and the organizers' appreciation, became an incredible experience for the girls. Financial constraints and unpaid wages were eclipsed by the genuine affection the Mexicans had for them. They were invited to watch the final between Denmark and Mexico.

## Memories of Mexico

In retrospect, Louise acknowledged a lack of full appreciation at the time, especially concerning the privilege of playing in the iconic Azteca Stadium. The gravity of the experience, perhaps lost in the focus on football, now resided in the recesses of memory. The blend of regret and nostalgia marked the end of their remarkable journey on the Mexican turf. 'I'd love to go back. It would be an absolute dream.'

Trudy's frustration bubbled to the surface whenever she encountered reports dismissing their team as 'just a club team'. While the core of the squad hailed from Chiltern Valley, Harry had diligently scouted players from various teams, although his efforts were hampered by the proposed ban on participants. Their collective ambition transcended mere participation; they yearned to secure victories for Harry, for their loved ones, for themselves, and, above all, for England. The notion of being mere spectators, there to fill a numerical quota, was not their purpose. Their mission was clear – to play with intensity, compete fiercely and emerge victorious.

What is clear is that the commercial sponsors played a pivotal role in generating continuous revenue for the tournament. The collaboration between Mexico City, Martini & Rossi and other partners exemplified a concerted effort to promote women's football. They skilfully ignited curiosity among fans, who, drawn by reasonable ticket prices, discovered a brand of football that exceeded expectations in terms of skill and speed. The matches, far from being relegated to the sidelines, captured the public's imagination, dominating television broadcasts and newspaper headlines. The success of the tournament marked a turning point, as women's football transitioned from a mere curiosity to a serious and enthralling spectacle, leaving an indelible impact on the sporting landscape.

*'All the time we were there, Harry was saying,*
*"This could be done in England."'*
Jan

Val's homesickness, a familiar companion on her travels, took an unexpected backseat during her time in Mexico. Contrary to her usual longing for home, she found herself reluctant to bid farewell to the vibrant country. The allure of the Mexican experience had cast its spell, and if given the choice, Val would have extended her stay indefinitely.

The generosity of Martini & Rossi, who covered all expenses, left an enduring impression on Val. Grateful for their kindness, she continued to commemorate the memories by purchasing a bottle of Martini & Rossi every Christmas. The parting gift of a sports bag, complete with two bottles, became a cherished memento. While some younger teammates bemoaned the absence of a bag – this being due to the alcohol content from the sponsors in said bags – Val appreciated the sentiment, savouring one bottle upon her return and reserving the other for a special occasion – her wedding day.

Chris, amid the whirlwind of Mexico City, navigated a pivotal coming-of-age period. The trip served as a catalyst for personal transformation, prompting her to confront the realities awaiting her back in the UK. No longer could she hide behind a rebellious facade; it was time to embrace the person she aspired to be.

Navigating the unfamiliar terrain of Mexico City, Chris found herself overwhelmed by the unusual attention and the prospect of meeting new people. The World Cup arrived at a particularly tumultuous juncture in her life – transitioning from school to work and grappling with her emerging identity as a gay woman. The yearning for self-discovery unfolded against the backdrop of a whirlwind Mexican experience, encompassing a maiden flight, unexpected fame, the iconic Azteca Stadium, and the staggering presence of a 90,000-strong audience. Chris marvelled at the sheer improbability of it all, acknowledging that without experiencing it first hand, the remarkable tale would remain unbelievable.

The allure of the English women's football team in Mexico

extended beyond the pitch, sparking unexpected romantic interests. Lillian found herself at the centre of a sweet proposal when the manager of a local store presented her with an enormous box of nougat, asking, 'Will you marry me?' Amused by the unconventional gesture, Lillian opted to share the sugary delight with her teammates, avoiding any awkward declines. Her heart already belonged to John.

Yvonne, engaging in casual conversations with a waiter named Jesus, inadvertently attracted his interest. Their rooftop rendezvous, accompanied by English lessons for Jesus, led to friendly correspondence upon her return to the UK. However, when Jesus hinted at visiting her with friends, Yvonne, feeling uneasy, decided to bring their exchanges to an abrupt halt.

Jan encountered a charming admirer named Manuel, a hotel employee with whom she engaged in daily conversations. Their interactions were respectful, abiding by Harry's evening curfew. A handsome photographer also captured Jan's attention, leaving her with a heartfelt note expressing everlasting memories. Tearful goodbyes ensued as the photographer, enchanted by her presence, documented their every move.

Paula, too, found herself at the centre of affection, with Alberto, a singer at their hotel, later expressing intentions of matrimony through postcards. Unprepared for such proposals at her young age, Paula had to gently rebuff Alberto's visions of a honeymoon in Acapulco. A photo from a hotel party revealed another admirer, Gilberto, who wrote a sweet note complimenting Paula's beautiful eyes.

As a result of their intense World Cup experience in Mexico, Gill and Marlene found unexpected connections that transcended cultural and language barriers.

Gill's encounter began at a theatre owned by actor Manolo Fabregas, where the team was invited to watch a play. Post-performance, they headed to a diner, and a young admirer tapped Gill on the shoulder, requesting a photo. Little did she know, this chance encounter would lead to a surprise visit from the young suitor at their hotel the next day. Despite the language barrier, Gill, Chris and Leah managed to communicate with him in the hotel lounge. Exchanging addresses, Gill and the young man became pen pals. The photograph he sent had a heartfelt note on the reverse, expressing love and affection. A subsequent letter revealed his plans to study in England, but nervousness led Gill to regretfully end the correspondence. In a twist of fate, he later became a renowned actor in Mexico, even making appearances in Hollywood movies, under the name Rafael Sanchez Navarro.

Marlene's story unfolded against the backdrop of nightly mariachi performances at the hotel. Intrigued by the guitarist in the mariachi group, she struck up a connection during their time in Mexico. Their bond extended beyond the tournament as they became pen pals upon Marlene's return to England. Exchanging letters detailing their lives and dreams, their correspondence grew into a romantic connection. Despite doubts about marriage due to the swift pace, the excitement of receiving letters kept the flame alive. The only challenge was the language barrier, as the guitarist wrote exclusively in Spanish. Determined to overcome this obstacle, Marlene embarked on a journey to learn Spanish, enrolling in night school to unravel the sentiments expressed in those heartfelt letters.

There were tears when the girls said their goodbyes. But it was time to return home and carry on the momentum of women's football that all of them had just experienced.

# Chapter 6
# Back on British Soil:
# The Storm and the Fallout

———

The WFA and FA had not supported the venture of sending a team to Mexico.

Pat Dunn, the referee and chaperone of the team, was highly critical of the WFA on her return saying, 'Any organization that denies to the women of Britain the opportunities that we have had presented to us over the past five weeks, must be mad.'

FIFA and UEFA were outraged by the success of Mexico '71 despite all their efforts to deter nations from entering and ordering the Mexican FA not to host the tournament. To try and regain some control, at the end of 1971, UEFA passed a resolution recommending that member associations control women's football and integrate it into their existing structures. However, not all followed suit immediately. And with this announcement, it meant the end of FIFF and it was disbanded.

When Harry and the girls returned home, having been used to a media circus in Mexico City, they arrived back to nothing.

No media, no TV cameras, just a couple of lines in the newspaper mentioning that the girls had lost. The articles had headlines of: *'Soccer girls limp home to a rumpus'* and, focusing on Yvonne and Carol in plaster casts, *'Football mayhem as women are hurt'*. The articles were tongue and cheek and there was even a hint of cynicism with a reporter writing, *'Don't laugh – one day there may be a female Arsenal'*.

For Harry, the consequences of defying the FA and WFA started. And they started with a bang.

Amid a flurry of daily correspondence from the FA, Harry found himself inundated with letters bearing restrictions, charges and summons. Each seemed to carry the weight of opposition to his endeavours. Despite this barrage, Harry, undeterred, pressed on with his unwavering dream of propelling women's football to new heights. Undoubtedly, he was not merely dealing with challenges, but also nurturing aspirations of orchestrating the inaugural Women's World Cup in 1972, an ambitious vision that centred on hosting the prestigious event at the iconic Wembley Stadium in London.

Harry was enthused and inspired after what he had witnessed in Mexico. He expressed his aspiration to secure a sponsor for Chiltern Valley Ladies within the next two years in an interview with a local newspaper. In a separate article, June conveyed her conviction that full-time professional women's teams would emerge in the country's future, expressing hopes for their team to be among the pioneers.

These comments didn't help the already fragile relationship

between Harry and the WFA, who then accused him of attempting to present his team as the official England team, as the 'British Independents' were called 'Inglaterra' in Mexico. The WFA also alleged that Harry enticed players with a spot in the 'England team' and used the term 'England manager' in correspondence.

The WFA also faced limitations in pursuing professionalism due to a lack of funding, consisting only of a small government grant designated for amateur sports.

The PR manager for the England men's team at the 1970 World Cup was a man called Ted Hart. After hearing about the success of Mexico '71 and the crowd attendances, Ted approached Harry to help with the idea of hosting a Women's World Cup at Wembley the next year, 1972.

Hart made a few phone calls, and an exciting meeting took place at Harry's house.

A knock on the door heralded an unexpected and surreal moment as Geoff Hurst, the legendary figure from the 1966 World Cup-winning team, and his manager walked into the Batt residence. The hero of England's historic triumph was now seated in the front room of a house in Luton to young Keith's amazement. Geoff, clearly intrigued by the success story emanating from Mexico, had brought his chequebook, poised for investment. The allure of being part of this burgeoning venture was too compelling for him to resist.

Along with Hurst's teammate Bobby Moore and other businessmen, there was a pledge of £150,000 sponsorship.

The idea was that there were would be two England teams taking part in the tournament, one team entered by the WFA and the other by Harry. However, the WFA and Harry would have to settle their differences first.

The WFA did at least vote on the matter. There were two conditions set in place, one of them being Harry Batt could not be involved, nor could any teams connected to FIFF. FIFA had effectively banned them. The FA, having heard the planned proposal, warned the WFA to vote no, saying the plan was an attempt at 'blatant exploitation' by the sponsors.

The WFA committee found itself divided on the matter. Initially, in the first vote, the idea received approval with a 6-5 majority. However, the vote underwent two controversial reruns, resulting in a deadlock with a final score of 6-6. WFA chairman Pat Gwynne utilized his casting vote to reject the plan. Subsequently, those dissatisfied with the handling of the process called for a vote of no confidence, which concluded with a 5-5 tie, resulting in another deadlock.

There would be no Women's World Cup to be staged at Wembley.

Ted, Geoff and Harry eagerly sought a dialogue with the FA to engage in discussions, but the FA displayed a resolute lack of interest post-vote. The ensuing fallout from this ambitious initiative resulted in severe consequences for Harry and June. The FA, seemingly threatened by the unconventional vision, imposed a ban, prohibiting Harry from managing any football team within the UK, a sanction that also extended to June. The documented evidence, including conversations and meeting minutes, captures the contentious aftermath of a proposal that sought to reshape the landscape of women's football.

Chiltern Valley Ladies had to be disbanded.

The FA even banned the girls who played in Mexico. Every woman that was over 16 years old was banned for six months and those under 16 got a three-month ban.

Harry was furious when he heard the girls were to receive a ban for going to Mexico. When confronted with the severe penalties imposed on the Chiltern Valley Ladies by the FA, Harry launched an immediate and impassioned defence. He adamantly argued that the players were undeserving of such harsh punishment and took a bold stance, asserting, 'If you want to punish someone, only punish me.' Harry contended that the girls, having committed no wrongdoing, should not bear the brunt of the FA's retribution. However, it became apparent that the FA's approach was akin to wielding a sledgehammer – a ruthless eradication of both Harry and the Chiltern Valley Ladies from the football landscape.

The FA's actions went beyond mere disciplinary measures; they sought to obliterate any trace of the team and their historic venture in Mexico. The entire episode became a forbidden topic, and even the girls themselves refrained from discussing their remarkable experiences, a collective silence born out of a perceived transgression. The team felt as though they had committed a grievous offence, and the memories of Mexico were taboo.

In a determined effort to reverse the bans, Harry tirelessly appealed to the FA, hoping for a reconsideration. However, facing an organization that seemed to have predetermined its stance, Harry experienced the heart-wrenching reality of a futile pursuit. The appeals were met with an unyielding resistance. For Harry, the aftermath was one of profound loss – a shattered dream, dismantled by what Keith perceived as jealousy on the part of the FA.

Patricia Gregory had assumed the role of the WFA's honorary assistant secretary, eventually progressing to become its secretary and chairperson. In the early days of the organization, she talked about striving to act in the best interests of everyone involved saying,

*'We were working with a fledgling organization, doing our best for everyone. Our approach relied on maintaining fairness for all. It was crucial to prevent any individual or team from operating independently, misrepresenting itself, and using titles it wasn't entitled to. This wouldn't have been fair to the other players we aimed to represent and care for.'*

According to Patricia, the decision to intervene in cases where a team falsely portrayed itself as England or Great Britain, as seen in two competitions staged in Italy and one in Mexico, was essential to maintain fairness for all participants, while the WFA was assembling an inclusive and representative England team.

For a while, Harry talked about the unfairness constantly and kept writing letters, pursuing his vision of making women's football great. Then slowly and surely, the typewriter noise became less and less, until the machine was closed off and put away in the corner.

The authorities had taken everything from Harry – his pleasure and purpose in life. A character like Harry Batt needs optimism, needs to see goals, and looks ahead. Take away their dreams and you take away their soul, their reason for living because they can't thrive, and they can't be their true self.

It was all over by 1972. The FA had taken everything away. Harry tried to find something to get his passion back, but he'd been hollowed out.

> *'The typewriter gradually went silent. My dad stopped believing, and it was never spoken about again.'*
>
> Keith

In the aftermath of the Football Association's harsh penalties and the subsequent erasure of Chiltern Valley Ladies and their groundbreaking venture in Mexico, a heavy silence descended upon Keith's family. The once-vibrant topics of Chiltern Valley, the historic Mexico '71 expedition and women's football became strictly off-limits within their household. The mere mention of these subjects served as a painful reminder for Harry, prompting a collective decision to shield him from the anguish associated with those memories.

The family, bound by an unspoken agreement, chose to shroud these significant chapters in silence. The taboo extended to the point where Harry and June, who were once avid spectators of matches, abruptly halted their engagement with the sport. The pain inflicted by the FA's actions lingered in the air, casting a shadow over the once-celebrated achievements and groundbreaking journey of Chiltern Valley Ladies.

It was a similar story for the girls . . .

## Leah

Leah's return from Mexico carried with it a blend of emotions – sadness over bidding farewell to the unforgettable experience, yet eager anticipation to share the tales with her family and friends. The prospect of reuniting with her parents, sister Mary and brother Derry, heightened the joy of her homecoming. An immediate return to school awaited her, presenting an opportunity to regale her schoolmates with the remarkable journey she'd undertaken.

Upon reaching home, however, the reception was bittersweet. Newspaper articles, despite a few positive ones, predominantly veered towards the negative. The recognition and credibility Mexico '71 deserved was eclipsed by critical narratives. Undeterred, 13-year-old Leah meticulously compiled a scrapbook of her collected memorabilia, photos and newspaper cuttings.

The imposition of a three-month ban on Leah and her teammate Chris dealt a blow to their innocence. At just 13 and 15 years old, respectively, the girls found themselves banned from playing for Chiltern Valley.

*'June's brother Reg told Chris and me that we needed to leave Chiltern Valley and play for another club because we were banned for three months. I wish that had never happened. I was young, still 13 years old and somebody told us that we had done something wrong. Now we can't play football for our team.'*

Prompted by this restriction, they briefly joined a team in Northampton before settling with Luton Daytels, where they continued playing alongside Janice and Val for six years – until Val stopped playing to start a family. Eventually, their football journey led them to Aylesbury United in 1978, sharing the pitch with Gill.

The ban, a consequence of the association with Harry's team and their participation in Mexico, left a lasting sense of injustice. In retrospect, the gravity of the situation dawned on them, but their ignorance at the time left them unable to challenge the decisions. The repercussions, however, only deepened the significance of their experiences and the need to rectify historical oversight.

After Mexico, some of the girls carried on playing football while others gave up for a while. Life carried on, and most of the team lost touch until Leah started the search to reunite them in 2018.

'We never really allowed ourselves to celebrate and acknowledge Mexico '71 until now, 52 years later. We can still feel the camaraderie when we talk about it together. I haven't been back to the country, but if someone mentions Mexico, the first thing I think of is being there as a 13-year-old and those wonderful experiences I had. It brings a huge smile to my face which is wonderful to say about somewhere you visited all those years ago.

'I don't know if that resonates more now [2023] since we got back together as a team. We didn't talk about the World Cup for all those years because people weren't interested. Nobody could grasp that we'd played in front of 90,000 people, regardless of the result.'

Leah is passionate about Harry and June's legacy for what they did for women's football and herself as a player. Finding out in 2018 that there was an opportunity to stage a World Cup at Wembley in 1972, with Geoff Hurst wanting to invest in it, along with the FA voting no and the WFA refusing to do anything that Harry was involved with hurts Leah immensely and, in her opinion, is a massively missed opportunity, again highlighting the inequality she endured playing football as a girl during this time.

*'Tarnishing players because they played for Harry's team, putting a ban on the girls for going to Mexico, and Harry himself being completely ostracized, in an amateur sport, for me is unjustifiable. Due to our ignorance of what happened, we couldn't fight back.'*

Leah's philosophy in life has come from the confidence she has gained from football and standing up for what is right, helping her forge a career in the NHS as a surgical manager, dealing with high-pressure situations.

## Chris

Chris, in particular, faced additional challenges. Back at school, a presentation on her Mexico football expedition left her classmates and teacher astounded. Despite the initial shock, the English media's scant and negative coverage reflected the attitudes towards women's football during that era. A three-month ban disrupted her involvement in the sport and Chris was back to playing with the boys.

A persistent knee injury, with which Chris battled through in Mexico, led Chris to undergo an operation, disrupting her football journey temporarily. Music, notably David Bowie's, became her solace during this challenging period. The revelation at the reunion in 2018 that Harry had faced a lifelong ban from football left her with a profound sense of guilt and regret for not knowing earlier. 'After all Harry had done for us . . . I feel so guilty as I had no clue about this. I should have gone to see Harry at his house. I feel so bad,' she said.

Despite Harry's resilience in the face of adversity, the FA's ruthless actions stripped him of a game he loved. For the girls, they had a choice to play football again once the ban was over, but for Harry Batt, that choice was taken away from him.

*'I still can't get my head around why the FA banned us girls. The shame I felt because of it was horrendous. The word "ban". To be told you have done something wrong like a criminal offence. My "criminal offence" was to play football representing my country.'*

Chris

As for the debates surrounding the legitimacy of the Mexico '71 tournament, Chris stands resolute. To her, the intricacies of 'Official/Unofficial' classifications fade in the face of the opportunity they seized and the representation they provided for England's football. They played not for titles or recognition but for the love of the game and the honour of representing their country.

Chris's narrative is a testament to the power of sports to transcend barriers, foster a sense of belonging, and shape identities. Her story is a reminder of the value of embracing one's true self, the equality offered on the sports field, and the enduring legacy of those who dare to pursue their passions, against all odds.

## Yvonne

Yvonne's return from Mexico was marked by a sense of melancholy as the team bid farewell to each other at the airport. Despite a brief spotlight due to her broken leg, with a newspaper article documenting her injury, the attention swiftly faded, and life resumed its usual course. Back at work, the surreal experience in Mexico began to feel like a distant dream, fading away in the routines of daily life.

The broken leg, an unexpected consequence of the journey, led Yvonne to deal with hospital paperwork upon her return. Initially faced with resistance from the nurses who were not happy about the plaster being cast in Mexico, Yvonne insisted it had to come off. Eventually, the plaster was removed, and her leg showed no lingering issues.

Disappointment set in, particularly because the team was celebrated on Mexican soil, only to return to England with minimal acknowledgement. The pedestal they occupied in Mexico quickly crumbled, and a conspicuous silence overshadowed their achievements. While close friends and family were aware of the momentous experience, the rest of the world remained oblivious. The team members scattered, each going their separate ways.

Yvonne, oblivious to any ban, continued playing football for the Yellow Scorpions. The lack of awareness of consequences stemmed from her team's status as a local, unregistered entity not under the scrutiny of the FA. Reflecting on the potential impact of knowing about the ban, she emphasized the team's innocence and the focus on competition without considering external ramifications.

'As a young player, I did nothing wrong. We as a team did nothing wrong,' she said.

After the Mexico World Cup, Yvonne soon met her husband Keith, and started a family. Although she attempted to resume playing football after having children, the challenges of juggling responsibilities led her to make the decision to retire from the sport.

Recalling the context of their football journey, Yvonne highlighted that they played during a significant period, with the England men's team winning the 1966 World Cup and losing in the quarter-finals of the 1970 World Cup in Mexico. Despite a new World Cup competition for women with commercial support from FIFF, the FA displayed disdain towards it.

She questioned the FA's negative stance, wondering what they did wrong. The team aspired to play well, represent English women footballers, and showcase their capabilities to the world. However, instead of support, they faced criticism and were labelled 'Harry's Girls' by the FA. Yvonne was frustrated at the FA's failure to recognize Harry's valuable contributions, emphasizing that his multilingual skills facilitated communication with foreign teams and secured their participation in international tournaments. Yvonne believed that if the FA had embraced Harry's forward-thinking approach, women's football might have reached a level comparable to the Premier League. She felt the need for maverick characters like Harry, but the FA's reluctance to support him hindered the progress of women's football.

*'For years, I wouldn't talk about Mexico '71, wouldn't even have got my ceremonial medal out or anything like that, just tucked away in a box of memorabilia.'*
Yvonne

## Paula

Paula was unaware of the restrictions that had been imposed upon her for playing in Mexico. Being younger than 16, the ban was supposedly set for three months – a period during which she, obliviously, continued playing the game she loved. 'No one did anything wrong. No one committed any crime.'

When Chiltern Valley Ladies disbanded, she became a part of the Arland Ladies in Luton, embarking on two seasons with them, from 1972 to 1974. It was a time of adventures and new challenges, including a memorable three-way tournament in Gibraltar, where she crossed paths with Gill, former teammate and now opponent.

The winds of change blew once more, and Paula found herself joining Aylesbury for the 1974–75 season, eager to team up with Gill. However, destiny had grander plans for her. In 1975, at the age of 20, Paula joined the Royal Air Force. Her commitment took her to RAF Wittering, near Peterborough. Despite her duties, she managed to return home on weekends to play for Aylesbury, though she soon realized it was unsustainable and unfair to her teammates. Reluctantly, she stepped back from playing regularly, leaving behind the camaraderie and competition she cherished.

Life took another turn when Paula moved to Germany in 1977 to join her husband, requiring her discharge from the RAF.

In Germany, her passion for football was reignited in an unexpected match between civilians (whom Paula was now representing) and RAF Officers where she astonished everyone with her skill. This led to an offer to join a local team . . . language barriers mean little when a shared love for football prevails. She played until the arrival of her family in 1980 marked a new chapter in her life. Even in Germany, her past caught up with her in the most delightful way when she encountered Big Jean watching and supporting her during a match.

Paula's legacy in the family lived on through her younger brother, Stephen, her most ardent supporter. At a social club watching a Liverpool match, Stephen shouted out a question: 'Who here has scored a goal in the Azteca Stadium?'

Paula became a mother to four boys. Tragically, her second son was born with spina bifida and hydrocephalus, and he only lived to 16 weeks, so three boys, Ricky, Nick and Mike are with her now. Her second husband, Colin, has two boys, Luke and Lewis, to carry on the tradition of lots of boys in her family (along with the four brothers too!)

Post-Mexico, where she had once shone on the 1971 Women's World Cup stage, Paula spoke little of her footballing past, its memories tucked away like relics in a forgotten cupboard. Life, as it does, marched on, with football playing a quieter role.

Years later, while working at Southport College, an icebreaker activity unearthed Paula's hidden legacy. Her casual mention of playing football in Mexico ignited curiosity and admiration, revealing a piece of history that her colleagues were eager to explore.

Upon retirement, the call of the pitch beckoned once more. Discovering 'walking football', Paula ventured back into the sport with a mix of nostalgia and trepidation. Decades had passed since she last played competitively, but her love for the game burned as brightly as ever. Her return was not without its challenges – in the first training session a suspected broken toe, a painful reminder of the sport's demands. Armed with determination and a new pair of boots, Paula persevered, her spirit unbroken.

As Paula's prowess became more evident, so did the curiosity among her new teammates. Her humble beginnings in the south and the mystery of her past piqued their interest, leading to a revelation that would once again bring Paula's footballing legacy into the spotlight. 'Look up "Lost Lionesses" on the internet,' she told them with a cheeky wink and a smile.

## Trudy

Trudy's return from Mexico was marred by heartbreak as the atmosphere in England starkly contrasted the vibrant spirit of her time in the tournament. The silence that followed was deafening, with minimal interest from the press and a sombre mood prevailing. Everyone bid their farewells, going back to their homes, and the abrupt halt to football activities came with the unexpected ban imposed by the FA.

Unaware of the ban initially due to her family's relocation to Lincolnshire, Trudy found herself in an area devoid of girls' teams, marking the end of her football journey. Reflecting on the potential fury and devastation she might have felt had she known about the ban, Trudy acknowledged her father's commitment to justice. 'If I'd have known, I would have been so upset. My dad would have fought for me, for all of us. I know he would have.'

Trudy saw the severity of the FA's ruling as a testament to the authorities' true colours. 'Harry got banned for life. For me that says everything about the FA.'

Several years ago, Trudy looked at all her memorabilia and thought, 'Who's interested in all this because I'm not.' It was her mother's interception that kept these precious mementoes from the bin. She gathered them all up and hid them from her. Trudy's truly thankful to her now.

## Jean

For Jean, the return to England was marked by a disheartening indifference towards the team's achievements. That Jean had not been banned might have been linked to her unofficial status with Chiltern Valley Ladies, as an 'unregistered' player, but she vehemently disagreed with the punitive measures imposed on her teammates. 'We were amateurs. Girls that just loved playing football and loved the freedom of doing so. To ban us wasn't right. You can't say "You can't play football!"'

Jean had a job to go back to. She was posted to Brize Norton in Oxfordshire where she carried on with her RAF duties.

*'I never felt that connection again with another team like I did with Chiltern Valley Ladies and the Mexico team.'*

Jean

## Carol

A few weeks after Carol had returned home, she received an invitation to a Newcastle United dinner as a guest speaker. Despite her father's dislike of social events and his minimal alcohol consumption, she decided to bring him along. The event took place at Gosforth Park, a prestigious venue at the time, where they were seated at the head table. Carol's father found himself next to Ron Guthrie, a former forward for Newcastle United. Despite not being a drinker, he ordered a pint of Guinness, only to accidentally spill it over Guthrie's light beige suit within five minutes.

Later, Carol was announced onto the stage.

*'I walked up to lots of applause, and I thought, "At last, people are recognizing women's football!" A compere was hosting the evening, and he started speaking. "Carol, you were at the Azteca Stadium, Mexico City. I read in the newspaper that you broke your leg. Tell us all about that."*

*'And I said, "It was against Argentina, she tackled me, and I've broken a small bone in my foot. And it's got to be in plaster."*

*'And he then cheekily said, "So it was a bunfight, was it?" grinning to the audience. I didn't understand what he was doing at the time, he just went on and on about fighting on the pitch and putting the team down. I came off the stage and thought, "What's the point? What is the point?" It was then we got the bus home'.*

*'I remember being sat on the bus, next to me dad and he turned to me and said, "Don't worry, Carol. It will not be today [that women's football gets the respect]. It will not be tomorrow. But one day it will be." '*

Subsequently, Carol faced a six-month ban from playing, a consequence of her engagement to a man who vehemently opposed the idea of women playing football. 'He was adamant about that. I was told not to play football again.'

Posted to a different RAF station far from her family, she refrained from investigating other local teams as per her fiancé's wishes. Only during a reunion did she learn about the prohibition on playing.

Keeping her Mexico experience a secret from all but her parents, Carol adhered to the RAF's instructions not to reveal her real name to reporters upon her return. With that chapter closed, she returned to work. 'I missed the camaraderie . . . we had a purpose. And I missed that bonding. There was talent in our team,' she said. Despite the undeniable talent within their ranks, circumstances beyond her control had abruptly ended her football journey.

Carol, considering Mexico '71 as a brilliant celebration of women's football, hates the 'unofficial' tag attached to their World Cup experience. To her, they represented England on the global stage, even if the official label didn't acknowledge it. 'I don't like that word "unofficial". When we were out there, we represented England. That's how it was.'

She attributed the lack of official recognition to a personality clash within the FA, fuelled by Harry's visionary approach. Even after the ban was lifted, Carol believed that progress in women's football could have been expedited if the FA had acted promptly. 'Women's football could have been in a better place earlier if the FA and WFA got their finger out.'

## Jill

When Jill returned home, she brought back with her two large bottles of tequila tucked away in her suitcase. Her uncle picked her up from the airport, and they headed to Euston station, where her sister awaited. Excitement filled the air as Jill revealed the tequila bottles, a secret celebration waiting to unfold. With their parents away in Cornwall staying in the caravan, the sisters seized the opportunity. Disembarking in Birmingham, they found themselves alone at home, mischievously exchanging knowing glances. Jill retrieved one of the bottles, fetched two glasses, and poured a toast to the memorable Mexican experience. Had their parents been present, such partying wouldn't have been possible, but it was a perfect way to commemorate the adventure and share stories between the sisters. The next day, nursing tequila hangovers, they boarded a train to Cornwall so Jill could regale her parents with tales of Mexico, wisely omitting any mention of the tequila celebration.

Jill discovered her ban only later, a confusing revelation considering she was so young. The ban was disheartening and impacted her football activities. 'The FA made us feel like we had done something wrong. It was unfair. And Harry, he was brilliant at what he did. He loved women's football and they took it away from him.' Despite continuing to train and play, it wasn't the same, and it marked the beginning of the end of her football journey, and the silence about Mexico persisted. The team, once closely knit, lost touch with each other.

Post-Mexico, Jill continued playing for a while, but a knee

operation, although a routine meniscectomy, sidelined her for two weeks. She later joined a team in Leicester. However, her mother's words echoed in her mind – she needed a stable career. Pursuing nursing training at college became the next chapter in Jill's life. The demanding nature of nursing, with its unpredictable shifts, clashed with the structured training required for team football. Jill found herself torn between her passion for football and the realities of her profession. Frustration set in as she returned to a world that seemed indifferent to the momentum generated in Mexico. Despite the absence of professional opportunities, Jill remained committed to playing, albeit with a different feel. Once qualified, she managed to carve out time for football, albeit in a more measured and constrained manner.

Reflecting on the composition of the Mexico team, Jill acknowledged that while there might have been more skilled players in the country, the 14 young women who said 'yes' to the opportunity became the ambassadors of women's football in Latin America at that time. Despite their youth and the potential existence of a more formidable team if circumstances were different, the girls out there in Mexico played to the best of their abilities, seizing the chance to represent their country on the global stage.

Jill pointed out the missed opportunity to push women's football forward with exceptional players like Paula and Louise. As children, they were unaware of the complexities behind the scenes with the FA.

*'If we didn't have Harry Batt, what would have happened?*

*I wouldn't have gone to Italy, Sicily and Mexico that's for sure. Fred Gibson was the manager at Nuneaton, and he was a fantastic supporter of women's football. Fred was easy going, a completely different character to Harry. Fred used to go and meet with the FA as the Nuneaton League was affiliated. I think Harry was full steam ahead if he wanted to do something and that didn't go down well with the authorities, but at least he did something.'*

Jill recognized the existence of pockets of affiliated women's football, noting that her experience differed from that of the other girls. 'I wish there had been more options and opportunities for girls to play back then.'

> *'I could get bitter and twisted about it all, but that negative energy ruins your life. There's no point.'*
> Jill

## Lillian

Lillian found herself grappling with an emptiness upon returning home from Mexico. While she briefly shared snippets of her experience at work and with family and friends, the acknowledgement was limited. Newspaper coverage, confined to a small article in the *Daily Express*, failed to capture the nation's attention, as women's football went unrecognized.

Lillian, not an official member at the time, continued playing for a non-FA affiliated club in Northampton. Life took a joyous turn as she married John in 1972, and has been with him ever since. Even during her pregnancy with their daughter Jane,

Lillian, devoted to football, tried to play despite her manager's reluctance!

The revelation of Harry's ban came as a surprise to Lillian, who learned about it when the team was reunited years later. She couldn't understand the FA's reluctance to work with someone like Harry, who invested considerable time and effort into promoting women's football. Given his extensive contacts and success in securing team sponsorship from Martini & Rossi, Lillian found it perplexing that the FA wouldn't embrace such a valuable ally. 'Why wouldn't someone want to know more about what happened in Mexico? Why wouldn't they want to work with Harry?'

*'I had a moment in Mexico. I'm with my girls. This is where women's football should be. We have a great manager who's been pushing it. This was our time. Harry shouldn't have been kicked out. Who knows where we'd be now with him in charge?*

*'I don't think we will ever find out the true story. I want the FA to say sorry about Harry. They will go back to 1972 when "apparently" it all started. Well, it only started because the teams in 1969, 1970 and 1971 played. Somebody had to start the wheels in motion. Yet none of the members of those teams were asked to trial for England either. NO trial. Nothing.'*

*'There was something special about us as a group. You look around and there's another girl like me. She likes football. She plays football. We were Musketeers.'*

Lillian

# Jan

For Jan, the return home after the thrilling tournament brought mixed emotions. Excitement to reunite with family and share extraordinary experiences contrasted with the sadness of leaving behind the camaraderie and adoration they had found in Mexico. The prospect of returning to playing in near-empty stadiums after the vibrant Mexican crowds weighed heavily on her mind. 'In Mexico, I felt more appreciated – for my football, for my skills, as the country loved women's football!' she said.

The realization of a six-month ban, delivered by the FA for representing British Independents in Mexico, hit hard. Unable to voice dissent, the unfairness of the situation was felt. With Chiltern Valley Ladies disbanded, Jan moved on to join the Daytels, captained by Marlene, seeking solace and continuity in the sport she loved.

Football was more than a game to Jan; it was a part of her soul. However, as the tides of life shifted, so did the chapters of Jan's story. In 1976, she married Tony, and together they embarked on a new adventure, welcoming three children into their lives: Gail, Lisa and Adam.

Gail, the eldest, was a spark of energy from the start, inheriting the athletic prowess that ran deep in Jan's veins. Yet Jan chose a different path for Gail's talents. Despite her own love for football, Jan never passed the baton of the sport to her daughter. Instead, she guided Gail's innate athleticism towards badminton, a decision that would see her daughter soar to incredible heights. Gail blossomed under her mother's encouragement, her dedication and skill propelling her to become an Olympic silver medallist, a World, European and Commonwealth champion. Jan watched with pride as Gail's name was etched into badminton history, a testament to her extraordinary talent and the nurturing guidance she had received.

While Gail's journey took her to the global stage, Jan's heart remained anchored to the grassroots of sport. Her love for football found a new expression in the playgrounds of the school where she worked in Bedford. Here, Jan became more than a staff member; she was a mentor, a friend and a football companion to the school children. The playground became a field of dreams where Jan shared her love for the game, playing for hours with a joy that was contagious. These moments transcended the boundaries of a simple game, weaving memories that would last a lifetime for the children who had the privilege to play alongside her.

Even as the years passed and those children grew up, the legacy of those playground matches lived on. Jan's impact was not measured in goals scored or matches won but in the laughter, the camaraderie, and the love for football she instilled in the hearts of those young players.

Jan's story is a celebration of the diverse paths that passion and love for sports can take. From the football fields with the Daytels to the badminton courts of the Olympics, and back to the school playgrounds of Bedford, Jan's life has been a beautiful tapestry of dedication, love and the transformative power of sport. Through her, many have been inspired to pursue their dreams, whether with a football at their feet or a badminton racket in hand, carrying forward the spirit of sportsmanship and the joy of play that Jan embodied so fully.

## Gill

Upon returning from Mexico, 14-year-old Gill promptly resumed her routine at Mandeville Secondary School, as the term had already begun. Surprisingly, there was no mention during school assemblies of her remarkable summer escapade playing football in the World Cup. Despite local press coverage before her departure, the school seemed oblivious to her achievements. Gill couldn't help but wonder whether the reception would have been different had a male pupil represented the country in football or rugby.

Reflecting on the flight home, Gill, having experienced the Azteca Stadium's electrifying atmosphere with 90,000 spectators, harboured hopes for the advancement of women's football. However, post-World Cup, progress was disappointingly minimal. Although the 50-year ban on women playing on affiliated FA grounds was lifted, a new ban prevented her from playing for her club teams upon her return. Gill faced a three-month suspension, and her manager at Thame Ladies was fined £5 for 'allowing her to go'.

Subsequently, Gill chose not to broach the topic of Mexico. The ban left her with a sense of wrongdoing, causing her to shut off the memories. While her parents proudly mentioned it to others, Gill avoided discussing the experience. Storing all her memorabilia in a cupboard, she occasionally revisited the contents, reassuring herself that it did indeed happen and it wasn't all a dream.

*'After the ban, I started playing for my club again. I did go to regional trials but never got picked for an England squad. In my opinion, it was because I went to Mexico. My punishment for going with Harry. I was one of "Harry's girls".'*

Gill

Gill's journey in women's football continued after the ban was lifted. In 1976, Thame Ladies faced a split, leading to the formation of Aylesbury Ladies, managed by Gill's father, who later became a Director of Aylesbury United FC. The lifting of the FA ban on women playing on affiliated pitches allowed Aylesbury Ladies to thrive, attracting players from various regions. The team flourished as Aylesbury Ladies from 1976 to 1987.

A significant turn of events occurred when Ali Clement, an Aylesbury Ladies player and Arsenal FC community officer, discussed the idea of starting a women's team at Arsenal with her manager, Vic Akers. Gill's team was seeking a new manager due to the impending move of their current manager abroad. The proposal to adopt Aylesbury Ladies as Arsenal's women's team was accepted, leading to the foundation of Arsenal Ladies in 1987. Gill, now commuting from Stoke Mandeville, trained at Highbury twice a week, despite the late hours and additional expenses required to play. 'We had to pay back then!'

*'I am so proud to be a founder member of the Arsenal Ladies team of today.'*

Gill

Reflecting on Harry's visionary perspective, Gill recounted his 1971 prediction in a national newspaper that one day there would be an Arsenal Ladies team. Despite scepticism and mockery at the time, his vision came true, posthumously. Gill proudly donned the Arsenal shirt for the first time in July 1987, with her five-month-old baby daughter on the sideline. Despite considering a move to Menorca with her parents in 1989, her passion for football led her to stay in the UK and continue playing for Arsenal Ladies.

Gill played until the age of 34/35, an anterior cruciate ligament (ACL) injury ending her career. Despite the setback, she praises Vic Akers for his belief in women's football, a belief that propelled Arsenal Ladies into the spotlight, attracting notable players and pushing boundaries in the sport. Gill remains an avid supporter, attending Arsenal Women and Lionesses matches. She expresses joy at the evolution of women's football and its newfound acceptance and popularity, with young girls now able to pursue their passion without fear of derision. 'It's great to see so many young girls wearing football kits and not be ridiculed for wanting to kick a ball.'

*'I feel immensely proud as I was one of the 14 who went to play for Arsenal Ladies. Firstly, Harry Batt picked me to be part of his Mexico '71 squad and helped give me confidence and belief that I was good enough to be there. And secondly, for Harry to have that vision to believe there would be a women's Arsenal team, I am proud to have proved him right.'*

Gill

## Marlene

Marlene had already booked her holiday for September when the team received an invitation to stay longer in Mexico for the 5th/6th playoff match against France. She had to navigate the situation of informing her parents without them having a phone at home, relying on her next-door neighbours to tell them about the change in plans. Upon landing at Heathrow, she was pleasantly surprised to find her parents, Dennis and Margaret, waiting with a new ticket and a suitcase filled with holiday clothes. They seamlessly exchanged suitcases, and Marlene jetted off to Corfu to join her friends. The gesture left a lasting impression on her, and despite exhaustion from travel and jet lag, she revelled in the beachside football sessions, still buzzing from her Mexico experience.

Unbeknown to Marlene, a six-month ban had been imposed on her. Jean, the manager of the Daytels, failed to relay this information, and she learned about it later through other channels.

Upon returning to work, Marlene received a warm reception from colleagues eager to hear about her Mexico adventure. However, interest waned, and within a week or two, the topic faded away without further mention.

Meanwhile, there were constant letters from Marlene's love interest from the summer and she made the decision to fly out to see him.

*'I was so nervous but excited at the same time. I told him I was coming, and he was there when I arrived at the airport thankfully! However, due to miscommunication and probably language issues, he hadn't booked me a hotel, so we were in a taxi driving around trying to*

*find somewhere for me to stay! I had all day, for the week I was there, to myself as he worked in a bank. He wasn't just a guitarist in a mariachi band! Then we would meet up in the evening and hang out together. I flew home after a week and that was the end of our romance – I didn't go back to Mexico. I was still 24 years old, but I'm glad I made the journey back to Mexico to see if it could work out.'*

Her football journey continued with the Daytels, and some teammates joined after Chiltern Valley disbanded. Chris, Janice, Val and Leah played for a while, but Marlene hung up her boots at the age of 27 as family life took precedence.

Marlene regretted not talking more about her Mexican experience, attributing her reticence to her upbringing that discouraged bragging. Surprisingly, her husband often took the initiative to share her football past with others, expressing pride in her achievements. 'He always turns to me when we meet new people and says, "Can I tell them? Tell them what you used to do?"'

### Louise

For Louise, articulating the essence of Mexico proved challenging, as the surreal experience had transformed into a dream-like memory. The persistent resistance from football authorities like the FA and FIFA against women's tournaments and the participation of women in football fuelled her frustration. The lack of support from those in influential positions contributed to her decision to step away from the sport at a young age. The belief instilled by her Mexican journey slowly waned, leaving behind a bittersweet taste of unfulfilled potential.

*'I came back from Mexico with hopes and dreams,*
*and they slowly died.'*
Louise

Louise has the biggest 'what if?' story. Recognized as an exceptional left winger with natural talent – and after Mexico, playing with Southampton Ladies, many of whom made up the 'official' team selected by the WFA in 1972 – the future was bright for her as an 18-year-old. With experience in international tournaments in Italy, Sicily and Mexico, she would be a first on many a manager's team sheet today. Except she wasn't. Louise Cross never made any England trial.

Louise, reflecting on her football journey, reveals the sting of hurtful comments about her early exit from the sport. People express disbelief at her decision to step away at a young age. Rumours circulated that her name was proposed for an England trial post-Mexico, but a mysterious letter that allegedly never reached her house clouds the truth.

*'I have had comments such as, "I can't believe that you gave up so young" and "You were such a good player, why did you walk away?" and these do hurt. Rumour is that my name was put forward for an England trial after Mexico, but the letter to me "never made it" to my house. I wasn't good enough to be considered for the 1972 England team apparently, even though many people told me I was.'*

Whatever the truth of it, Louise suggests her association with Harry, as one of 'Harry's girls', cast a shadow over her name.

*'My name was tarnished. All for being associated with Harry.*

*A research team looking into minutes of the meetings from the WFA's
trial selection was told there was nothing to be found as all the records
were destroyed in a fire. I have heard some people saying that maybe
I was banned when they did the trial. I don't know, this may be true,
but without official letters, it's hard to know for definite. We came back
from Mexico in September 1971 and then I was banned for six months,
yet I didn't know about the ban surprisingly.*

'*I am always told – especially by the 1972 England team – that
Mexico '71 was an "unofficial" tournament. We as a team know that
now, but we were completely unaware of all that "unofficial/official"
debate at the time. Women should champion other women. We need to
support each other and hearing a comment saying, "It was an unofficial
event" from another sportswoman from around the same era as you,
does hurt.*

'*You know what, we went out and competed. We didn't know
we weren't official. It wouldn't have bothered me anyway, but I didn't
know. And it wasn't our fault they called us England in Mexico, and
not "British Independents". The Mexicans didn't know the
ramifications of what they did.*'

Louise's regret surfaces as she contemplates the lost opportunity
to continue playing professionally. If she could turn back time, she
would relive her teenage years with dreams of becoming a
professional footballer, a dream hindered by the lack of
opportunities for women in England at that time. The recognition
afforded to the 1972 team further intensifies her sense of missed
chances, feeling that they took away a potential trial opportunity.

Despite the passage of years, Louise's sadness endures, fuelled by the belief that her football journey could have been so much better. The lingering confusion over her trial exclusion and the contrasting fate of her Southampton teammates who went on to represent England evoke a deep sense of disappointment.

*'I understand that the 1972 team is recognized, but I feel they took a chance away from me and I would have played football for longer.*

*'If I could go back in time, if I had a chance to, I would go back to being 15 years old, because I wanted to be a professional footballer. That's all I wanted to be. There were no opportunities here in England for women. And if I were to go back in time, I would like to have an England trial. It's an easy convenience for them to say that I was banned at the time, or that the letter didn't get to me – I can't prove it, but I was good. I was good enough to have a trial. It doesn't mean to say I would have been selected. I appreciate that, but I could have walked away and said, "You know what, thank you for the opportunity, I gave it my best shot."'*

Louise retired from football aged 22 because all the behind-the-scenes politics got to her. It had nothing to do with football. It was an incredible talent lost.

## Val

Val seamlessly slipped back into the routine of daily life the week after her return from Mexico. 'I just went back to work, came home, ate dinner, then watched *Coronation Street*.' Despite her mother's apprehensions about her potential return to Mexico, Val knew it was an unlikely prospect, primarily due to her aversion to flying and 'I couldn't blooming afford it anyway!'

Upon learning about the six-month playing ban imposed on her, Val remained nonchalant. To her, everything else seemed like an anticlimax after Mexico '71. Post-ban, the dissolution of Chiltern Valley Ladies left Val with few options and she found herself playing for the Daytels.

Despite the bans and the politics, Val continued to enjoy playing football. The camaraderie and the sense of belonging to a team were unparalleled joys for her. The experience in Mexico had set a high standard, making subsequent challenges seem less significant.

Val bluntly calls the FA 'pathetic' for not accepting the team's efforts and commending them for giving it their all to promote English women's football. She senses envy within the FA even after more than 50 years, describing it as 'sad' and expressing sympathy for those having such feelings. Val believes that had the FA appreciated and supported the Lost Lionesses, the women's game would be further advanced today. 'We as a team made Harry and June proud, which really matters,' she says.

Reflecting on the past, Val recalls feeling a clique forming within the 'official' England team, particularly favouring Southampton Ladies. She notes that Louise, who played in that team after Mexico, never received an England trial despite being of the same standard as other girls receiving call-ups. The lack of transparency regarding trials, along with a sense of being tarnished, is a recurring theme among the Mexico '71 girls. Despite these challenges, Val remains grateful for the unique experiences and support she received, knowing that not many people had the chance to pursue such opportunities.

*'I was happy playing for a team locally, but it's incredible how you can be tarnished by something you've done that wasn't your fault.'*

*'I miss being part of something, something magical.'*
Val

Val's football days gradually faded as the demands of life took precedence. Balancing parenthood with playing on the pitch proved challenging, so Val reluctantly hung up her boots in 1974. Though she occasionally visited Harry and June, her work and family commitments led to inevitable gaps between visits.

## Harry

Keith Batt looked around the room at the National Football Museum in Manchester when he was asked to do a speech about his dad, Harry. It was a function celebrating women's football in 2019. Feeling incredibly humbled to be in the company of some great football experts, he put his cue cards to one side and the speech he had prepared went out of the window. Keith felt this enormous desire to talk from the heart. To talk about Harry, his dad, and the wonderful women who played in his teams. He got emotional and the hurt poured out.

*'Dad bought this crappy old minibus so he could transport the team around the country. He crammed everyone into this bloody thing. He had this passion. I'm sick and tired of this word "unofficial"– call it what you like.*

*Be as negative as you want. Call him a chain-smoking bus driver. But that "unofficial chain-smoking bus driver from Luton" did more than the whole of you lot put together, could accomplish in 50 years.'*

Keith

The girls have struggled with the persistent disbelief and dismay that lingered when they were made aware of the news of Harry's ban. The devastating revelation has struck them deeply, and their emotions continue to ache even in the present. Reflecting on the past, Leah wonders if, as a united team, they might have navigated the tense situation had they been privy to the impending ban. The idea of collectively engaging with the FA, addressing differences or fostering communication, makes her wonder if there wasn't a solution back then. Right now, she can't fathom the fairness in the process that ultimately transpired. The very notion that Harry, a stalwart contributor to an amateur sport, had been treated with such disregard, fills her with sadness.

*'If we had known back in 1972 about Harry's ban . . . I would like to think as a team, we would have spoken to the FA and tried to smooth out the differences, talk to each other, just anything to stop that action from taking place, because I cannot imagine how that process happened and was deemed fair! It's devastating for me to hear how it broke Harry. We were playing an amateur sport and to hear that someone who gave so much to it had been treated that way, I have struggled to come to terms with that.'*

The girls speak so highly of Harry. He was their rock and light when they were seen as outcasts and unsure of where they fit in society. Yet the treatment he received for wanting a world that was fairer for women, a place where sport and business could meet, and ultimately opportunities and pathways for talented young female footballers, was dreadful.

Keith recalls that the ban for life from the Football Association took a toll on Harry's spirit. Already unwell at the time, the ban further added to his despair. Harry had envisioned a future for women's football, inspired by what he saw in Mexico, but repeated setbacks crushed his aspirations. The dream turned into a heartbreak, leaving him feeling hopeless and eventually leading him to say, 'I give up.'

Each time Keith recounts that chapter of his life, a fierce determination to defend Harry surges within him. Keith has consistently advocated for recognition for the girls who participated in Mexico '71 and for his family. The deafening silence from those in official positions spoke volumes to him. Keith believed that this silence was an acknowledgement of their wrongdoing – an admission that they knew they had treated the participants unfairly. 'The facts are there,' he said, 'it happened. What the authorities did was destroy a great man and it could be argued that the FA set women's football back 30 years.'

In the 1970s, especially within the confines of his school, Keith encountered a resounding message that football wasn't a game for girls. A particular incident stands out from his school days when a teacher confronted Keith about an essay he had written about his five-week stint in Mexico during the summer holidays. After school, the teacher requested a few minutes to discuss his work.

Accusing him of fabricating events, the teacher asserted that Keith shouldn't lie. Keith vehemently defended himself, repeatedly stating, 'I haven't lied! I haven't lied!' The teacher's frustration grew. Ultimately, Harry intervened, visiting the school about the issue. Presenting the essay as evidence, the teacher claimed Keith was making things up. Unperturbed, Keith's father calmly read the essay and, with unwavering confidence, affirmed, 'Everything that is written here is 100 per cent true and more.'

> *'I saw the pain, the anguish and the hurt my dad went through. I saw the other side of being part of a football team, where every spare penny found went into funding the team. All to Chiltern Valley Ladies, because it was just what the Batt family did.'*
> Keith

Keith views Harry as an incredible man with an extraordinary vision who achieved the seemingly impossible. While he wishes he knew the exact details of how his father achieved such success, he only witnessed the struggles, arguments and fights, usually about money for the team and funding at home. Keith and his family actively participated in fundraising to support the team's needs.

For Keith, an apology from the FA and WFA would hold little value; he wants all the trophies and memorabilia to be displayed in a museum, ensuring the Harry and June Batt story is seen and heard repeatedly. He believes it's never too late to showcase their achievements and inspire others. If he can make a difference by addressing the events of 50 years ago, Keith sees it as a personal achievement that brings him happiness. Despite starring as a ten-year-old mascot, he hopes to demonstrate his care for the cause and feels privileged to have been part of the remarkable journey.

*'I was talking to a reporter one time, and they asked me, "How would you describe your dad?" And I said, "Well, when I was a kid, all the other kids, the friends I had, were into the Marvel, DC comics and all the superheroes like Superman, Batman and Spider-Man. I live with my superhero. It's my dad."'*

Keith

Harry Batt died on 16 September 1985 from a battle with cancer, aged 78 years old.

# Chapter 7
# Alternate Realities: 'What If?'

As the sun set on the Copa del Mundo Mexico in 1971, and with FIFA and UEFA still issuing stern advisories to national associations endorsing women's football, cautioning against participation in unauthorized competitions or those organized by the once-prominent FIFF, it seemed that women's football was back in the shadows. Having incurred the disfavour of these paramount governing bodies, FIFF found itself on the outskirts of legitimacy, unable to rally any teams for a third Copa del Mundo in 1972, ultimately leading to the federation's dissolution that very year.

There lingered a suspicion that financial gains enticed the Italian entrepreneur group steering the federation more than a genuine passion for women's football. Still, between 1969 and 1971, these audacious businessmen orchestrated three major competitions – an enticing European Championship in 1969 and two exhilarating World Cups in 1970 and 1971.

These tournaments served as a platform for women to thrust

their talents into the spotlight, creating ripples of awareness in the echelons of FIFA, UEFA and various national football federations. Over time, Mexico '71 has been blurred in women's football history, but it undeniably merits a distinguished place – be it men's or women's – for its incredible achievements and ultimately asks the question, 'What if?'

Imagine the trajectory of women's football had the FA not imposed a ban in 1921. What if progress had accelerated in the 1970s? The potential for a professional league in England during the early 1970s was apparent, so why did the FA staunchly dismiss its feasibility?

Italy had successfully established a professional league, supported by seasoned businessmen, drawing sizeable crowds to major stadiums. The economic argument was validated by this Italian model. Additionally, the commercial triumph of Mexico '71 highlighted the financial opportunities in women's football. So, why did England lag behind in embracing these possibilities?

If it hadn't been for Harry and June, kickstarting the English presence in women's football – in Italy for the Women's European Championship in 1969, the first Women's World Cup in 1970, the Sicily qualifiers for Mexico '71, and finally the Mexico World Cup itself – there would not have been an 'official' England side in 1972, organized by the WFA. What is amazing today is the access to information on the internet and for those who partake in social media to allow this story to be told. There would be no way of burying it in archives if it were to happen in the present day. It is indeed incredible that people did not want to believe the real story, especially those who were an intrinsic part of it. Or was it because they were women, and it was acceptable not to be heard?

Harry Batt had that vision for women's football – he could see the potential and the growth opportunities when others said no. Italy had a professional league for women, with some clubs offering up to £100 per week to play. Harry wanted that in England. He knew it could be done with the right backing and support. Women's sport needs men to champion it. It does today and it did more than ever back then. The likes of Harry Batt, the fathers of daughters and the male supporters for their sisters and mothers, were all so important to start the momentum of women's and girls' football and were gaining more and more support as time went on. All it needed was the support from the men at the top. The men who made the crucial decisions. Then together, women's sports could have had the freedom to grow exponentially, providing pathways and opportunities aligning with society's recognition in the 1960s and 1970s of women's social rights.

There is a recurrent pattern within sporting associations in sporting history – committees grappling for control, power struggles overshadowing progress, and an inability to comprehend the impact on the future. In the eyes of the Lost Lionesses, grassroots sports thrived under the guidance of individuals like Harry and June, yet the WFA seemingly failed to grasp Harry's unique personality. It appeared that the FA also, at that time, held no genuine interest in propelling women's football forward. Harry, characterized as a maverick and visionary, became a casualty of a situation where the FA, driven by a need to regain control, clashed with the WFA's resistance to his involvement. The Lost Lionesses believe that the inability to overcome personality clashes and political hurdles stalled the progress of women's football, with individual egos impeding the collective goal of advancing the sport. As Keith comments:

*'If the FA, WFA and Harry had worked together there would have been a Women's World Cup at Wembley in 1972. It may or may not have been a success, but with Harry at the forefront leading the way, with the contacts and sponsorship already in place, it would be hard to think it wouldn't have been. Plus, he had the experience from Italy '70 and Mexico '71 behind him too. Harry would have known how to make it work. There was raw talent in the 1960s and 1970s just as there is today. Yet those talented girls were told when they were growing up, they cannot play football because of their gender.'*

Let's talk hypothetically and imagine a world today when the FA, WFA and Harry Batt joined forces after the squad returned from Mexico. Six main points are discussed from the perspective of all parties working together for the positive future of women's football.

## The Media

The media likely played a significant role in shaping the public's perception of women's football and its slow progress from 1971 as well. After the Mexican media giants Televisa did a stellar job with full promotion of the Copa del Mundo, the girls returned to negative headlines such as 'Soccer girls limp home to a rumpus'.

Had these articles been crafted with a more positive tone,

emphasizing the talent of the women, the support they received abroad, the enthusiasm of the fans, and their overall experience, women's football might have gained wider acceptance among those previously unfamiliar with it. Instead, the coverage often resorted to mockery. Harry, who proposed starting a professional women's league, was ridiculed, and there was a misplaced emphasis on traditional notions of femininity over the genuine desire of women to play football on a muddy pitch.

In exploring picture archives from the era, the first photo of a woman in relation to football in the 1970s depicts a young lady being escorted out of a stadium by police during a fight among fans at an Arsenal–Chelsea match. It seems as if the decade began with women being unfairly characterized as too delicate for the sport.

One of the few action shots from the Copa del Mundo 1971 shows two women on the turf injured, reinforcing the narrative of women's frailty once again.

A 1972 Reuters story discussing the growth of women's football began: 'After years of regarding women soccer players as something of a joke, the world's exclusively male official soccer organizations are now prepared to take them seriously.' And it asserted that the staging of officially sanctioned world and European tournaments 'seems now only a matter of time'. However, the focus of the article was on trivial clichés rather than the legitimacy of the sport. Concerns were raised about potential rule changes such as using lighter balls, smaller fields and shorter matches, or replacing the term 'ungentlemanly conduct' with something like 'unladylike conduct'. The author bemoaned the idea that the tradition of exchanging jerseys after matches would have to be abandoned. However, these were not genuine concerns but rather attempts by some men to undermine the legitimacy of women's football.

This article could have been written and reported in a completely different tone about the impact these tournaments would have on inspiring young girls, the health benefits of sport, the resilience learned from playing team sports, and the commercial opportunities for potential sponsors. But no, it was focused on the language and minor details of adding women to the footballing programme. And using the word 'joke' in the high-profile article informed the reader of the journalist's view of women's football *before* he revealed news of the competitions and tournaments being considered.

## 1972 World Cup, Wembley

The news that there could have been a Women's World Cup at Wembley will be a shock to many. There was interest from sponsors. There was investment – Bobby Moore and Geoff Hurst wanted to put their own money into the event. There were players – not only from the Lost Lionesses squad as all were young enough to keep playing, but also enough talent within the women's game to field *two* teams, as proposed to the FA. With established teams such as Fodens, Manchester Corinthians and Southampton Ladies, this was the perfect time to showcase the state of the sport and inspire the next generation.

There was support in the FA and WFA with the voting. Ted Hart (the PR manager for the England men's team at the 1970

World Cup) and Harry were passionate about the tournament and knew how it could be done. Harry had the experience of Italy and Mexico, and England had the experience of hosting a World Cup six years earlier, which was a much bigger tournament.

Yet the members voted 'no' and the reasons why are unclear.

Imagine if the answer had been affirmative. Harry and Ted would have led the charge in the organizing committee, collaborating closely with FIFF and the FA to ensure revenue was fairly distributed and all stakeholders remained content. Supported by the media, as previously discussed, with positive coverage in major newspapers and players making appearances on TV shows and in magazines – mirroring the enthusiasm seen in Mexico – the event would likely have captured the British public's imagination. Given that Wembley in 1972 could hold more than 100,000 people, surpassing the capacity of the Azteca Stadium, filling it would have been challenging. However, with a united effort and lessons learned from the previous year, it seems entirely plausible that this goal could have been met.

Even if Wembley Stadium had been only partially filled, the event would have been considered a triumph. Hosting a modest affair that featured two English teams, as suggested, along with participants from the Mexico event and extending invitations to nations absent from previous tournaments, would undeniably have been preferable to having no event at all. The presence of new fans and supporters, coupled with comprehensive media coverage of both the tournament and its athletes, would have sent a powerful message from the FA: the prohibition on women's participation in football had been lifted, and the organization was wholeheartedly in support of its growth. Although the event might not have received FIFA's official sanction, it could have marked the beginning of what was possible in the sport.

However, the FA and WFA chose a cautious approach, opting not to challenge the existing norms or to be the catalyst for change. This decision, influenced by a single vote and the change of heart of one individual for reasons unknown, meant that what could have been the most significant tournament in the history of women's football never took place. There was silence, no progress, just a return to casual games and the highlight being a local tournament in Deal during the summer. This situation meant there were no role models for young, athletic girls to look up to.

Yet the potential for a triumphant Women's World Cup was evident. With the collaborative efforts of FIFF, Harry and Ted, and set against the backdrop of England's fervent football culture, the 1972 Women's World Cup at Wembley had all the makings of a landmark event. Such a tournament could have accelerated the sport's growth, elevated its standards sooner, spurred greater investment, and led to the creation of a league club system decades earlier than it materialized, moving the timeline from the 2000s to the 1980s.

*'If there had been a World Cup in Wembley in 1972, with the calibre of players we had in this country, we could have won it. What an event that would have been. If only . . .'*

Jill

## WFA

The combination of a positive media and a successful 1972 Women's World Cup at Wembley, would have been the perfect set-up for the WFA. They would have had adequate funds due to the demands of the fans to support grassroots football.

When established in 1969, the Women's Football Association was set up to play a crucial role in reviving the women's game in the country, even before the ban was lifted. Despite being predominantly managed by volunteers and grappling with financial constraints, the passionate individuals involved in the WFA have become an integral part of English women's football history for their efforts in rekindling the women's game.

Patricia Gregory, who led the WFA for over a decade, has been quoted in a BBC article as disliking Harry Batt's ways, saying that there needed to be a more conservative and inclusive approach to selecting a team to take to Italy and Mexico.

In 1981, the WFA opened its own administrative office, but the sport continued to rely heavily on volunteers. Without serious backing, progress was limited. The FA began to show more interest, but it took until May 1984 to affiliate the WFA with the same status as County FAs. This did open the door to more central FA support, including funding, however, much more still needed to be done and the women were always playing catch-up to the men. This affiliation laid the groundwork for the FA to create its women's football division, taking charge of the game in 1993 following the dissolution of the Women's Football Association. The administration of the sport was once again under the purview of the Football Association, marking a return to its control 70 years after the initial ban.

From the moment of the WFA's formation in 1969 and the lifting of the ban in 1971, to the FA taking over in 1993, in comparison to what was happening in other countries, in particular, the USA, it could be suggested that progress in England was slow. Even after the WFA selected the first England women's team in 1972, opportunities for women to represent England in international competitions were still scarce with only 25 international matches played between then and 1978. The WFA's efforts to integrate women's football into the national sport did not seem to make a significant impact.

In 1984, England lost to Sweden 4-3 on penalties in the two-legged final of the first UEFA competition for national women's teams, the precursor to the Women's Euros. But insufficient funds yet again continued to stunt the growth of the game for the women.

In 2000, the FA boldly announced that there would be a professional women's league by 2003. Fulham Ladies became the first professional club in 2000, spurred on by the backing of the FA's declaration, but went back to semi-professional status three years later.

In fact, it wasn't until 2009 that the FA introduced central contracts, meaning women were finally able to make a career out of the sport. But in England, there was not a professional female football league until 2018 when the Women's Super League went fully professional.

Looking at the timeline and how events could have shaped

women's football, it is shameful to think about the missed opportunities.

## USA

The USA does not have a rich history of men's football, historically having chosen to concentrate on baseball and American Football. However, it is one of the leading nations in the growth of the women's game. Looking at how this came to fruition makes it inexcusable how this was not capitalized on in the UK.

It all started in the USA with the declaration of Title IX in 1972, which states:

*'No person in the United States shall, on the basis of sex, be excluded from participation in, be denied the benefits of, or be subjected to discrimination under any education program or activity receiving Federal financial assistance.'*

The impact on America – its society, education system and attitudes towards women's sports – has been truly transformative. Title IX, from a sporting standpoint, mandated colleges to offer scholarships to female athletes if provided to their male counterparts. This pivotal shift turned football into a gateway for higher education, consequently boosting participation and elevating the level of competition.

Title IX became federal law a year after the ban on women's football was lifted in England, even though it was still illegal to play football if you were a girl in countries such as Brazil. As the world sluggishly changed its stance on women's football, Title IX granted the US a significant head start.

While traditional football powerhouses worldwide began investing in women's football relatively recently, the well-established machinery of the US has been producing athletic talent for decades. The result: a substantial lead in nurturing and developing female athletes on the football field.

In 1978, 17,970 girls were participating in football across 597 schools, according to that year's survey. In 1982, the year the National Collegiate Athletic Association (NCAA) started sponsoring women's sports, across all three NCAA divisions 1,855 participated in women's football on 80 teams.

'Soccer' became a pathway to higher education, consequently increasing participation in the game. The more players, the greater the competition. The bigger the battle, the better the quality.

To bring these statistics up to date, in the 2021/22 school year, soccer was the third most popular girls' programme with 374,773 participants, according to the USA High School Athletics Participation Survey.

The turning point for the success of the US women's national team appears to be Anson Dorrance's appointment as the head coach. Dorrance, a man with a mindset akin to Harry Batt's, assumed leadership in 1986 at a time when training camps were rare, victories were scarce, and the idea of winning trophies seemed absurd – there were limited competitions for trophies to be won! In the late 1980s, female national players would stitch badges onto their hand-me-down kits from the men's national team, purchase their football boot studs, and earned a mere $10 a day during national duty. With limited tournaments for female soccer players and no financial incentives, the concept of world domination was a distant thought, held by only a single individual, Dorrance.

Dorrance sought the thrill of the adventure and the challenge of competing on the global stage. He wanted the USA to take 'soccer' to the football-loving world. Despite the numerous shortcomings the national team faced in its early years – lacking facilities, support, history and expectations – Dorrance possessed a blueprint for a more promising and successful future. A wave of young talent joined the team, several of whom he had coached at the University of North Carolina, where he was and remains the head coach.

Perhaps most crucially, there was a shift in mentality. A 'go get it' attitude, similar to Harry Batt.

Dorrance is quoted as saying, 'We went in there with absolute reckless abandon. We had an amazing opportunity to make a mark in a sport the world invented, that they thought we couldn't play. We tried to make every team we played against suffer for 90 minutes, and that was our specialty.'

He made the USA team 'aggressive on the pitch, enjoying every moment of the battle' which, unsurprisingly, his players excelled at. The team's playing style was, as Dorrance put it, 'reflective of the American spirit. The players injected it into our team. We found comparable alpha female warriors that also embraced that.'

The absence of soccer as a firmly ingrained element of American sporting culture may have initially posed a challenge for the team, but it provided the female soccer players in the country with a blank slate of opportunity. Dorrance was determined that this team would rise to become the best in the world.

A considerable influx of players entering collegiate training environments characterized by high standards, elite coaches possessing a profound understanding of the game, and excellent facilities implies that the entire structure surrounding collegiate soccer is finely tuned. Every crucial element that significantly influences performance is carefully considered, allowing each player to realize her full potential.

England missed a significant opportunity to lead the development of women's football, a path Anson Dorrance and the United States embraced with open arms. England's more cautious and conservative approach has held back its progress. This hesitancy and the slow pace of women's football progress professionally, has meant that England lagged behind the US and delayed the creation of a vibrant, competitive environment that could have attracted talent, sponsors and fans. As a result, the US women's national team soared on the international stage, capturing multiple World Cup titles and Olympic gold medals, while England has been playing catch-up, only more recently beginning to close the gap through increased investment and attention to the women's game.

## FIFA and UEFA

If national football associations were impeding the growth of women's football, then the responsibility to promote female participation arguably fell to the global and continental governing bodies. Witnessing the triumph of FIFF should have been a catalyst for both FIFA and UEFA to spring into action. The commercial success alone, coupled with their obligation to half the world's population, not to mention the evident enthusiasm of fans and the strong desire among women to play the sport, should have motivated these organizations' leaders to spearhead the movement for women's football. The elected presidents and board members had an unparalleled opportunity to be pioneers, to forge a lasting impact by championing women's football – a sport long marginalized and deemed unsuitable for women. This was their moment to correct historical oversights and champion a cause that would not only advance women's football but also signal a broader commitment to inclusivity and equality within the sport.

In 2004, Sepp Blatter, then FIFA president, was asked for advice on expanding the women's game's global audience. Despite the pressing issues of women's football, such as the fight for professionalism, increased investment, sponsorship and better TV broadcasting, Blatter chose to focus on an unconventional aspect – shorts. The head of the world's largest sports organization suggested that women should wear 'tighter shorts' to enhance the sport's appeal.

Blatter, seemingly inspired by beach volleyball attire, remarked, *'Let the women play in more feminine clothes like they do in volleyball. They could, for example, have tighter shorts. Female players are pretty, if you excuse me for saying so. And they already have some different rules than me, such as playing with a lighter ball. That decision was taken to create a more female aesthetic, so why not do it in fashion?'*

Despite these regressive comments, Blatter remained in his position for a further decade. The reluctance and resistance of the

FA and FIFA towards women's football during that time reflected a stark contrast to the enthusiasm and growth happening at the grassroots level. This disconnect persisted through generations, hindering the progress of women's football, but now, finally, the sport is gaining the recognition it deserves.

It took until 2019 for UEFA to launch its first initiative in women's football. In a 'historic' move, UEFA introduced its inaugural strategy exclusively focused on the women's game. This initiative outlined a five-year strategic framework, demonstrating UEFA's commitment to fostering, guiding and elevating both women's football and the role of women in football throughout Europe.

UEFA president Aleksander Čeferin said:

*'Women's football is the football of today. It is not the football of tomorrow. It is UEFA's duty as European football's governing body to empower the women's game. UEFA will put significant financial investment into the sport, underlining that it dares to aim high and make European football as great as it can be. The actions that we propose and commit to in 2019 will lead to a greater, more professional, and more prosperous game by 2024. Time for action.'*

One can only wonder why it took until 2019 for the president of Europe's footballing authority to come up with this strategy. While many European countries have been the big forces in women's football – Denmark, Sweden, Norway, Germany, England, Spain and France to name but a few – and also big names in men's football, the women's development has been largely ignored until recent years. With the men's game so popular, why was there not a UEFA strategy to implement the development of the women's game until 2019?

During the 1980s, the Mundialito – 'Little World Cup' – took place on five occasions. In 1988, FIFA decided to organize an international women's football tournament, a pivotal step that eventually paved the way for the introduction of the Women's World Cup in 1991.

Yet, it was only after that inaugural Women's World Cup in China, initially named the FIFA World Championship for Women's Football for the M&Ms Cup, that FIFA granted women the privilege to officially refer to the tournament as a 'World Cup'. No one seems to know the reason why.

The 1991 World Cup was modest, featuring only 12 competing teams, and marked by instances of sexist disparities – such as matches being held on AstroTurf instead of grass, and the duration limited to 80 minutes instead of the customary 90. These measures echoed outdated notions that women were not physically suited for football, which had led to the initial ban on females from the sport.

In 1995, women were finally granted the recognition they deserved, ending decades of marginalization, as the Women's World Cup was played in Sweden under its official name.

## European powerhouses

In Scandinavia, unlike other regions in Europe, women's football found a welcoming environment, which explains the strong presence of Danish, Norwegian and Swedish teams in major tournaments. There's a perspective that Italy and Denmark were pioneers, leading the charge in women's football before UEFA and FIFA fully recognized the sport's potential. By the time these organizations began to take women's football seriously, the early dominance of these countries had started to wane. Denmark would not reach another Euro final until 2017, often overshadowed by their Scandinavian counterparts, Norway and Sweden.

As Italy and Denmark's influence diminished, Norway emerged as Europe's sweetheart for a time, boasting talents like Linda Medalen and Hege Riise. These stars shone brightly at the inaugural 'official' World Cup in 1991 and the first official European Championship in the late 1980s. However, Norway's prominence was fleeting, as they struggled to maintain their standing against the rising power of Germany.

Germany established itself as a dominant force, becoming the first country to win consecutive Women's World Cups, a feat the USA would achieve 12 years later. Despite their victories in 2003 and 2007, Germany could not sustain this momentum into the 2011 World Cup hosted on their soil, and they have not secured a World Cup medal since 2007. Nonetheless, Germany has enjoyed considerable success in other significant women's football competitions, such as the Euros and the Olympics. Their three Olympic bronze medals between 2000 and 2008 were surpassed when they defeated Sweden 2-1 in the Rio 2016 final to win gold.

Countries like Denmark and France initiated their domestic leagues in 1974, while others, including Sweden and Spain, had to wait until 1988. Even in Germany, a prominent footballing nation, the Frauen-Bundesliga wasn't established until 1990 and required significant restructuring to evolve into the league we recognize today.

## What if . . .

Had FIFA taken a proactive stance in promoting women's football back in the 1970s, the landscape of the sport today would likely be dramatically different and far more advanced. Such early support would have catalysed the development of professional leagues across the globe, leading to a more competitive and high-profile international scene much sooner. Investments in infrastructure, coaching and youth development specifically for women's football would have accelerated the growth of talent, creating a richer, more diverse pool of players and teams. This, in turn, would have likely led to earlier professionalization and commercialization of the women's game, mirroring the men's but with its own unique appeal and fan base. By now, women's football would not only be enjoying equal status and support but could have also been pioneering in areas such as governance, player welfare and community engagement, setting standards across the sport. The ripple effect of such early support from FIFA would have resulted in more countries having established women's leagues, greater media coverage, larger fan bases, and significantly more opportunities for girls and women in football worldwide.

Even today, it can still be a 'shock' to see a woman skilful at football. As Louise comments:

*'There are a few misogynists when I'm playing walking football.*

*It has taken a good few years for some of them to pay me a compliment. It's strange isn't it, that men think that football is "their sport" and a woman playing, and being very good at it, just doesn't sit well with them. I have got a great "drop shoulder and go" skill and it works a lot of the time, even against the men. I guess I will still have to keep surprising the old men that an old woman can play just as well, maybe even better than them!'*

The United States has demonstrated how to champion a sport across genders, raising the question of why there was such hesitancy and uncertainty elsewhere. Figures like Harry Batt and Anson Dorrance approached the game with determination, achieving notable success and fostering recognition and commercial viability for women's football. Had there been a similar mindset earlier, it's conceivable that the landscape of women's football might have been spared derogatory comments like those from Sepp Blatter about tight shorts, and initiatives like UEFA's plan to promote grassroots sports for girls could have been introduced sooner. It prompts speculation on whether figures like Baroness Sue Campbell (see Chapter 8) might have collaborated with the Women's Football Association sooner, and whether trailblazing women could have been welcomed into the Football Association to further advance women's football without being constrained by it.

There was a time when being 'a girl' in the football world meant being relegated to a second-class status. The prevailing attitude dictated that women should remain quiet and consider themselves fortunate just to be allowed to play. This is a significant factor that contributed to the delayed recognition of girls' football. Despite the passage of time, there is still frustration at the refusal by those at the top to acknowledge past mistakes and instead, choose to repeatedly sweep women's issues under the carpet.

The crux of the issue was financial; the Women's Football Association, under the sway of the Football Association, was stifled. Had it been an independent entity, it might have thrived, free from the restrictive oversight that curtailed its growth.

But no matter what FIFA, UEFA and the FA achieve, nothing can compare to the moment when a group of mostly inexperienced teenagers ran out onto the Azteca Stadium turf in front of 90,000 deafening Mexican fans.

# Chapter 8
# Harry's Legacy and the Evolution of English Women's Football

———

There are many untold stories of women who persevered, often unnoticed, in pursuing their passion for sports. The resilience of women who, with no other alternatives available, managed to balance work, family, partners and children while still dedicating themselves to sports, cannot be spoken of highly enough. 'Women just did it. If we wanted to do sport we just had to find a way,' Leah so rightly put it.

Progress has been made and there are expanding opportunities for women in football beyond playing roles. From pundits and TV presenters to coaches, managers and referees, women are now making their mark across various football-related professions. However, the Lost Lionesses all stress the need for continued investment and mentoring support to nurture this growth.

There is a need for a comprehensive approach by football authorities, including the development of grassroots initiatives for women's football alongside the promotion of high-profile tournaments with a collaborative learning environment, where men and women work together to propel football in the right direction.

There is optimism for the future, with the ongoing efforts by football associations to address gender equality. However, it is important to retain elite sportswomen in football, because the still-present limitations in post-playing opportunities lead to the loss of valuable talent. With encouragement, maintaining the passion and providing diverse options for a smooth transition, this will ensure that the wealth of experience and knowledge possessed by these athletes is tapped into and utilized effectively.

Jean strolled into her village recently, and a friend, curious about her plans, enquired about her evening activities. Jean casually mentioned heading to Manchester for a presentation at the National Football Museum. Her friend, seemingly unaware of Jean's football past, expressed surprise, exclaiming, 'I never knew you were interested in football!' Jean, with a twinkle in her eye, revealed, 'I used to play for England, a long time ago, mind.' The friend's astonishment was palpable and she admitted, 'I used to talk to you outside school most days, and you never told me?!' Jean simply replied, 'No, because there was no point in telling you. You wouldn't have believed me!'

It has been the same for Louise. Grappling with the notion of self-promotion, she recognized the need to share her untold story and shed light on the treatment she and her teammates endured. Over the years there has been disbelief regarding her experiences in Mexico, and if she mentioned playing at renowned stadiums it often garnered laughter and suspicion instead of acknowledgement. A poignant moment occurred when, in her forties, Louise engaged in a kickabout with her son's teenage friends. The boys, stunned by her skills, couldn't fathom a woman exhibiting prowess on the pitch.

*'I know you're not supposed to blow your own trumpet, but who else is going to do so? It has taken so long for our story to be told and for people to know how we were treated afterwards. I have always struggled with people not believing that I have played in the San Siro and Azteca stadiums. All of that has ground me down over the years.'*

This sense of 'unfinished business' also motivated another member of the team. During her stint at after-dinner speaking engagements, Trudy was billed as an 'England footballer', and created some amusement when she appeared in an elegant black dress and heels. The audience, often unfamiliar with Mexico '71, expressed incredulity about the untapped commercial opportunities for women's football in the UK. Trudy, like her teammates, refrained from discussing her experiences initially due to people's responses. Now, with age and wisdom, all the women feel a sense of pride and a responsibility to share their insights.

*'I think like all of us, I didn't and don't talk about my experience. At one stage it would have been because people would have belittled it and made a joke of women's football, because that's what it was like in those days. I know differently now. I'm so proud of what we achieved, and I don't care what people think any more. We, as a team, have things to say now we're older and wiser. We are a lot more critical of the people*

*who decided to ban us and halt the progress of women's football in this country when they could have been more encouraging.'*

Slowly but surely, the story of the Lost Lionesses is being told and known, unfolding as a revelation to start with, but now unravelling as a rich tapestry of history previously kept in the shadows.

The significance of the blue plaque at Crawley Green Sports and Social Club extends beyond a mere commemoration. It stands as a testament to the legacy of Harry and June's teams from 1967 to 1972, with a particular nod to the Chiltern Valley Ladies as their esteemed club team. This historical period is etched into the annals of women's football, marked by the remarkable achievements these teams secured on the international stage in a mere five years.

Reflecting on this era evokes a flood of cherished memories for all the girls who proudly adorned the jerseys of Harry and June's teams. The camaraderie, the victories and the indelible experiences form a tapestry of moments that continue to resonate through time. In acknowledging this pivotal chapter in women's football, a resounding and collective thank-you reverberates from each player, a heartfelt expression of gratitude to Harry and June for steering them through an era that was, by all accounts, nothing short of incredible.

On 16 September 2023, a blue plaque was unveiled at the entrance of Crawley Green Sports and Social Club in recognition of Harry and June Batt and their commitment to women's football. It followed months of work from Lost Lionesses' Leah Caleb, Chris

Lockwood and Gill Sayell, along with mascot and Harry Batt's son Keith, in collaboration with Luton Heritage Forum and the FA. The plaque reads:

> '*Chiltern Valley Ladies, FA & British*
> *Independents (1967–1972)*
> *Pioneers of international women's tournament football in*
> *England, Europe and across the World.*
> Led by Harry and June Batt and their female players.'

Interestingly the FA have added their name to this plaque.

Many of the women came to pay tribute to the tireless work Harry and June had put in over the years, to develop a place where girls and women could play the sport freely, feeling safe, wanted and coached. Harry gave these women hope and dreams when they were shut down in so many ways.

The Lost Lionesses were overjoyed about the blue heritage plaque at Crawley Green Sports and Social Club. It stood as a symbol of recognition for a man who had been mistreated for his forward-thinking nature, his authenticity and his commitment to a cause. It was the first real acknowledgement of Harry and the Lost Lionesses' place in history.

Keith was overwhelmed with emotion, and struggled to put into words the profound significance of the moment to him and his family. Over half a century ago, his parents set in motion a movement that paved the way for girls and women to embrace football in the Luton area. The arrival of recognition at Crawley

Green Sports and Social Club held a deep and emotional meaning. The pitch, shared with boys and men in the early days – the team occasionally offered access to a modest room ('Most of the time the girls were locked out') – was where it all began. The club, thanks to Harry and June, was a place where dreams were nurtured, and possibilities unfolded.

While recounting their story during an interview with Craig McLean for *The Telegraph* in July 2021 at Crawley Green, a surge of emotion unexpectedly hit Chris. During a group conversation about Harry, she nearly lost composure. Keith, turning to her, offered reassuring words, stating, 'My dad wouldn't want you to feel like this; it wasn't your fault.' The enormity of the experience of Mexico, the impact of Harry, the feeling of helplessness against the officials, and how it shaped her life, was all hitting Chris at once.

Adding to the poignant moments, the renowned fashion designer Martine Rose crafted a 'Lost Lionesses' England shirt for the entire group, documented by the acclaimed *Face* magazine. As Chris donned hers, there was immense gratitude for Martine Rose and her team, who took pride in commemorating what they had accomplished. 'When I put that shirt on, I'm telling you now, it was the best feeling,' said Chris.

At a reunion in 2018, Keith told the team that Harry (and June) had been banned by the WFA from any form of football for life in 1972. The emotions and the hard work of campaigning for Harry were apparent as tears flowed from all in attendance. Many there were finding out what Harry had been through and his treatment by the FA for the first time.

Navigating the complexities of what seems right, all the girls strongly believe that Harry deserves recognition for propelling women's football forward. The ban imposed on the girls had a heartbreaking consequence: some never returned to the sport. Some were fortunate to continue playing for a couple more years, thanks to the impact of Harry's contributions.

*'You can't go back in time, but you can appreciate and value contribution. We could all dwell on what could have been, but maybe now's the time to say thank you.'*
Marlene

Some of the Lost Lionesses, on the other hand (Paula especially), advocate for an official apology from the FA to Harry and June Batt. Expressing her strong disapproval of how Harry was treated, Paula contends that, even though those who made the decision may no longer be present, an acknowledgement of the unfair treatment would hold great significance, especially for Keith and the rest of the Batt family. The devastating impact of Harry's ostracism took its toll on him. The ban not only stripped him of his ability to manage and be involved but also snatched away his passion. He was a broken man after being banned for life.

The more events that the Lost Lionesses are asked to attend and talk at, the more pressure is mounting on the FA to acknowledge the girls' achievements in Mexico. At the National Football

Museum event, where Chris remarked, 'If only Harry could see us now,' it was emotional for everyone involved. The occasion prompted more questions from those unaware of the lack of promotion for women's football after Mexico '71, igniting curiosity and trying to bring the pieces of the puzzle together.

While some outsiders to the team have suggested that the girls should receive caps from the FA, it has never been a pressing matter for many of the players. The FA has consistently labelled them as an 'unofficial' team in an 'unofficial' World Cup. With a broader perspective, it would be noted that if recognition were to be granted, it should extend to players from the 1969 and 1970 tournaments, as well as acknowledging the women who played in the 1920s.

It also asks the question of the desire for recognition from the FA now. There is uncertainty about what the FA might say. An apology is a hard ask since the individuals who made those decisions are no longer part of the organization, but Trudy, for instance, is just happy with the gradual improvement observed in women's football. There would be little meaning in a retrospective apology. The suggestions of a simple statement acknowledging their achievements would be acceptable, yet the FA refrains from doing so, persistently branding their team as 'unofficial'.

*'I would like the FA to say that our team was instrumental in the journey of women's football in England, the same as the people before us and after us.'*
Trudy

On 7 October 2022, the FA did extend an invitation to the Mexico '71 team to Wembley for a friendly match between England vs USA , promising a pitch walk in front of the crowd. The women were led to believe this was in recognition of their achievements in Mexico. However, the event did not unfold as expected. The team found themselves forgotten – again. The women's excitement was dashed by an apparent oversight that left them unacknowledged during the anticipated walk onto the pitch.

The Lost Lionesses were left in the stadium while the 1972 'official' England women's team walked out to the cheers of the fans. Jean says:

*'The FA did invite the Mexico '71 team to Wembley, and we had a lovely time in a hospitality box with food and drink. We were told that someone would get us as we would be invited out onto the pitch and our achievements announced to the crowd. We were all so excited. Well, that didn't work out, as apparently, they "forgot" about us. How can you invite somebody and then forget about the walk out onto the pitch?'*

## Lionesses 1991 to 2022

The emotions etched on their faces spoke volumes: despite the sting of a narrow defeat in the 2015 World Cup semi-finals, the Lionesses clutched their bronze medals with exuberant pride after securing a victory against Germany in the third-place playoff. This team had defied expectations, surpassed goals and won over the nation's hearts: 2.4 million viewers had tuned in for the midnight kick-off of the semi-final on the BBC, drawing the attention of the Football Association's top brass.

The surge in interest caught the FA off guard; they hadn't anticipated such a wave of support with the viewing figures of matches, website enquiries for local girls' teams, and initially missed the chance to harness it. However, change was on the horizon. In January 2016, Baroness Sue Campbell stepped into her new role as the head of women's football for the organization. A little more than a year later, the FA issued an apology for the nearly half-century-long ban on women's football and introduced its 'Gameplan for Growth'.

Featured on the report's cover, the image of the players donned in their red away kits, joyously brandishing their bronze medals, encapsulated their triumph. The report set forth three ambitious goals:

1. To double participation rates,
2. To double the fan base, and
3. To secure consistent success on the global stage.

Tucked away within these objectives was the audacious aim of winning the 2023 FIFA World Cup.

Campbell's foreword to the report underscored the significance of these aspirations. She hailed the team's third-place finish at the 2015 FIFA World Cup as a significant milestone but stressed that they were aiming even higher for 2023. Her vision involved close collaboration with the FA Women's Super League clubs to forge a future for women's football that was both mutually supportive and unrivalled globally. 'The time is right, and the time is NOW!'

Campbell declared, setting the stage for an ambitious journey towards global dominance.

The dynamism brought by Sue Campbell's leadership was undeniable. By the end of its three-year Gameplan for Growth in 2020, the FA had achieved nearly all its set objectives, save for one looming question: Had their efforts positioned England to win the 2023 World Cup? The unfolding events answered resoundingly in the affirmative. The England women's team, reaching their first-ever World Cup final, was set to face Spain for the ultimate accolade. We will tell the story of their challenge for the trophy in Australia and New Zealand in Chapter 10.

But for now, let's start at the beginning. This milestone was the culmination of a prolonged journey, one that spanned decades, even a century, crafted by the relentless efforts of pioneers who pushed for recognition and reform within the sport. The 2017 strategy marked a pivotal moment, laying the groundwork for the Lionesses' success by surrounding the players with the necessary support and conditions for excellence.

The strategy's promises were ambitious: professionalizing the top leagues, creating roles dedicated to performance and coaching development, and providing comprehensive support for players across all age groups, from world-class coaching and healthcare to lifestyle and well-being guidance. These initiatives paved the way for players like Lucy Bronze, Bethany England and Laura Coombs to embrace professionalism fully. For younger talents like Georgia Stanway and Lauren Hemp, juggling work and play was a non-issue.

The Lionesses had been floating around at the 'average' mark since the 1990s. After missing out on opportunities to grow the game, in contrast to what was happening in the USA, England women had been hovering around the quarter-finals and semi-finals in European Championships – but yet to make a mark on the world stage before that third place at the 2015 World Cup in Canada.

Martin Reagan's tenure as England women's coach came to an abrupt end following England's 6-1 defeat to Germany in the quarter-finals of the UEFA European Championships in 1991, a loss that also dashed their hopes of qualifying for the first-ever FIFA Women's World Cup. It wasn't until five years later that a significant milestone was reached for women's football: the International Olympic Committee officially recognized it as an Olympic sport, incorporating it into the 1996 Olympic Games in Atlanta. (An interesting note about Team GB's participation in women's football is that entry into the Olympics requires a consensus among the men's teams, meaning all Home Nations must agree to the terms for a men's team in order for a women's team to compete.)

In 1993 when the FA assumed responsibility for women's football in England from the WFA, they appointed Ted Copeland as the manager of the national team. Under his guidance, England succeeded in qualifying for the 1995 European Championship and made it to the semi-finals. This achievement earned England its first-ever berth in the World Cup. During the 1995 World Cup held in Sweden, England progressed beyond the group stage but faced a familiar foe in the quarter-finals, where they were defeated by Germany with a score of 3-0.

Hope Powell took the reins as England's first full-time head coach in June 1998, stepping into the role previously held by her mentor, Ted Copeland. Under Hope's leadership, the team nurtured a new sense of ambition, setting their sights on leaving a mark on the international scene. However, the journey in sports often involves a winding path rather than a direct ascent. England made it to the 2001 European Championship, yet their campaign ended without advancing beyond the group stage. In 2005, as hosts, England again fell short of reaching the semi-finals. Despite these setbacks, progress was evident, and England's path to the 2007 World Cup in China was marked by an unbeaten qualification streak. Their World Cup journey took them to the quarter-finals, where they were matched against the USA, ultimately concluding their run with a 3-0 defeat.

Under Hope Powell's guidance, a significant advancement occurred in May 2009 with the introduction of central contracts. This change allowed players to dedicate themselves to full-time training without the necessity of juggling full-time jobs. This strategic move bore fruit just three months later at the European Championship in Finland, where England reached the final for the first time in 25 years, although they were defeated 6-2 by the defending champions, Germany.

This achievement set the stage for England's participation in their third World Cup in 2011, where their journey concluded in the quarter-finals after a 4-3 penalty shootout loss to France.

In August 2013, following England's disappointing performance at the UEFA Women's Euro, which saw them exit the competition at the group stage, Hope Powell concluded her tenure as head coach.

Following Hope Powell, Welshman Mark Sampson took over as the England manager. Under his leadership, England secured their spot in their third consecutive World Cup, winning all ten of their qualifying matches and finishing top of their group.

The 2015 World Cup in Canada presented a formidable challenge as England faced the hosts in the quarter-finals. Despite competing against a robust Canadian squad and amid the fervour of a packed BC Place in Vancouver, England triumphed with a 2-1 victory, advancing to the semi-finals for the first time in their history. This achievement also represented the first time any England senior team had reached the semi-finals of a World Cup since the men's team in 1990. However, the journey was bittersweet, as England suffered a heart-wrenching own goal in the final moments against Japan, which led to Japan's advance to the final.

England secured a historic third-place finish by defeating Germany 1-0 after extra time, courtesy of a Fara Williams penalty. This victory over their longstanding rivals marked the first win against Germany in official women's football and represented the best finish by any England senior team since the men's team's iconic 1966 World Cup victory.

And from this came the desire to strategize. For the first time there was a belief that there was more to come. The plan . . . the desire . . . the initiatives . . . the backing. The time was right.

However, it was still a work in progress. During Euro 2017,

England secured a 1-0 victory over France in the quarter-finals, advancing to face the tournament hosts and eventual champions, the Netherlands, in the semi-finals. However, their journey came to an end when they were defeated 3-0.

There was another setback when in September 2017, Mark Sampson's tenure as England's manager came to an abrupt end. The Football Association dismissed him following the emergence of evidence pointing to inappropriate and unacceptable behaviour during his time at Bristol Academy and a new manager was sought.

Phil Neville, with his history as a player for Manchester United and Everton and caps for the England men's team, stepped into the role of England manager, marking his first high-profile managerial position. Under Neville's guidance, the team achieved second place in the 'SheBelieves Cup', an invitational tournament in the USA, marking England's highest finish in the competition to that point.

In the 2019 edition of the 'SheBelieves Cup', England clinched the title for the first time. They opened the tournament with a 2-1 victory over Brazil, followed by a 2-2 draw with the United States, and sealed their triumph with a 3-0 win against Japan.

The 2019 World Cup in France was next on the agenda. England's journey included decisive 3-0 victories over Cameroon and Norway, propelling them into a semi-final showdown with the United States in Lyon. This match marked England's third consecutive appearance in a major tournament semi-final. Despite their efforts, England was edged out with a 2-1 defeat. The team ultimately secured fourth place after a 2-1 loss to Sweden in the third-place playoff.

Following their World Cup departure, England's performance took a downturn, facing challenges across a string of friendlies that culminated in a 2-1 loss to Germany at Wembley Stadium on 9 November 2019. This match was notable not only for the outcome but also for setting a record attendance of 77,768 for an England women's match, the second-largest audience for a women's game in England, just behind the 80,203 spectators at the 2012 Olympic final at the same venue. The team's struggles extended into 2020, failing to retain their 'SheBelieves Cup' title in March. Defeats by the United States and Spain contributed to a tally of seven losses in eleven matches, marking England's most challenging period since 2003. This series of defeats piled on the pressure for Neville, who acknowledged his role in the team's 'unacceptable' performance amid growing media attention. In April 2020, Neville declared his intention to resign as manager at the end of his contract in July 2021.

The appointment of Sarina Wiegman as manager – the first non-British permanent manager of the England women's team – was heralded as the final piece needed for the national team's success. Kelly Simmons, the FA head of the women's professional game, lauded Wiegman's impressive track record and her role to elevate the Lionesses to new heights. 'Her record is absolutely astonishing . . . She can help take the Lionesses to the next level. She is a world-class manager, and we're very lucky to have her as our leader,' Simmons stated.

An FA budget restructure at the end of 2020 saw the women's team become independent from the men's team for the first time, allowing more strategic freedom. Under Wiegman's leadership, these professionally supported England players are now fully focused on their game, embodying the essence of football at its best.

In 2021, Sarina extended an invitation to Leah, Chris and Gill to share their experiences from the Mexico World Cup in 1971. Intrigued by a chapter of history unknown to them, the current England women's squad listened intently to the Lost Lionesses' stories, culminating in the presentation of England shirts. Jill Scott presented hers to Gill, Leah Williamson presented to Leah, and Beth Mead presented to Chris. Each one was adorned with the signatures of the entire Lionesses team. Following this memorable moment, they were graciously invited to share dinner with the team. This experience left an indelible mark not only on the three of them, but the current Lionesses squad, who understood the struggle and the resilience shown by these pioneering women who were the trailblazers for women's football during a difficult time.

Euro 2022, hosted by England and postponed due to Covid, saw the team make a remarkable comeback in the quarter-finals. Trailing by a goal against Spain, England clinched a 2-1 victory in extra time. The semi-final at Bramall Lane in Sheffield was a showcase of their prowess as they triumphed over Sweden with a stunning 4-0 scoreline. Alessia Russo's goal in this match, an instinctive backheel, earned a nomination for the FIFA Puskás Award for its brilliance.

On 31 July, the Women's Euro 2022 final at Wembley became a historic moment for England as they overcame Germany 2-1 in extra time. Chloe Kelly's decisive goal in the 110th minute, following a corner, sealed the victory after normal time goals from Ella Toone for England and Lina Magull for Germany. This victory marked the team's first major trophy and represented the first major international championship won by any England team, women's or men's, since the iconic 1966 win. The final attracted a record-breaking crowd of 87,192, setting a new attendance record for the European Championship for both women's and men's competitions.

It has been a whirlwind over the past few years under Sarina Wiegman's management, with the meteoric rise of England's current Lionesses. To be crowned European champions in 2022 shows that dreams can come true under the correct leadership and management.

Immediately after their triumph at Euro 2022, the England squad penned an open letter addressed to Rishi Sunak and Liz Truss, who were contenders in the Conservative Party leadership race at that time, stating their ambition to inspire a nation and viewing their recent success as just the start. But the letter highlighted a concerning statistic: merely 63 per cent of British girls have the opportunity to play football during school PE classes. It concluded with a call to action from all 23 members of the England Senior Women's Euro squad, urging the leadership candidates to prioritize the funding of girls' football in educational settings, thereby ensuring every girl has the option to play.

The team epitomizes the essence of women's football, encapsulating passion, belief, trust and fun. As narratives from different decades of women's football are being discussed and documented, a common thread of unwavering love for the game emerged, laying the foundation for the sport's current success.

The present Lionesses team recognizes the weight of legacy and its role in inspiring future generations. Sarina's poignant message to them emphasizes the collective journey, stating, 'This is for every girl, this is for every woman, who played football. You as the current England team are standing on the shoulders of giants.' Women's football now stands on a significant platform, instilling confidence in young girls and women, and equipping them with life skills to navigate setbacks.

# Chapter 9
# Reignited Roars:
# The Lost Lionesses Reunite

———

Leah was stuck in traffic in Bedford in the summer of 2017, when she caught a glimpse of a familiar figure. Despite over 40 years having passed since they last met, Leah instantly recognized her former teammate. 'I knew it was Janice on her bike! I would recognize her anywhere! She looked like a centre-forward footballer even when cycling!' Stirred by the memories of their strong connection as a team in Mexico, Leah contemplated the idea of reuniting the squad.

In February 2018, a pivotal moment occurred when Leah's brother forwarded an article about the history of women's football. To her delight, the Mexico '71 World Cup claimed the eighth spot among the ten significant points highlighted. Fuelled by the recognition, Leah reached out to the article's writers, revealing her role as one of the players in the Mexico squad. This initiated a series of email exchanges, eventually leading to Leah planning a visit to the National Football Museum in Manchester.

Eager to involve her former teammates, Leah called Chris, inviting her to join the trip. The two women conducted their first interview for the museum's archive, reliving the memories that had long been put away. Subsequently, Leah reached out to Gill, and the trio convened to discuss their shared goal of tracking down the remaining members of the squad. While Val and Janice's whereabouts were roughly known – in the Bedfordshire area – the others remained a mystery, so they set about reuniting the squad.

The momentum for the reunion gained traction through an unexpected avenue – *The Danny Baker Show* on BBC Radio 5Live. Chris took the initiative and wrote to the producers, proposing her participation in the game where listeners adopt a team, just ahead of the 2018 men's World Cup. When introduced to the show, she expressed her desire to adopt Mexico (accompanied by the lively tunes of mariachi music, of course). Danny was intrigued and asked why, and seizing the opportunity, Chris shared the story of her participation in the 1971 Mexico tournament.

Danny, taken aback by the revelation, admitted, 'Well Chris, I thought I knew everything there was to know about football, but I never knew that.' In a surprising twist, Chris learned she had adopted not only Mexico but also England because of her story and Danny's amazement. The impact of her interview reached Ian Youngs from the BBC, who contacted her through the show producers. Through this connection, they managed to locate all but two of the team members.

Chris continued her quest to reunite the entire squad by appearing on the Radio 4 *Saturday Live* programme with Richard

Coles on 6 April 2019. This effort bore fruit when they were invited to *The One Show* on BBC TV less than three months later, marking the full and joyous reunion of the entire squad, including Keith.

In the golden years of Val's life, a time when the world often shrinks to the familiar confines of neighbourhood routines and brief exchanges down at the local shops, a spark of excitement rekindled her spirit. It was the joy of reconnection, a vibrancy through the monotony of daily life, bringing back the warmth of old friendships that had once seemed lost to time. Val found herself cherishing these moments of reunion, a stark contrast to the predictable encounters that typically coloured her days. 'It gets a bit of a stalemate when you get older, so it's been nice getting back in touch with the team!' she said.

Among these cherished connections for Val was Chris; with her timeless humour and unchanging vivacity, she had a special place in Val's heart. A surprise encounter had unfolded in the most mundane of settings – in Tesco, where Val spent her evenings working behind the till.

The evening had been like any other, with Val scanning items and exchanging pleasantries with customers, when the unexpected happened. Chris appeared, as if conjured by the magic of yesteryear. The sight of her old friend in such an unexpected place left Val momentarily speechless, a mix of surprise and delight washing over her. 'Chris just appeared the other side of the counter that I was working! I was gobsmacked but so happy to see her!' Val recalled, her voice brimming with the joy of that serendipitous meeting.

★

As the team gathered in Boston, Lincolnshire, in 2021 for their 50th-anniversary reunion, Yvonne was struck by the immediate sense of connection that enveloped them all, as if the years apart had simply vanished. The long-suppressed memories of their time in Mexico bubbled to the surface.

To her, it's as though no one has really changed. Only Carol's and Jill's hairstyles seem different, yet their essence remains unmistakable. Jean's presence is as memorable as ever, and Leah, Gill, Louise – everyone retains the same spirit they had in Mexico. 'It's amazing how we've clicked and it's like we have always been in contact with each other,' Yvonne reflected.

In Norfolk, a new chapter unfolded for Yvonne and Carol, who now share a bond unimagined during their earlier days. Together, they attend Lost Lionesses meet-ups, a testament to their friendship and far removed from Carol's once authoritative role as PT and captain.

Carol's son, years later, uncovered his mother's hidden past in an unexpected way, calling her after seeing her on Sky Sports News discussing Mexico '71. 'I've just seen you on the TV – what's all this about you playing football for England?!'

Carol had kept those memories locked away, not wishing to stir up old feelings of anger and upset. Yet, Leah's initiative to reunite the team had reawakened those long-dormant stories.

Similarly, Gill had never shared the Mexico experience with her daughter, Courtney, until the reunion brought it to light. Despite Courtney's involvement in football, this chapter of her mother's life was one Gill had chosen to block out. Now, with the memories resurfacing, they explored this chapter together, much to Courtney's amazement.

'I love sharing the memories with her now,' she admits, embracing the past that has shaped their present.

Lillian is currently revelling in the warmth of reconnecting with her old football team, a journey made poignant by the passage of time and her own battles with ill health that have limited her mobility in recent years. Despite these challenges, the bond with her teammates remains unbroken, nurtured through regular updates from Leah, whose phone calls are eagerly anticipated by Lillian. These moments of connection are a lifeline, a bridge to the world and the people who still mean so much to her.

This bond was celebrated in a tangible, joyous manner when the squad came together on a five-a-side pitch in Boston for *The One Show* in 2019. Lillian, nearing 70 at the time but undeterred by the years, took her place as goalkeeper once again. Her performance was a vivid reminder of her enduring passion for football, marked by a save so remarkable it left onlookers, including a few journalists, in awe. Their astonishment at her agility and commitment for saving a shot at her age, alongside her mobility issues and health battles, only elicited a straightforward, confident response from her: 'Well, I was in goal. That's what I'm supposed to do!'

The Boston meet-up was more than just a game; it was a reunion of souls that had defined their younger years. The joy Lillian felt in seeing familiar faces, in recognizing each person despite the years that had transformed them, was profound. Leah and Gill, once young teenagers, were now grown women in their early sixties.

'I recognized everyone! Even though Leah and Gill were only 13 and 14 years old at the time. It's so lovely to see them now!' Lillian reflects, her voice filled with affection.

Louise had proved tricky to find, the challenge compounded by her change of surname from Cross to Gardner. A researcher from *The One Show* saw that her walking football manager, Tony, had written an article about the Women's World Cup in 1971, with a 'Louise' featuring heavily, on the AFC Tottons website and made the link.

The moment of reconnection was overwhelming for Louise, bringing with it a flurry of attention that initially left her feeling slightly embarrassed. However, any feelings of awkwardness swiftly dissipated the moment she was reunited with her former teammates. Being in their presence, sharing stories and reminiscing about their adventures together, reignited a sense of belonging and camaraderie that had lain dormant for too long.

Now, with the past and present converging, Louise is embarking on a new mission. She is keen on taking up the mantle of an ambassador, not just for the sport that has given her so much but also for the community she holds dear in the Southampton area. She aims to inspire, engage and contribute to the promotion of walking football and the broader message of inclusion and passion for the game that transcends age and time. This new chapter in Louise's life is not just a testament to the enduring bonds formed on the pitch in Mexico but also a beacon for the future.

Sparked by the curiosity and enquiries of journalists, the chance to reconvene after so many years has been a source of immense joy for the girls and in particular, Trudy. It's a rare fortune that their entire team from the Mexico 1971 World Cup remains intact, a stark contrast to other teams from the same era that have faced the loss of members over the years.

The initial gathering in Boston, the first since their days in Mexico, unfolded with a sense of surreal timelessness. For Trudy, it was as if the intervening decades had simply melted away, leaving them all as connected and close as they had been on and off the field all those years ago. Seeing Lillian, diving across the pitch with the same vigour and determination as in their younger days, left Trudy in awe.

> *'I would love to have a picture with us all together one last time in that stadium.'*
> Trudy

Amid the joy of the reunion filmed by *The One Show*, there were two absences. Trudy's defensive partner, Big Jean, and Paula were strangely missing as the girls didn't know what part of the country they were in. However, it may have been because of another factor as well . . .

Jean's elusive status during Leah and the BBC's Ian Youngs' quest to reunite the team was down to an amusing error. In their diligent search, the cause of the mix-up became evident when Jean revealed that her surname had been misspelled by Leah and Chris. The crucial 'K' in her surname was omitted, leading to the belief that it was 'Brecon' and not 'Breckon'. 'Leah and Chris bloody spelled my name wrong, didn't they? Missed the blooming "k" out!' However, *The One Show*'s research team displayed commendable detective skills, eventually tracking down Jean's brother, Alan. Perplexed by the sudden enquiry about his sister's football past, Alan confirmed Jean's involvement, prompting the reunion organizers to reach out.

Jean received the call from the number her brother provided, learning that her participation would be kept a surprise, making her the last to be found. After half a century apart, she stepped into the room where the others were gathered, and to her delight, she recognized the entire group immediately. The only delay in identifying Carol again was down to her hairstyle! It seems her transformation from once being a prim and proper Physical Training Instructor in the RAF to a woman with a long white ponytail, confused Jean.

Trudy couldn't contain her happiness when, in the eleventh hour of reuniting the entire team, Jean was finally found. Watching Jean walk into the room, Trudy's eyes widened in disbelief before she enveloped her in a warm hug. 'I love Jean! My partner in defence was found!' she said.

Paula was the other team member proving tricky to find, as she had joined the RAF and moved away. She even ignored a letter from the BBC sent to her place of work, initially, believing it to be a scam, but finally the missing piece of the Lionesses' jigsaw was in place.

*The One Show* captured their reunion. Adding to the secrecy and keeping it under wraps from friends and family until the broadcast, all the girls casually dropped hints to their friends and loved ones about tuning in to that show. The revelation to Paula's son, Ricky, took a more public turn as he shared the link on Facebook, proudly stating, 'To all my friends that didn't believe me when I said my mum played for England in the Azteca Stadium in Mexico City. Here you go!'

For many of the women, talking about their experiences has brought back many memories. In a recent interview reflecting on the Mexico '71 experience, Jill found herself overwhelmed with emotion. She confided in Leah, Gill and Chris, expressing how she hadn't delved into the memories of Mexico in great detail for years. 'We need to talk together more because everybody remembers different things.'

In early 2023, Jill embarked on a trip to Mexico City, driven by a deep desire to visit the stadium. It was a poignant encounter. Jill's journey also took her to the coast, where an unexpected serenade by a mariachi band on the beach stirred vivid memories of their time in the hotel. The mariachi band, clad in traditional attire, echoed the lively tunes that had followed the team everywhere during their Mexico adventure. The experience by the sea proved to be both emotional and uplifting, transporting Jill back to the vibrant moments at the World Cup.

Jill connected with Cecile, the Mexican player who played for England in the 5th/6th playoff match against France. The reunion, marred by family tragedies that life had thrown at Cecile, carried a bittersweet tone, but held a special significance, with both women moved to tears after 50 years. Jill promised to return.

The reunion of the Lost Lionesses unfolded as an incredible

testament to the enduring power of sports in forging lifelong connections. Beyond the reconnection of Harry's original England squad, the last few years brought them in touch with players from other international teams they faced, further expanding their network.

As the years advanced, the longing for simpler times and the onset of nostalgia became more pronounced for them. The joy of reuniting with the girls lay in the shared understanding and the ability to reminisce about a historical era. They remembered each other as they were back then; they relished the memories of the great times they shared and the sheer enjoyment they derived from playing football.

Reflecting on the past five years, the journey had been nothing short of amazing and incredibly emotional for Val and the rest of the group.

*'That's why I have enjoyed meeting up with the girls again because they understand, they get it. They knew me back then; we had a great time, and we loved every second. We enjoyed playing football.'*

Val

# Chapter 10
# Breaking Boundaries: England's Trailblazing Journey to the 2023 Women's World Cup final

———

Since its inception, the FIFA Women's World Cup has witnessed exponential growth and broader recognition, driven finally by FIFA's efforts to promote women's football globally and expand the number of participating countries. The tournament has seen a steady increase in the number of competing teams, growing from the original 12 teams in 1991 to 16 in 1999, and eventually to 32 by 2023, amplifying the stage for nations to demonstrate their skills at an elite level.

Efforts have also been directed towards enhancing the tournament's visibility and stature. With growing media coverage and global viewership, the Women's World Cup has not only raised the profile of women's football but has also inspired a new generation of girls to follow their footballing dreams.

To boost competitiveness and offer equal opportunities to all teams, the FIFA Women's World Cup adopted the group stage format starting with the 1991 tournament. In 1999 the tournament expanded from 12 to 16 teams. Teams are organized into groups to play in a round-robin format, with the leading teams from each group moving on to the knockout phase, promising an exhilarating contest.

With the rising popularity of the FIFA Women's World Cup, there was a growing call for more engaging matches in the later stages. In response, the 2015 Women's World Cup in Canada broadened the knockout phase to include a round of 16, alongside the existing quarter-finals, semi-finals and final. This expansion allowed for more teams to advance, heightening the tournament's excitement and intrigue.

These adjustments to the format have not only allowed for more teams to participate but have also introduced more nail-biting matches for fans to relish. The ongoing development of the World Cup format has elevated it to one of the most eagerly awaited and prestigious events in the game.

The FIFA Women's World Cup has been a stage for countless unforgettable moments that have left an indelible mark on the fans. From groundbreaking achievements to contentious calls and episodes, every iteration of the tournament has contributed to the sport's history.

Among the many highlights, the tournament has seen extraordinary performances that have become legendary. The 1999 edition in the United States featured one such unforgettable moment when Brandi Chastain clinched the trophy for the host nation with a winning penalty against China. Her celebratory gesture of removing her shirt and kneeling in triumph has become a symbol of women's football, with current England Lioness Chloe Kelly copying this celebration when she scored the winning goal in the 2022 Euros at Wembley.

In the 2015 tournament in Canada, Carli Lloyd of the United States made history by scoring a hat-trick in the first 16 minutes of the final against Japan, setting a record for the quickest hat-trick in a FIFA Women's World Cup final. Lloyd's remarkable achievement has cemented her legacy in football history.

Initially, the tournament faced challenges in achieving the same prominence as its male counterpart. However, concerted efforts over time have significantly raised the profile of women's football worldwide. A pivotal element in enhancing the visibility and acknowledgement of the FIFA Women's World Cup has been the growth in media coverage. As the tournament's popularity surged, a broader array of media outlets began to allocate resources for in-depth coverage. Nowadays, television networks, newspapers and digital platforms offer comprehensive reporting, including live broadcasts, detailed analyses, interviews and feature articles. This expanded media presence has played a crucial role in increasing awareness of women's football and the World Cup, thereby attracting a global audience.

And of course, this had already been done in Mexico City in the Copa del Mundo of 1971.

Additionally, the enhanced profile and recognition of women's football through the World Cup has attracted greater investment into the women's game. Sponsors, media partners and football governing bodies have acknowledged the appeal and commercial potential of women's football, resulting in increased financial backing and resources for the sport's development at every level. This influx of support has led to better training facilities, superior coaching and more competitive leagues, significantly elevating the quality of women's football worldwide.

With each iteration, the Women's World Cup not only continues to inspire and uplift young girls but also makes notable progress towards achieving gender equality in football.

England have qualified for the FIFA Women's World Cup five times prior to 2023, reaching the quarter-finals in 1995, 2007 and 2011, finishing fourth in 2019 and third in 2015. It was time to take on the world following the European Championship success in 2022. Australia and New Zealand were the joint host countries for this prestigious tournament.

The Women's World Cup 2023 was hailed a commercial success with stadiums packed with fans. Visa signed a £10 million deal to be the main sponsor, and over the period of the tournament, over 1.7 million tickets were sold. Attendances for the England vs Australia semi-final have been counted at 75,784. The fans turned up.

PR and marketing teams went full steam ahead pre-tournament, ready to showcase the female footballers' talents in adverts. TV adverts cleverly taunted the viewer to address bias with gender. One of the best was the partnership between the French national team, 'Les Bleues', and telecom company Orange. The advert starts with famous male French footballers using their skill and power to score incredible goals, then rewinding the footage to show that the reality is that it was the women French players who were creating this incredible play, but with the male players' faces computer-generated onto their bodies. Suddenly the viewer is forced to confront their views on women's football. The goals, the finesse and the skills were all acceptable when it was Kylian Mbappé, but now it is a girl, can the goals still be admired in the same way?

## Lost Lionesses on the current squad

A few weeks before the England squad for the 2023 World Cup was announced by Sarina Wiegman, Chris, Leah, Gill and Janice were sitting around a table drinking tea and eating biscuits, discussing the injury woes with Beth Mead and Leah Williamson, both out with anterior cruciate ligament (ACL) injuries. According to new research, a female athlete is up to seven times more likely to get this injury than a male athlete, and the four Lost Lionesses were putting their heads together to understand why. Over-training, packed scheduling and wearing football boots designed for the male anatomy were all ideas put on the table, as well as training correctly according to the menstrual cycle.

The women feel connected to the current Lionesses. Each in their own way. These women have played a World Cup, albeit in a very different time for women and women's football, but the build-up, the excitement as well as the Mexico '71 story having recently being uncovered, got them revisiting those memories of wearing an England jersey.

Marlene got to experience a triumphant moment live as she watched the Lionesses clinch victory at Wembley during the Euros in 2022. Pride surged within her as the team emerged from the tunnel, evoking vivid memories of her own entrance into the Azteca Stadium in Mexico. 'The emotion I felt then was overpowering, so I know how it feels for the girls,' she explained.

Jill, on the other hand, was a mix of pride and bashfulness when her football past became known. A photograph of her donning her football kit from the Mexico days is hung on the wall of the Cornish tearoom kitchen in which she works. Lorraine, her colleague, took delight in pointing out the picture to customers and proudly proclaiming, 'She's a Lioness!'

All the Lost Lionesses watch the England women's team. They go to the games; they know all the players and they all buy tickets and show support in the stands with everyone else. They each have a favourite current player and someone they think plays similarly to how they did 50 years ago.

And if BBC's *Match of the Day* is ever short of pundits, then all 14 would be happy to give their opinions on the players and style of football played. Let's just say that all are not keen on 'all this passing back nonsense', they all are fans of the long ball and always moving forward!

For Leah, it was a challenging task of pinpointing her favourite player in the modern football landscape or someone she used to resemble. Considering her old-fashioned playing style, and the qualities she admired in certain players, Lauren Hemp caught her eye for her speed and exceptional ball control. While Leah may not have possessed the same silky smoothness as Lauren James – though others may disagree – she appreciates James's style, particularly the dribbling around opponents and the constant movement, reminiscent of her own playing approach. In her mind, the emphasis was always on driving forward with the ball.

The girls all express their views on the current squad and recognize the wealth of talent it holds. However, the team faced setbacks with key players like Williamson, Mead and Fran Kirby succumbing to injuries in the lead-up to the World Cup. Additionally, the retirements of Ellen White and Jill Scott after the European Championship in 2022 meant the loss of two experienced players, a challenge that surely caused some concern for England manager Sarina Wiegman.

## The story of the tournament

In Australia and New Zealand, England finished top of Group D and on 7 August 2023, they faced Nigeria in the round of 16. Val was critical of England's play. 'My heart rate was going through the roof! England played awful. It was so negative with all that passing backwards!'

Trudy and her 95-year-old mum, Thelma, were in the lounge watching the match on tenterhooks. England didn't play well at all, but full credit to the Nigeria team who hustled the English players constantly. Lauren James is sent off as tempers start to flare and the nerves are hitting England, the expected winners of the match.

Extra time was survived by ten-woman England and then it was down to penalties. The dreaded 'P' word. England missed the first penalty, but then it was down to Chloe Kelly to send the team into the quarter-finals. She scored. Not only does she score but kicks the ball at a recorded 69mph and the ball smashes into the back of the net. Trudy and her mum scream and shout as the net bulges and the whole of England take a huge sigh of relief.

England moved into the semi-finals after beating Colombia 2-1 to set up a clash with the joint host nation Australia for a place in the coveted World Cup final. However, the organizers scheduled the match at the same time as Southport FC's walking football practice.

Paula, an active participant in veteran walking football on Wednesday mornings, found herself as the sole woman among a group of supportive men who relished hearing her tales of the Mexico World Cup. Faced with a scheduling conflict, Paula decided to record the Lionesses' match.

Upon returning home, Paula's husband had to resort to watching the last five minutes in the garden on his phone so as not to disturb his wife as she nervously watched the TV. There was relief after the Lionesses secured a 3-1 victory over Australia, and a challenging final against Spain awaited.

For obvious reasons, Paula drew parallels between the current Lionesses' experience and her own memories of playing in Mexico, especially the impact of the crowd's presence. The England team, even with some support in the crowd, were up against the majority of Australian fans screaming and cheering for their girls. 'It reminded me of when we played against Mexico and the crowd was more for the other team!' she said. Despite the initial shock, the noise faded into the background as the focus shifted to the game at hand as it does with many sportsmen and women.

England lost the World Cup final to Spain 1-0. Both teams entered the final brimming with confidence, having improved their performances throughout the tournament. England started brightly, challenging Spain's defence with balls over the top and behind the back line. Lauren Hemp created England's best chance when her curling effort from 15 yards struck the crossbar. However, Spain soon imposed their quality, figuring out how to counter England's high press. They dominated large portions of the game, exploiting the spaces left by England's attacking full-backs. Spain cleverly switched play to their left, allowing Olga Carmona to latch onto a simple pass from Mariona Caldentey and calmly slot the ball low past a diving Mary Earps. It was a deserved victory for Spain, but it will feel like a missed opportunity for the Lionesses. Despite often finding ways to win under Wiegman, they couldn't find the answers in the biggest game of their history.

But, European champions in 2022 and World Cup runners-up in 2023, the current squad can be called a success, reflecting the investment into the women's game.

There is a mixed feeling of awe tinged with disappointment when reflecting on England women's journey to the World Cup final. The team's resilience in navigating diverse playing styles throughout the group and knockout stages was impressive. Millie Bright, in her role as captain, emerged as a standout performer, earning Leah's admiration. But there should be praise for the entire squad, as well as singling out players like Jess Carter, Alex Green and Chloe Kelly, whose focused mindset and ability to switch gears when it mattered impressed on the world stage.

> *'The recent World Cup 2023 showed that Harry knew*
> *it could be done. He was proved right in Mexico.*
> *The proof was there all the time.'*
> Trudy

> *'I could hear dad's voice in my head when I was watching the*
> *Lionesses in the World Cup final, saying "I told you, son."'*
> Keith

The Women's World Cup of 2023 has held a more significant role for Leah and the team, who have found immense joy in witnessing more teams from various nations compete. The expanded group stages allowed new countries, especially those from Africa, to make their mark on the global stage. There is still progress to be made, but the perception of women's football has notably evolved in the last five years, signalling to inspire girls and women that they are welcome in the sport and that football is for everyone.

> *'There was a stigma attached to us all those years ago because*
> *we loved playing football. I feel it has only been really lifted in*
> *the last five years. Finally, girls and women feel accepted*
> *playing the sport. It's OK to do so.'*
> Leah

The ongoing success of the current Lionesses has created the emergence of a lasting legacy. The nationwide support and momentum surrounding the team, particularly from diverse family groups and various age groups, have left the Lost Lionesses heartened. It is reminiscent of the fans and support from Mexico.

Perhaps most importantly, the impact on young girls can now be celebrated. This is so important for the Lost Lionesses and marks a pivotal moment, as the current squad's success finally provided young girls with female football role models to look up to.

*'At last there are female role models!'*
Leah

## Controversies

But this alludes to one of the big talking points to come out of World Cup 2023. For years, football fans, especially young and impressionable supporters, have proudly sported the names of their heroes on their jerseys. However, if Mary Earps is your hero, then tough luck. Despite her rising fame as an England goalkeeper and numerous individual accolades, such as being named the world's top goalkeeper at the FIFA Best awards, winning the Golden Glove in Australia and New Zealand, and taking the title of BBC Sports Personality of the Year in 2023, fans were disappointed to find that replicas of her goalkeeper jersey were unavailable to purchase in the lead-up to the tournament.

In the summer, Earps revealed that fans couldn't buy one due to Nike's alleged decision not to make women's goalkeeper kits available for public sale as part of their commercial strategy. Earps said it was hurtful that fans could not buy a replica of her goalkeeper shirt. Interestingly, a quick online search revealed the ready availability of England men's goalkeeper jersey for purchase. Additionally, replicas of Earps's Manchester United kit, produced by Adidas, had sold out the previous season.

Nike responded, stating that they were working towards solutions for future tournaments. Fan power took over and after a petition signed by over 100,000, Nike released a limited number of Earps goalkeeping jerseys for sale. Funnily enough, they all sold out. Those fans unable to purchase official replicas resorted to using fabric pens to create their own versions of Mary Earps's goalkeeper jersey.

But a row over replica jerseys wasn't the only controversial moment surrounding World Cup 2023. Sitting watching the final, supporting her nation to victory, was the Queen of Spain, yet there was no appearance from the British Prime Minister at the time Rishi Sunak, nor Prince William who is president of the Football Association. The reasons given for their non-attendance were 'climate impact' but the question was raised whether both would have turned up if the England men were in the World Cup final.

Social media videos supporting the Lionesses were in abundance. Big names such as David Beckham posted his daughter Harper with England flags and signs saying, 'Go Lionesses!', yet his sons were not in the post. The same for Prince William. There was a video with Princess Charlotte supporting the England women, but her brothers were nowhere to be seen. There were the obligatory 'girl supporting girls' photo or video, yet it seems that boys supporting girls wasn't deemed necessary.

With the lack of influential male celebrities supporting the Women's World Cup, it would have been a perfect time for the current president of FIFA, Gianni Infantino, to step in with some powerful words to set the tone.

In a World Cup conference, Infantino addressed 'all the women' and told them they 'have the power to change'. Advising them to choose their battles wisely, he asserted that women could influence men and FIFA, encouraging them to take action.

*'Pick the right battles. Pick the right fights. You have the power to change,' he said. 'You have the power to convince us men what we have to do and what we don't have to do. You do it. Just do it. With men, with FIFA, you will find open doors. Just push the doors.'*

However, this speech also faced criticism, with the *Guardian's* Marina Hyde describing his words as 'patronizing women beyond belief' and BBC presenter Gabby Logan deeming the comments 'ridiculous and reductive'. Commentator Jacqui Oatley labelled them 'nonsense'. Even players, including Norway forward Ada Hegerberg, expressed discontent, sarcastically mentioning she was 'working on a little presentation to convince men' in a social media post. The way Infantino said 'women must pick the right battles . . . to convince us men what we have to do', seemed to suggest that women themselves were responsible for action over equality, and not the president of FIFA.

The women's game of football *is* different to the men's game. Men are physically stronger and faster, but that doesn't mean that both styles of football can't be appreciated in their own way. The Lost Lionesses are adamant to stress this, and they don't want it to be the same. It would be impossible anyway. Leah, an avid enthusiast of both men's and women's football, relishes the distinctive styles each gender brings to the game. There is a uniqueness to women's football that should be embraced and the diverse approach that sets it apart celebrated.

Mexico '71 was a chance to showcase this. But it begs the question, if more fans had had the chance to see women's football in the run-up to World Cup 2023, would there still be the sexist and misogynistic comments that keep re-emerging? Comments such as:

- Women's football is so slow.
- Women goalkeepers are dreadful.
- Women should be in the kitchen and leaving the football to the men.

Which unfortunately brings us on to *the* biggest talking point of all at the 2023 World Cup, which took place during and after the final between England and Spain – the behaviour of then-Spanish football president Luis Rubiales. There were several reports of indecent behaviour, leading to a FIFA investigation.

Three incidents involved Spanish women footballers. Rubiales was seen to forcibly kiss Jenni Hermoso on the lips at the trophy ceremony, as well as carrying striker Athenea del Castillo over his shoulder. He is also alleged to have given Olga Carmona an unwanted kiss on the cheek. Two Lionesses also complained as

Rubiales stroked the face of Laura Coombs and gave a 'forceful kiss' to Lucy Bronze. Added to the above, Rubiales couldn't contain his excitement when the final whistle went and grabbed his crotch while he was next to Queen Letizia and her 16-year-old daughter Infanta Sofia.

Sadly, it seems, 52 years after Jaime de Haro's comment of 'focusing on the femininity', still women have to endure a deep level of unnecessary sexism and misogyny from the men at the top of football's federations.

## A new hope

Given all the factors mentioned, this tournament instilled a considerable amount of hope and confidence, suggesting that the trajectory of respect for women's football is indeed moving in the right direction.

At the World Cup in Mexico, the foundations had been laid. Record-breaking crowds and robust media support showcased the potential, especially with the strategic decision to host the women's tournament a year after the men's, utilizing the existing infrastructure. The emergence of female football talent and rising stars, fuelled by professional leagues in certain countries, indicated positive progress.

Harry Batt attended the 1971 World Cup at the Azteca Stadium, witnessing the final between Denmark and Mexico. All that was required was the authorities' attention, backing and investment.

Chris and the other Lost Lionesses make it clear that they are not after fame. Their involvement in women's football was not driven by a desire for personal recognition. For Chris, the reason for this journey was to ensure that young girls understood the history of women's football and that it extended far beyond recent England successes.

The Lost Lionesses are aware of the significant sacrifices made by women in the sport even before their own playing days. In the 1960s and 1970s, there were many challenges faced by other talented girls who never had the chance to showcase their skills due to societal restrictions. 'I am very lucky because there were girls just as good or equal to my football talent that never got the chances I did,' says Chris. 'The Lost Lionesses had the chance to show what could be done.'

The word 'legacy' is thrown around all the time when there is a huge sporting competition like a World Cup or Olympic Games to justify the billions that are spent on hosting these spectacular global events. Phrases like, 'It's for the future generations', and 'It will inspire the children to be active!' are shouted out everywhere. Of course, you have to see it to be it.

In 1971, it seems that the future generations of girls playing football were not on the minds of those in charge, nor were they thinking about the women battling away just to be able to do something they were passionate about. Those women did all the hard work, with no money, no recognition and no support. To not think about the future demeans those women like the Lost Lionesses.

England's remarkable success in recent years is largely attributed to an outstanding group of players. Their gracious victories and compassionate gestures towards their opponents have solidified their status as true role models for the nation. This not only reflects positively on their characters but also shines a light on the exemplary leadership of coach Sarina Wiegman. Since her arrival in 2021, Wiegman has elevated the team beyond the disappointments of semi-final losses in the previous two World Cups.

This achievement is also a testament to the significant investment made in women's football over the last decade. Initiatives such as the establishment of St George's Park as a national training centre in 2012, talent identification programmes that have nurtured these stars, and the professionalization of the Women's Super League (WSL) in 2018, have all played pivotal roles.

For many, reaching the World Cup final marks the culmination of a transformative journey for the sport in England, a journey that began in earnest when the FA's 50-year prohibition of women playing on league grounds was rescinded in 1971.

The Lionesses have significantly advanced both the sport and the broader cause of women's rights. Their victory at the Euros, achieved on home soil, significantly elevated the sport's visibility and participation levels. This success translated into a notable increase in both registered players and WSL attendance and viewership. Beyond their achievements on the field, the team played a pivotal role in advocating for equal access to sports for girls in England, leading to a government pledge of £600 million in funding.

Despite the strides made with England's journey to the final, it's clear to many that the path towards recognition in the sport remains lengthy. The players expressed dissatisfaction with the Football Association's position on performance-related bonuses, highlighting this as an ongoing issue and a facet of broader grievances regarding the governing body's approach to commercial matters. In their statement, the team emphasized that their advocacy was motivated by a strong sense of responsibility to grow the game. Also, Wiegman is only paid around a tenth of the salary of the men's team boss, which prompts conversations about the lack of female representation off the pitch in the sport overall.

Of the 32 nations involved at the last World Cup, only 12 had a woman as head coach. The prize money was a quarter of what was on offer in the men's version of the tournament. And the comments of the FIFA president, who seemed to suggest that women were responsible for taking action to bring about equality, hasn't helped the quest for equal opportunities and recognition.

In a domestic context, the examination of women's football by former England player Karen Carney recently underscored the ongoing issue of women and girls being significantly less active than their male counterparts. This disparity is often attributed to persisting gender stereotypes and inadequate facilities, which deter female participation. Among several recommendations put forth, Carney highlighted the necessity for establishing minimum standards within the professional realm, advocating for increased funding, addressing the diversity shortfall, introducing a specific broadcast time for women's football, and professionalizing the second-tier Championship.

The present Lionesses have the potential to revolutionize the sport and influence cultural perceptions in contemporary society. They are attracting larger audiences, inspiring new players, garnering increased respect, and drawing in new sponsors. Such momentum is essential for addressing the remaining challenges the sport faces and is set to grow even further. This team has the capability to enact even more profound transformations, leading to greater positive impacts for future generations of Lionesses than has already been achieved.

*'The way I see it going forward, which is what we're seeing with the Lionesses of today, is the power football and sport in general has for women. It was frowned upon for me.'*
Leah

For now, football is still a man's world. But watch out boys, as here come the girls.

# Epilogue:
# A Fitting Conclusion

My connection to this extraordinary chapter in the history of women's football began with a personal inspiration – my mother, Janice Barton is the formidable centre forward for the Lost Lionesses. Her journey and those of the 13 other inspirational girls, have been hidden from the world for far too long. Their stories need to be told.

As I reflect on the journey of unveiling the remarkable tale of the Lost Lionesses, a narrative tucked away in the folds of time, I am reminded of a poignant moment that underscores the enduring impact of Mexico '71.

Fast forward to a sunny afternoon in Milton Keynes, where my son Ollie attends a local primary school. Ollie has a close friendship with a boy named Miguel, who is of Greek and Mexican heritage. It was the Year 2 sports day in 2017 when my mum, Jan, journeyed from Bedford to witness Ollie's budding sportsmanship. Miguel's mother, Linda, originally from Mexico, introduced us to her father, Miguel Herrera Lopez, who was visiting from Mexico City.

I immediately turned to Miguel Snr. 'Oh, my mum has been to Mexico – she played in the Women's World Cup there in 1971!' and looked to my mum to explain in more detail.

In a twist of fate, Miguel Herrera Lopez made a stunning revelation – he had been present in the crowd at the Azteca Stadium that year, witnessing the England women play in the World Cup.

The connection of two boys – two best friends and schoolmates, both playing on the same football team, with one's granddad having witnessed the other's nan on the grandest stage 50 years prior – sent shivers down our spines.

Miguel Herrera Lopez's animated recollection of the excitement that engulfed the city during the tournament painted a vivid picture. It was a celebration that resonated for weeks, a collective joy that transcended time. Sadly, Miguel Herrera Lopez passed away in March 2023, leaving behind the memory of a moment that united two individuals who shared the same experience in August 1971.

His passing served as an emotional reminder of the urgency to immortalize the Lost Lionesses' legacy. This book stands as a testament to the linking of 14 lives – a testament to the resilience, courage and impact of these unsung heroines.

I find myself still astounded that the experiences of some of the players in Mexico – Gill, Carol and Jill especially – were kept hidden from their children. The surprising revelation that they never spoke of their time in Mexico leaves me pondering the layers of untold stories that exist within many women in the history of female sports.

Growing up, my grandparents often told me the tales of visitors, all amazed at the number of football trophies adorning their house. The assumption, invariably, was that these accolades belonged to their sons. Yet, my nan, with a twinkle in her eye and huge pride, would correct them, asserting that the true football prowess resided in her daughter, Janice. Moments like these were accompanied by the unveiling of Mum's scrapbook, a treasure trove of newspaper cuttings and photographs chronicling her time in Mexico. I vividly recall images capturing her skilful manoeuvres around defenders and the exhilarating moments of goals scored in the Azteca Stadium.

What baffles me is the assumption that everyone shared my awareness of the Women's World Cup. I naively believed that this significant part of women's football history was common knowledge. It's a perplexing revelation that this chapter in history, particularly one set in the iconic Azteca Stadium amid the passion of Latin American football, has been overlooked and neglected.

One memory that is etched in my childhood recollections revolves around my mum playing a football match. I must have been about four or five years old, my little sister nestled in a pushchair, and my dad, nan, granddad and I found ourselves at the sprawling green fields of what I believe to be Luton (perhaps Stopsley). The expanse was dotted with numerous pitches, and in the midst of it all, there was my mum, energetically sprinting up and down the field. It struck me as peculiar, her running up and down the pitch, a sight I couldn't quite understand at that young age. Holding onto my nan and granddad's hands, I could hear their spirited cheers of 'Come on, Janice!' resonating in the air. However, my dad, less enthused, grumbled about the prospect of 'watching the match' and 'looking after the kids'. Despite the mixed reactions, that singular memory lingers, a cherished fragment of a moment in time. I wish I'd had more such memories to share, but juggling football and motherhood became too much, and my mum's football stopped.

Since retiring from elite badminton in 2008, I've joined the motivational speaking circuit, where I frequently share the sources of my inspiration. Foremost among these is my mother, who has always been my primary role model.

Growing up, having a sporty mum felt entirely ordinary to me. I assumed all mums donned tracksuits, played football and were perpetually active, engaging in some form of exercise. Our household seemed like a live scene from *The Fast Show*'s 'Competitive Dad', with my mum energetically playing sports, leaving me to tirelessly retrieve balls. Rest was a foreign concept; my mum was always rallying me to engage in another activity, whether cycling, tennis or swimming. Television, especially children's shows, was a nonentity in my childhood, overshadowed by a constant immersion in sports.

At the tender age of four, my mum introduced me to badminton in a tin hut near our home in Bedford, a relic from the Second World War that became a sanctuary with its three badminton courts. My summers were filled with collecting tennis balls for players on the grass and clay courts in the surrounding area, and winters were spent observing my parents and their friends play badminton. Eventually, the desire to join in became irresistible. Despite my initial lack of coordination, Mum's encouragement led me to persevere, and with each successful hit, my affection for badminton grew.

My mum, proficient in both badminton and football, challenged me to a game when I was seven. The excitement was incredible; I was about to compete against my hero. Predictably, she outplayed me thoroughly, a pattern that continued with every match. I lost 11-0 over and over again.

Some might find this approach surprising, and I often jest about needing therapy to cope with my mum's competitive streak on the badminton court. However, in her unique way, she recognized a familiar determination within me – a reflection of her own resolute spirit.

At the age of ten, I gave a presentation at school about my mother – in my mind, a pioneering figure in sports. I brought in a scrapbook and her participation medal to share her achievements and her role in Mexico '71 as a trailblazing footballer. I had imagined a grand applause at the end, expecting my classmates to swarm me with praise about how incredible my mother was. Instead, the presentation was met with puzzled looks and scepticism, leaving me to wonder if even my teacher believed my story – similar to how Keith and Lost Lioness Chris felt when they too presented in school about Mexico '71. This incident took place in 1987. It was the first time that I began to question how women were perceived in the sporting world.

★

It's crucial for girls to have strong female role models in their lives. While boys may easily look up to famous actors, athletes or even fictional characters, girls often draw inspiration from those closer to home. Family members like mothers, aunts, sisters and cousins, along with teachers, tend to have a more significant influence on a girl's life than celebrities. However, as I shared this narrative with an audience during one of my after-dinner engagements, it prompted me to reflect on the scarcity of female role models in the media during my childhood.

Beyond the unique challenges of growing up as a sporty girl who felt out of place for her ambition, muscular and 'stocky' physique, and preference for sport over shopping for clothes, the 1992 Barcelona Olympic Games stood as a pivotal inspiration in my life.

As I approached my 15th birthday, I found myself at a critical juncture in both my life and sporting career. With badminton newly included in the Olympic programme, I was competing in national tournaments and had made it onto the England Junior B team. Despite my enjoyment of the game, doubts clouded my belief in being able to reach the pinnacle of the sport.

Then came 5 August 1992, the day Sally Gunnell raced in the 400m hurdles final, finishing in 53.23 seconds. Watching that race alongside my mum, I was engulfed in excitement, cheering for Sally as she clinched the gold medal for Great Britain. Our joyous celebration was memorable, not just because I shared it with my mum, but because it was the moment I saw a strong female athlete on television. Sally was a woman of muscle and sheer determination, embodying the very qualities I saw in myself and aspired to emulate.

That moment was transformative; it ignited a passion and determination within me to elevate my sporting ambitions. Inspired by Sally's example, I resolved to intensify my training and commitment to achieve my Olympic dreams, even as my peers were drawn to parties, boys and fashion. Mum stood by me every step of the way, offering unwavering support, motivation and inspiration, especially during moments of doubt or desire to quit.

Reflecting on that defining experience, I often wonder: without witnessing Sally Gunnell's triumphant race, would I have taken that leap to the next level in my sporting career? The saying, 'If you can't see it, how can you be it?' was so apt at that moment.

I had always thought I knew the story of the Lost Lionesses, but it turned out I only knew my mum's version, and even then, not in its entirety. It wasn't until my 46th year that I took the time to sit down with my mum for a few days and truly delve into her life story. The realization that I was hearing about her childhood and her beginnings in football for the first time filled me with a profound sense of guilt. My mother, Janice Barton, had a deep love for football, a passion that often led to her feeling isolated and friendless because it was deemed inappropriate for a girl to be so engaged with the sport – a notion unthinkable today.

Despite her love for the game, my mum never passed on her football skills to me. I don't recall ever having a casual kickabout with her in the garden. However, I spent countless hours watching her play with my younger brother, Adam. From his first steps, she was there in the garden, guiding him as they played football, transforming our backyard into a miniature pitch, complete with imaginary stakes of playing for Spurs or England.

While my younger sister Lisa and I watched from the sidelines, I never felt envious or a desire to join in. Football was the special bond between my mum and Adam, a domain where her talents shone. Reflecting on those times, I recognized that during the 1980s, societal norms strictly divided sports by gender, leaving little room for girls in football. At my junior school, there was no encouragement for girls to play football; gymnastics and dance were the preferred activities.

Curious, I asked my mum why she didn't involve me in football, especially when she noticed my competitive spirit and potential in sports. Her response was always the same: 'There were no opportunities for you to continue with football if I taught you.' This acknowledgement was a stark reminder of the era's limitations – a talented individual refrained from passing on her skills and love for the game due to a lack of faith in the system and opportunities for women in football during the 1980s and '90s. She added, 'I didn't want you to endure what I had to – the misogyny, the lack of respect. So, I encouraged you to find another sport to channel your energy.' Her words shed light on the sacrifices made and the paths altered in the hope of sparing the next generation from the same battles she faced.

My mum's approach to parenting indeed steered me towards significant achievements in badminton, including an Olympic silver medal in Athens 2004 and becoming World Champion in 2006. Yet, I sometimes ponder whether, had there been accessible pathways in football for girls during my youth, I might have found similar success on the football pitch.

Admittedly, my football skills leave much to be desired, even now in my forties. While my mum didn't teach me the art of dribbling past defenders or scoring spectacular goals, she imparted invaluable lessons on overcoming the obstacles and barriers inherent in pursuing sports. Among the most impactful lesson was the importance of competing against boys. Reaching a point where I was not just the best girl in badminton but was also challenged to play against boys, pushed me to elevate my game. Boys, knowing they were up against a girl, would play harder, forcing me to dig deeper to overcome them. This resonates with the experiences of the Lost Lionesses, who honed their skills by playing alongside boys, significantly enhancing their gameplay. My specialization in mixed doubles badminton, competing with and against men, was driven by a fearless desire to prove my capabilities and relish the competition.

Writing this book has reignited my interest in playing football, albeit often as the goalkeeper while my sons, Harry and Ollie, practise their shots. Despite my quick reflexes, I've grown more inclined to dodge the ball rather than save it, leading to my mum stepping in as my substitute. Consequently, I find myself in the role of referee, a task akin to being a UN peacekeeper, navigating the spirited dynamics of grass field football with my family.

I sometimes wish my mum had passed on just a bit of footballing skill to me, if only to have impressed the boys a bit more during my teenage years. It wasn't unusual for a boy who had come over to see me to end up in the garden, showing off his keepy-up skills to my mum instead, engaging in conversations about the latest football scores and Tottenham Hotspur's prospects for the season. At times, it seemed like these boys were keener on talking football with my mum than hanging out with me. There was even an instance when my friend Mat Aram dropped by, spent an entire hour chatting with my mum about football, and then left without so much as a hello to me.

Conducting interviews with the ladies during the 2023 World Cup was an enchanting experience. We delved into discussions about the present Lionesses, analysing tactics, the team set up, and their objectives in the tournament.

I had planned to visit Trudy in Lincolnshire on the morning of the England vs Nigeria last 16 match, anticipating that the game would have concluded by my arrival. However, I arrived just as the penalty shootout was about to commence, and I was immediately drawn into the tense atmosphere in Trudy's living room, alongside her 95-year-old mother, Thelma. The air was thick with anticipation, and when Chloe Kelly scored the decisive penalty, Trudy and I leapt up in jubilation, screaming in victory. I believe Thelma shared our enthusiasm in spirit. The undying passion and emotional investment were palpable.

It's heartwarming to see all the Lost Lionesses ardently following the England women's team. They attend matches, familiarize themselves with each player, and join the sea of fans in the stands. Each of them has a current favourite player whom they feel mirrors their playing style. Listening to Jean, at 70, passionately identify with Millie Bright's game brought a tear to my eye. It's disheartening, however, to learn that these women have to purchase their tickets to the games. When I offered to secure complimentary tickets for them, their humble refusal – 'Oh no, we don't want to cause a fuss. We don't mind' – only added to my admiration for their graciousness and love for the game.

Reading and listening to the way journalists and reporters addressed sportswomen in the 1960s and '70s can be incredibly frustrating. In the 2023 *Copa 71* documentary, archive footage reveals a TV reporter posing a question to Trudy McCaffery: 'So what is a nice girl like you doing playing football?' Newspaper articles from that era often unnecessarily emphasized the feminine aspects of female footballers in their coverage. It's challenging to come across an article from 1969 that comments on a male footballer's physical attributes, such as their calves – a modern exception being Jack Grealish – or includes a caption under a photo of Harry Kane scoring, that divulges his hobbies like playing chess or enjoying long walks, as hypothetical examples.

I have a similar example of this sexism from the end of my badminton career. Beijing 2008 marked my final Olympic appearance for Great Britain. Aware it would be my last, I felt emotionally and mentally exhausted. The demands of elite sport were overwhelming, and at 31, I was prepared to embrace life's next chapter.

In the first round, Nathan Robertson and I managed an upset

against China's Gao Ling and Zheng Bo, the gold medal favourites. Our confidence was high as we faced South Koreans in the quarter-finals, a team we had defeated previously. Despite our efforts, the Koreans outperformed us, winning 21-19, 21-11, and eventually securing the Olympic gold, leaving us with a fifth place finish.

The sting of defeat is profoundly disheartening for an athlete. In those moments, flooded with thoughts of what could have been, the reality that I wouldn't achieve gold felt like a bad dream I desperately wanted to escape. The objective of competing is to win, making the experience of loss feel like a detour from the intended path.

Post-match, facing the media is obligatory, as stipulated by the IOC and Team GB. The BBC team, including Sir Matthew Pinsent, was the first to approach me, broadcasting live. When asked how I was feeling, I found myself speechless, overtaken by tears, comforted by Nathan and Matt as I struggled to articulate my disappointment.

The ensuing hour was a haze of repetitive questioning about the match. However, one reporter's enquiry stands out starkly in my memory. Aware of my impending retirement, he bypassed sports-related queries to ask, 'Are you going to have babies now?' This question, posed in 2008, shockingly reduced my identity to my reproductive capabilities, ignoring my athletic achievements and personal circumstances.

Throughout my professional badminton career from 1998 to 2008, I've encountered sexism and misogyny, just like the Lost Lionesses and many other women in sports and beyond. I've been scrutinized for my appearance, instructed on how to dress or behave to please sponsors, and faced inappropriate advances – all because I am a woman. Despite these challenges, I wouldn't hesitate to relive my sporting journey for the successes I've achieved. However, this acceptance doesn't mean such treatment is right or should continue to be the norm for women in sports.

Watching the reunion of the Lost Lionesses has been incredibly heartwarming and has brought a significant amount of joy to my mum and the rest of her teammates. The sense of unity that comes with being part of a team is profound. Despite the fact that the girls were only together for a brief period of four to five weeks, the experiences they shared have created bonds that will endure a lifetime. It would be truly magnificent to see the girls reunite on the Azteca pitch once again. Thank you to *The One Show* for being instrumental in this reunion.

I'd like to extend a heartfelt thanks to all the men who supported the Lost Lionesses in any capacity. Additionally, my gratitude goes out to the boys who shared the football pitch with these pioneering girls. It's noteworthy that few of the girls reported any form of mistreatment from you; instead, they felt welcomed into the game and the teams within the community, albeit after proving their mettle.

A special acknowledgement to Mexico for the overwhelming love and support from the fans, including the men. Hearing stories about how my mum might have fallen for someone else besides my dad during her time there adds a humorous twist to our family narrative, suggesting there was a slim possibility I might not have been born.

And of course a huge thank you to the 14 Lost Lionesses and Keith Batt for their time talking with me and sharing their personal stories. Throughout my conversations with the remarkable Lost Lionesses, I discovered a piece of my own story in each of theirs – whether it was their initiation into sports, the hurdles they encountered along the way, or simply their unbridled passion and zest. Each of the 14 women, while distinct in personality, shared a pivotal sliding doors moment with the Mexico '71 tournament, after which their lives diverged onto separate paths, with the event seldom spoken of again.

I was deeply moved by Marlene's return to Mexico in pursuit of her romantic interests. Val's dry wit and her fascination with Hitchin Town's football field had me laughing endlessly. Leah, who was the youngest member of the team, has since taken the helm on numerous projects involving the squad. It's astonishing to think she was only 13 at the time. Gill, with her quiet yet determined demeanour, left a lasting impression during our conversation. Hearing about how Harry instilled confidence in Yvonne and how the Mexico trip was a transformative experience for her was truly heartwarming. For Chris, the journey prompted a moment of self-acceptance, confronting her sexuality and life choices head-on upon her return. Louise and I could have talked for hours and I love how she and Paula are still playing football. Paula had me laughing many times as her memory was vague on most of the events in Mexico, only remembering her antics! Lillian, even with her current health issues, was entertaining and inspiring and I saw the fire burn inside her when she talked about football. The dynamic between the formidable Big Jean and spirited Trudy was a joy to discover, underscoring the need for a Big Jean in everyone's life. Jill's dedication to the team, despite limited opportunities, and Carol's exemplary leadership, revered by her teammates, spoke volumes of their characters.

Lastly, learning about my mum, Jan, and the experiences that shaped her has brought us closer, forging a bond that extends beyond familial ties to one of mutual respect between two sportswomen. Mum, I am immensely proud of you.

Life has thrown all sorts at these women, but the lessons learned in sport have got them through. Jill sums it up perfectly.

*'I do believe that I have learned a lot as a woman in a team sport and those learnings have passed on to my children. I like to think that I have taught them to not be afraid of going out of their comfort zone and putting themselves out there.*

*'In sports or life, you might lose of course, but you'll learn something from it. And with that attitude, I think that's a fantastic way to live life. Because of sports, these attributes have been instilled into them. It's coming through with them as well to their children, my grandchildren.*

*'Now I live in Cornwall and swimming is a big part of my life as it was when I was a kid growing up. Sport has kept my kids and myself sane when times have been tough. It was hard as a single mum at times, but I knew sport would be the best for them. It's an outlet too, as well as teaching good discipline. Life has thrown all sorts at me, but I know*

*I have shown my kids and grandchildren how to deal with whatever obstacles get put in front of them.'*

Even today, sport is still a man's world. And a bigger battle awaited these 14 trailblazers upon their return home from Mexico – a struggle that transcended the boundaries of the pitch. The impending challenge revolved around the very future of women's football, thrusting them into a pivotal role as pioneers in a cause larger than themselves and they were unequipped to fight. Yet now is the time to show the world what they, along with Harry and June Batt, against all the odds, achieved.

> *'If I could go back to the Azteca Stadium, to stand on that pitch . . . I'd probably cry me bloody eyes out, you know.'*
> Jean

For the first time, the Lost Lionesses can finally celebrate and acknowledge Mexico '71 more than five decades later. The camaraderie is still there and will never leave.

Thank you, Lost Lionesses. Thank you, Harry and June Batt.

# Index

restrictions on women 179, 219
slowness to promote women's football 232–3, 234–5, 238
Women's Euros 228, 236, 252–3, 254–5, 257–8, 273, 274, 276, 287
United States (USA), women's football in the 229–32, 236, 238, 255

**Vargas**, Alicia 'La Pele' 161, 170, 171

**walking** football 28, 194, 266, 278
Wembley Stadium, London
  1972 Women's World Cup
    FA/WFA voting 'no' to hosting 182, 187–8, 224–6
    Harry's vision for hosting 180, 181–2, 222, 224–5
    'what ifs' 224–6, 227
  2022 FA snub 249
  2022 Women's Euro 257–8, 273, 276
  friendlies 249, 256
Whitbread Breweries 49, 128
White, Ellen 277
White Ribbon 80–1
Wiegman, Sarina 256–7, 258, 259, 275, 277, 286–8
William, Prince of Wales 282
Williams, Fara 254
Williamson, Leah 257, 275, 277
Wilson, Carol
  introduction to 9
  before Mexico
    childhood 51–3
    Chiltern Valley Ladies 109, 110–11
    family bonds and influences 52, 68
    Harry and June's World Cup efforts 120
    RAF 107–8
    sports camp in Scotland 68
  Mexico, Coppa Mondial 1971
    British Embassy reception 148–9
    injuries 159, 163, 164, 180
    made captain 134

    matches 1–3, 160, 163
    Mexican fans 159–60
    opening ceremony 153
    press coverage 145–6, 180
    training 134–5, 143
  post-Mexico
    FA ban 197
    FA, views on the 197
    fiancé's ban 197
    Newcastle United speech 196–7
    RAF 197
    silence on experience 197, 264, 292
    team reunions 264, 268
Wilson, Raymond 51, 52, 68, 196
Wing, Bobbie 128
Women's Football Association (WFA)
  Batt's struggles with 94–6, 180–1, 182, 221–2
  Coppa Mondial 1970 90–1
  Czechoslovakia trip 81–2
  dissolution 227
  Dunn's criticism of 179
  FA affiliation 227
  FA ban on Harry and team 184
  formation 80
  lack of vision 220–1, 222, 228
  mission 227
  refusal to endorse 1971 team 179
  selecting 1972 team 209–10
  Steering Committee 80
  voting 'no' to 1972 World Cup at Wembley 182, 187–8, 224–6, 227
Women's Super League (WSL) 228, 250, 287
World Cup (FIFA), Women's
  1972
    FA/WFA voting 'no' to hosting at Wembley 182, 187–8, 224–6, 227
    Harry's Wembley vision 180, 181–2
    Louise not considered 209, 210–11
    recognition received 210, 211, 249
    'what ifs' 222, 227
  1991 235, 236, 252, 271–2
  1995 235, 252–3, 274

# Author's Acknowledgements

———

I would personally like to thank all 14 of the Lost Lionesses for giving up their time to talk to me about their story. You have been honest, brave, and authentic and I couldn't have asked for more. It has been hard for you to remember an event that was over 50 years ago, but you all were so lovely and accommodating. You are all inspirational trailblazers. Thank you.

Leah Caleb – you are an elephant with your memory!! Thank you thank you thank you – you have been so helpful with photos and the finer details.

To Keith Batt – your passion for your mum and dad's work is incredible, and it was fascinating to hear your story knowing you were living it and seeing the emotions that they went through. You are a credit to your parents.

I hope I have told your stories well and made you proud.

To my mum… I wish I had known more of your story earlier, and I wish women's football had been recognized so you could have shone like the talented footballer I know you are. I loved learning about your childhood, and I thank you for teaching me to overcome obstacles and show the world you can do something when you put your mind to it. I love you.

To my literary agents, Rick and Beverley Mayston at Agent Fox Media for giving me the belief that this was possible.

To Trevor Davies at Octopus Publishing Group for saying yes, and for talking on the phone to help guide me when I have been completely out of my comfort zone.

To my boys Harry and Ollie for putting up with me spending a lot of time on a laptop. You have been incredibly supportive and I love you.

# Picture Acknowledgements

———

*Inset pages 1–8*

Page 1 above: Home Counties Newspapers, courtesy Keith Batt.

Pages 1 below, 2 below, 4 below, 6 below and 7 above: Mirrorpix via Getty Images.

Page 2 above: El Heraldo de México, courtesy Leah Caleb.

Page 3 above: courtesy Gill Sayell.

Pages 3 below, 4 above: courtesy Leah Caleb.

Page 5 below: *Material proporcionado por la Fototeca, Hemeroteca y Biblioteca Mario Vázquez Raña/Organización Editorial Mexicana S.A. de C.V.*

Pages 5 above, 6 above,: Cine Mundial Archivo/National Football Museum.

Page 7 below: courtesy Keith Batt.

Page 8 above: UEFA Together #WePlayStrong, courtesy Frame Creates.

Page 8 below: courtesy www.saveourtown.co.uk.

# About the Author

———

Gail Emms MBE is a retired English badminton player who has achieved international success in doubles tournaments. First chosen to represent England in 1995, Gail went on to become a world champion – winning a silver medal at the Athens Olympic Games with mixed badminton doubles partner Nathan Robertson. Gail retired from the sport in 2008. Since then, she has forged a successful media career, becoming a recurring presence on esteemed platforms such as *Fighting Talk* (5Live) and *Question of Sport*. She also focuses on PR and event management with her own successful company. She is the daughter of Janice Barton, centre forward of the Lost Lionesses.